THE CARIBBEAN BASIN

The Caribbean basin has been the scene of international rivalries and conflict throughout the modern period. *The Caribbean Basin* provides a study of the entire Caribbean region, including Central America and the Caribbean coast of northern South America, as well as an analysis of the role of international intervention.

This history of the modern Caribbean includes discussion of the complex interaction among major world powers in the area, from the British, Dutch, French and Spanish clashes through the Latin American wars of independence to the emergence of the United States as a colonial power in the late nineteenth century. The book also surveys conflicts over colonial possessions, trade routes and Soviet–American confrontation in the Cold War years.

This study integrates the region's recent political, economic and social history with its military and diplomatic past. *The Caribbean Basin* charts this zone's emergence from colonialism during the course of the twentieth century.

Stephen J. Randall is Professor of History and Dean, Faculty of Social Science, University of Calgary, Canada. **Graeme S. Mount** is Professor of History, Laurentian University, Ontario, Canada.

THE NEW INTERNATIONAL HISTORY SERIES
Edited by Gordon Martel
Professor of History at the University of Northern British Columbia, and Senior Research Fellow at De Montfort University.

EXPLAINING AUSCHWITZ AND HIROSHIMA
History writing and the Second World War, 1945–1990
R. J. B. Bosworth

IDEOLOGY AND INTERNATIONAL RELATIONS IN THE
MODERN WORLD
Alan Cassels

GLOBAL COMMUNICATIONS, INTERNATIONAL AFFAIRS AND
THE MEDIA SINCE 1945
Philip M. Taylor

THE CARIBBEAN BASIN
An international history
Stephen J. Randall and Graeme S. Mount

Forthcoming:

WAR AND COLD WAR IN THE MIDDLE EAST
Edward Ingram

NORTH EAST ASIA
An international history
John Stephan

RUSSIA AND THE WORLD IN THE TWENTIETH CENTURY
Teddy Uldricks

REVOLUTIONARY ARMIES IN THE MODERN ERA
J. P. MacKenzie

THE CARIBBEAN BASIN

An international history

Stephen J. Randall and Graeme S. Mount

with David Bright

London and New York

First published 1998
by Routledge
11 New Fetter Lane, London EC4P 4EE

Simultaneously published in the USA and Canada
by Routledge
29 West 35th Street, New York, NY 10001

© 1998 Stephen Randall and Graeme Mount

Typeset in Times by Keystroke, Jacaranda Lodge, Wolverhampton
Printed and bound in Great Britain by TJ International Ltd, Padstow, Cornwall

British Library Cataloguing in Publication Data
A catalogue record for this book is available from the British Library

Library of Congress Cataloguing in Publication Data
Randall, Stephen J., 1944–
The Caribbean Basin : an international history / Stephen J. Randall
and Graeme S. Mount.
p.   cm. – (New international history)
Includes bibliographical references and index.
ISBN 0–415–08999–9 (hbk.). – ISBN 0–415–08998–0 (pbk.)
1. Caribbean Area–History. 2. Americans–Caribbean Area–
History–20th century. 3. Caribbean Area–Relations–United
States. 4. United States–Relations–Caribbean Area. I. Mount,
Graeme S. (Graeme Stewart), 1939– . II. Title. III. Series: New
International history series.
F2176.R36 1998
972.9–dc21   97–40734

ISBN 0–415–08999–9 (pbk)
ISBN 0–415–08998–0 (hbk)

CONTENTS

ILLUSTRATIONS

Plates

The following plates appear between p. 114 and p. 115

without internationalism the proletariat would not have been
revolutionaries"

British Guyana:
11 Linden – bauxite production (1974)

Nicaragua:
12 Sandinista election banner for incumbent president Daniel Ortega:
caption reads "Everything will be better: Daniel President"
13 Sandinista campaign rally in rural Nicaragua near the town of Esteli

Dominican Republic:
14 Bonao school built by Falconbridge Dominicana (1971)

Puerto Rico:
15 Canadian Destroyers in San Juan harbor (1972)

Maps

ACKNOWLEDGEMENTS

Like all works of scholarship, this volume reflects the collective efforts of many individuals. The authors would especially like to express appreciation to the following people. Dr. David Bright at Mount Royal College in Calgary carried out much of the research on Caribbean labour relations and drafted the early outlines of those sections of the manuscript. His background in British labour history was invaluable in the preparation of the study. He also assisted extensively with the collection of bibliography on race relations, sport, religion, as well as trade and foreign investment data. We would like to extend our appreciation to all the archivists who provided assistance to us, and especially to John LeGloahec of the Rockefeller Center and Paulette Dozois of the National Archives of Canada, both of whom far exceeded the normal expectations. Other research assistants over the past several years who have contributed material include: Kevin Gloin, Paul Chastko, and Jiajie Li. Shannon Cornelius deserves special appreciation for her excellent and conscientious preparation of the index, as does Robin Poitras for his cartography. At Laurentian University, we would like to thank Ashley Thomson, whose retrieval skills in matters electronic saved considerable footwork; secretary Rose May Demore; and students Tom Tong and Chris Bartman, who forwarded documents which they had retrieved on Cuba and Panama. Dr. Michael Stevenson, now at Trent University as a post-doctoral fellow, did research on the Ford administration's policies towards Puerto Rico. He made his findings from the Ford archives and from telephone interviews available to the authors. We also thank Bob DuBose, retired U.S. diplomat, who proved a most obliging and helpful host at the Freedom of Information Room at the State Department in Washington and again at his home in Harpers Ferry, West Virginia. As well, we are grateful for the information provided by Lawrence Chewning, Panama's Ambassador to the Organization of American States (OAS). The staff at Routledge have been wonderfully professional and pleasant in guiding the manuscript to publication. Our thanks to all of them. Finally, as ever, the authors would like to express appreciation to their families.

SJR
GSM

INTRODUCTION

Historian Bruce Solnick observed in his study *The West Indies and Central America to 1898* that the region has been difficult for analysts to classify. The creature of competing imperialism in the seventeenth, eighteenth, and nineteenth centuries, one area of the modern Caribbean basin owes its heritage to the legacy of the Spanish Empire; other segments were traditionally British preserve; a third area was French, and a final area, more diminutive, was dominated by the Netherlands in the colonial years. It is not surprising, therefore, as Solnick notes, that "often the history of the region is treated solely as a function of European colonial expansion."[1] Traditionally, one thinks of the modern Caribbean as the island nations, the descendants of the Spanish, English, French and Dutch Empires: Cuba, the Dominican Republic, Haiti, Puerto Rico, the U.S. Virgin Islands, the Netherlands Antilles (the main ones of which are Aruba and Curaçao), the French *départements* of Martinique, Guadeloupe, and Cayenne, and the main British colonies of Jamaica, Trinidad and Tobago, and Barbados. These areas, as one scholar observes, have had a common historical past rooted in European colonialism and economic dependency, combined with a heavily Afro-Caribbean population. This volume takes a broader approach, including not only those traditional island countries and dependencies but also the Caribbean basin, those nations of Central and northern South America whose shores touch the Caribbean and whose social, economic, political, and diplomatic history have been to a large extent intertwined with the island nations. Hence, the volume touches variously on Mexico, Guatemala, Honduras, Belize, Nicaragua, Costa Rica, Panama, Colombia, Venezuela, Guyana, and Surinam as well as El Salvador, whose history, although the nation does not border on the Caribbean, has generally intersected with the larger region (Map 1).[2] This is not to suggest that there is a unity to the basin; rather it tends to be a geopolitical entity; nonetheless, especially in the course of the twentieth century as U.S. hegemony displaced the older European colonialism, and the Caribbean became an American lake, that U.S. hegemony in itself has provided a unity to the area. At the same time, one must be cautious not to exaggerate the impact of the United States culturally, politically, and economically or to ignore the significant and lingering legacy of both Europe and Africa in the Caribbean basin. Significant

1

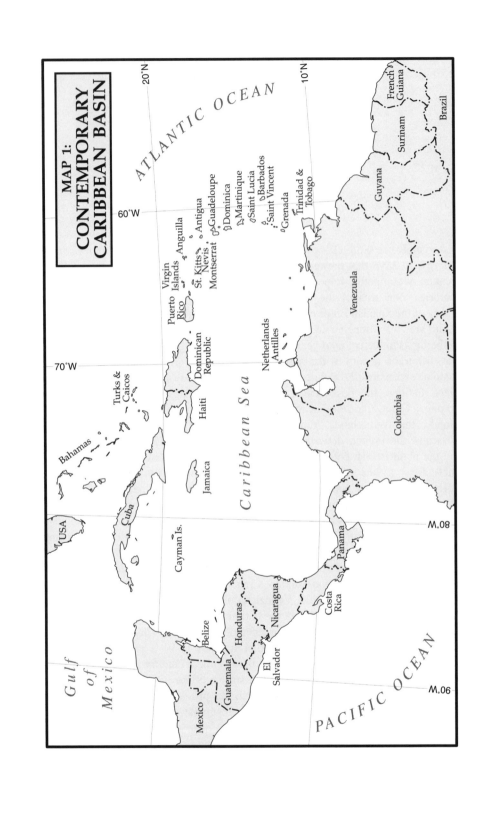

MAP 1:
CONTEMPORARY
CARIBBEAN BASIN

ATLANTIC OCEAN

Gulf of Mexico

Caribbean Sea

PACIFIC OCEAN

20°N

10°N

60°W

70°W

80°W

60°W

USA

Bahamas

Turks & Caicos

Cuba

Cayman Is.

Jamaica

Haiti

Dominican Republic

Puerto Rico

Virgin Islands

Anguilla

St. Kitts
Nevis
Montserrat

Antigua

Guadeloupe

Dominica

Martinique

Saint Lucia

Barbados

Saint Vincent

Grenada

Trinidad & Tobago

Netherlands Antilles

Venezuela

Colombia

Panama

Costa Rica

Nicaragua

Honduras

Belize

Guatemala

El Salvador

Mexico

Guyana

Surinam

French Guiana

Brazil

as well have been the intra-regional developments, from efforts to achieve federations and common trade blocs on the positive side to the history of human migrations and conflict on another side.[3]

Clearly, a one-volume study of the "new" international history of the Caribbean basin cannot do full justice to the remarkably rich and varied domestic cultural, economic, and political history, let alone the international history, of the region. Formidable as the task may be, this volume nonetheless is intended as an attempt to bridge that gulf between the domestic and international history of the Caribbean from the eighteenth through the late twentieth centuries.

As Solnick suggests, such an analysis must go beyond the obvious dominance in the twentieth century of the United States, even though any international history of the Caribbean basin will, of necessity, stress the presence of the United States during the past hundred years. The tendency has been, however, for foreign policy analyses of the region to be undertaken largely as bilateral studies: the United States and Cuba, the United States and Haiti, etc., rather than attempting to examine the more complex international dynamic that has often been at the root of relations in the region: the rivalry among European empires in the pre-Napoleonic period; the Haitian revolution in the 1790s; the impact of the wars for independence against Spain and Portugal in the post-Napoleonic period; the decline of Spain and the rise of the United States in the course of the nineteenth century; the brief arrival of Germany in the region in the decade prior to World War I; U.S. hegemony in the course of the twentieth century; decolonization in the British and Dutch Empires; and the challenge from the Soviet Union following the Cuban revolution. Beyond the involvement of the major powers in the region has been the important dynamic among the Caribbean basin nations and colonies themselves, including foreign trade, competing territorial ambitions, human migrations, and cross-border cultural/ intellectual linkages, among other activities that have interwoven their common histories. It is often difficult to narrowly distinguish between the domestic and international dimensions of many of these issues. Certainly this volume is not intended to be a history of the domestic developments of the nations of the basin except to the extent that such domestic developments have impacted on the international dynamic.

Imperial tensions have shaped the broader contours of the area; yet that international history has to be viewed within the context of both indigenous political, social, intellectual, and economic transformations in the region and those developments that lie on the intersection between domestic and international history: the rise of capitalist economic systems, colonial–metropolitan dependency, decolonization movements, human migration. It is difficult to separate entirely from the international arena even more traditionally domestic issues, including slavery and race relations; the rise of political party systems; the emergence of anti-colonial nationalism; the development of labour movements, among other features of the "domestic" history of the area. The world systems conceptual model, originally advanced by political sociologist

3

Immanuel Wallerstein and subsequently adapted to foreign policy analysis, is an especially useful tool to examine the international history of the Caribbean basin.[4] The Wallerstein model, which places its primary emphasis on the impact of capitalism on the relationship between the periphery and the metropolis, and which is remarkably valuable for understanding both great power relations and the relationship with dependent nations, may not be sufficiently nubile to explain all of the intraregional and indigenous developments in the area. Yet, as one senses from a reading of the literature of, for instance, V. S. Naipaul, the *mentalité* of the Caribbean basin has been overwhelmingly shaped by those colonial-dependency relationships as well as the ubiquitous factors of race, class, ethnicity, and religion.[5]

This study traces the international history of the Caribbean basin from the late eighteenth century to the present, beginning with an overview of the independence movements in the era of the French Revolution and the Napoleonic wars. The wars for independence against Spain and the Haitian revolution of the 1790s against French control represented major watersheds in the history not only of the Caribbean basin and Latin America more generally but also of the western world. The independence movements between 1790 and the 1820s were considerably less of a watershed in the British and Dutch Caribbean, and frankly for the French Empire, which remained intact except for the important loss of Haiti. As well, Great Britain had already deprived France of New France on the North American continent in the Seven Years War in the mid-eighteenth century, and the fledgling United States had obtained the massive interior of the continent – the Louisiana Purchase – from a cash-strapped Napoleon in 1803, thus significantly reducing the French role in the region as the nineteenth century dawned. Weakened as it was by internal political turmoil and the wars for independence, Spain nonetheless retained dominion over Cuba – the jewel of the Caribbean – and Puerto Rico for the balance of the century.

The apparent stability among the European nations that followed the wars for independence and of the Napoleonic period – the Metternichian peace – obscured not only emerging conflicts in Europe but also continuing international rivalries over power and principle in the Caribbean basin. The imperial powers clashed over the slave trade as well as the efficacy of slavery between the 1820s and 1870s, access to markets and raw materials, strategic positions in the region, including those issues that combined major strategic and economic advantage, such as the Anglo-American, and briefly French, rivalry over an isthmian canal from mid-nineteenth to early twentieth century. The mid-nineteenth century witnessed the emergence of the United States as a major actor in the region, with increasing commercial and geopolitical competition between the United States and Great Britain. One focus of such competition was an isthmian canal. In 1846, the United States and Colombia concluded the Bidlack Treaty; in 1850, Britain and the United States signed the Clayton-Bulwer Treaty of 1850, preventing either power from constructing and fortifying a canal against the other in the region. In that imperial rivalry, the fact that the Panamanian canal route was

Colombian territory through the nineteenth century is easily overlooked. With stalemate on the canal front, American interests moved ahead in the aftermath of the California gold rush to complete a Panamanian railroad, with steamship connections to both California on the west coast and the major cities on the U.S. eastern seaboard. The period also witnessed U.S. filibustering expeditions into Cuba and Nicaragua, Anglo-American tensions over Texas and the Mexican–American war of 1846.

Regional powers such as Colombia clashed not only with the imperial powers in the area, of course, but also with the other lesser powers in the region, with conflicts centring on such issues as borders and territorial controls, and access to mineral and other resources. Among the major ongoing tensions of the period were those between Venezuela and British Guiana on the one hand and Venezuela and Colombia on the other over boundaries, as well as the persistent opposition by other Central American powers against the British control of British Honduras/Belize. Most of the independent countries also faced internal revolutionary and secessionist movements; one of the most important in the course of the nineteenth century provided the subsequent occasion for the secession of Panama from Colombia and the construction by the United States of the Panama Canal early in the twentieth century.

The late nineteenth and early twentieth centuries witnessed the industrial revolution in the United States and Germany and the maturation of industrial and finance capitalism in Britain. With expanded industrial production and increasingly mechanized agriculture in North America and western Europe the quest for markets for production as well as for raw materials to meet demands in the industrial sector further strengthened linkages between the largely Third World nations of the Caribbean basin and the industrial metropolises. The main expansion of the late nineteenth and early twentieth centuries was in mining and oil extraction and refining, railroads, plantations, public utilities, and banking, as the capitalist nations transformed the economies of the region in order to meet their own economic needs. The United States was not the only player, of course. Great Britain was a major investor in all sectors, particularly in transportation and banking, as was Canada, which was important in mining, transportation and banking, in the latter area well ahead of the Americans.

Just as the emergence of industrial and finance capitalism marked the major economic watershed in the region, so in the strategic and political arena the Spanish-American–Cuban War of 1898 marked a major turning point. The Treaty of Paris late that year, which brought Puerto Rico and Cuba into the United States' sphere of influence and control, and Spain's departure from the hemisphere ended a century-long historical development that began with the wars for independence in the early nineteenth century. The main loss was Cuba, which remained at that stage the most important colonial possession of the old empire but which had economically for decades been moving into the U.S. economic and strategic orbit. What was a watershed for Spain was also one for both the United States and Cuba, as the former moved toward a more externally oriented political culture and greater engagement with the international community, and Cuba moved formally into the U.S. orbit for three decades under a U.S. protectorate.

Following World War I and the economic decline of Europe, there was little challenge to U.S. hegemony in the entire region. European imperial powers remained in the West Indies and on the Central American and South American mainland, but they gradually became of less significance in shaping the history of the region as U.S. economic and military power increased. The 1920s especially witnessed remarkable capital expansion by the United States in the Caribbean region, an expansion that the European nations were in no condition to emulate following the devastation of World War I. There was a brief challenge to U.S. hegemony from Nazi Germany in the late 1930s and during World War II, and there was widespread European influence in the region in such sectors as the labour movement, where anarchists, socialists, and communists were influential during the interwar years, but on the whole the history of the period from 1900 through 1945 was one of steadily increasing U.S. dominance.

Indeed, one of the dilemmas that confronted the independent countries of the Caribbean basin in the interwar and early Cold War years was the lack of a balance of power to offset U.S. hegemony, leaving the United States with both free rein and self-determined responsibility to police the region. From the first occupation of Cuba following the Spanish-American War until the end of the American protectorate over the island with the abrogation of the Platt Amendment in 1934, the United States frequently used military force in an effort to maintain stability. In response to a perceived "loosening of the ties of civilization" in the Caribbean, President Theodore Roosevelt pronounced the Roosevelt Corollary to the Monroe Doctrine, asserting the right to exert a police power in the region. The Corollary was more specifically a direct response to the increasing indebtedness of Caribbean nations to European powers and the clear intent of the Germans, Italians and others to collect their debts. The result was both gunboat and dollar diplomacy over the next three decades: U.S. military occupation of Cuba (1898–1902, 1906–9, 1912, 1917–22); of Haiti (1915–34); of the Dominican Republic (1916–24, financial control 1905–41); of Nicaragua (1909–10, 1912–25, financial supervision 1911–24). During World War I, the Woodrow Wilson administration, otherwise committed to a moral diplomacy and non-territorial expansion, further expanded the U.S. formal empire with the purchase of the Virgin Islands in 1917. And in Mexico, the Wilson administration on two occasions committed military forces in an effort to shape the direction of the Mexican revolution.

Until a series of conferences of inter-American states elicited a commitment to non-intervention in the internal affairs of the countries of the region, and until the Franklin Roosevelt administration committed itself to the Good Neighbor Policy, the use of force remained a constant threat. The actual use of force also left behind a historical legacy which remained a major source of discontent, ill-will and friction between the United States and the countries in the region in subsequent generations. That was especially pronounced in – though certainly limited to – Nicaragua, where the United States a half- century later reaped the whirlwind of the lengthy conflict with Augusto Sandino.

It was not surprising that under those circumstances, the pre-1945 years should have witnessed the emergence of anti-colonial nationalism in the region. Not all of that nationalism was directed toward the United States, since the French, British, and Dutch remained important imperial powers in the area. In European territories, the emergent nationalism logically concentrated on efforts to acquire independence; in the case of the independent countries nationalism was reflected in a wide range of economic, political, and cultural developments, although economic nationalism was the most common and pronounced. Economic nationalism took several forms, including restrictions on foreign investment, particularly in the sensitive natural resource sector, and protection for indigenous workers and organized labour. Colombia, for instance, passed legislation in the 1920s designed to enhance national controls over its oil industry and, in the 1930s, President Alfonso López Pumarejo continued that trend as well as implementing protective legislation for labour. The major act of economic nationalism in the period was Mexican nationalization of most of the foreign-owned oil companies active in the country in 1938. As in Mexico, in Trinidad oil workers became increasingly militant during the 1930s. Cuba also passed through a number of revolutionary situations in the late 1920s and early 1930s until Fulgencio Batista emerged as the strongman of the next three decades. On the whole, the interwar years were ones of ferment in the region, but World War II muted that ferment and increased the need for hemispheric solidarity, political stability and U.S. access to and control over strategic bases and raw materials. World War II was also less of a watershed for the Caribbean basin in terms of the international power balance than the Spanish-American War had been at the turn of the century. By 1940, the United States was already pre-eminent in the region; the war simply served to consolidate that position, and there was no further challenge until after the Cuban revolution and the insertion of the Soviet Union into the equation.

Cold War, decolonization, and economic development have been the operative motifs in the post-World War II years. The east–west, Soviet–American polarization that characterized the Cold War made American and to a lesser extent European powers active in the region highly sensitive to the intrusion and perceived intrusion of Soviet and communist influences in the area, whether in the political, labour, or intellectual spheres. In the 1940s and 1950s, Cold War concerns focused on Colombia, Venezuela, Guatemala, Cuba, British Guiana, the Dominican Republic, and Haiti, although Panama remained a trouble spot for the United States because of ongoing pressures to improve the Panamanian advantages from the canal.

Prior to the Cuban revolution, Britain and the United States especially confronted a number of Cold War challenges in the region. An important concern for both powers was the perceived threat of a leftist leaning regime in British Guiana early in the decade with the 1953 election of the People's Progressive

Party under Cheddi Jagan, a situation that led to British military action. There were similar if lesser British concerns over Jamaica under Norman Manley and Barbados under Grantley Adams. For the United States, Guatemala proved to be a preoccupation during the Arévalo and Arbenz years, with the leftist government leading the United States to support a surrogate invasion and counter-revolution in 1954. Both economic development and persistent nationalist yearnings proved to be more important factors in Puerto Rico for the United States than the Cold War concerns that dominated elsewhere.

The Castro-Cuban revolution in 1959 marked the most significant turning point in the history of the region since the Spanish-American War had driven Spain from the area. The success of Castro's revolution, its rejection by the Dwight D. Eisenhower and John F. Kennedy administrations (as well as every U.S. administration since 1959) contributed to drive Cuba and Castro into the Soviet bloc, creating for the next three decades the most significant challenge to western national security in the hemisphere in the twentieth century. The final sections of this volume are thus concerned with the international impact of the Cuban revolution in the region since 1959 leading to the crises of the 1970s and 1980s in Central America, Grenada, and Guyana, the winding down of the Cold War, the withdrawal of the Soviet Union from the region and the isolation of Cuba.

Since the mid-1960s there has been a greater emphasis on decolonization throughout the region, emergent nationalism, and economic development. At the time of the Cuban revolution, only Cuba, the Dominican Republic, and Haiti among the island nations were independent; but by 1980, that had increased to thirteen island nations, and most of the French, British, and Dutch mainland dependencies had attained independence (Surinam in 1975 (subsequently called Suriname), Jamaica, Trinidad and Tobago in 1964), and Puerto Rico held Commonwealth status in association with the United States (Map 2). Belize remained a British crown colony with complete internal self-government after 1964. During the Cold War years, a number of Caribbean nations and colonies leaned heavily toward Cuba or the non-aligned movement. For Britain, a major challenge was the necessity to come to terms politically and psychologically with the reality of the nation's decline as a world power, although by the 1950s the West Indies were as much a liability as an asset.

The Caribbean basin has been characterized as much by diversity as by commonality. The major nations of the region – Mexico, Colombia, and Venezuela – have had little in common with their lesser island and mainland neighbours. Language – Spanish, French, English, Dutch, Hindi – has been as much a dividing as unifying element, as has the wide diversity of religion throughout the area. Yet, the countries of the region have shared a European colonial heritage; they have also been affected by the emergence of the United States in the twentieth century as the undisputed hegemon; they were all affected by the Cold War, east–west tensions and the Cuban revolution; they have all experienced, in varying degrees, the process of decolonization and the challenges

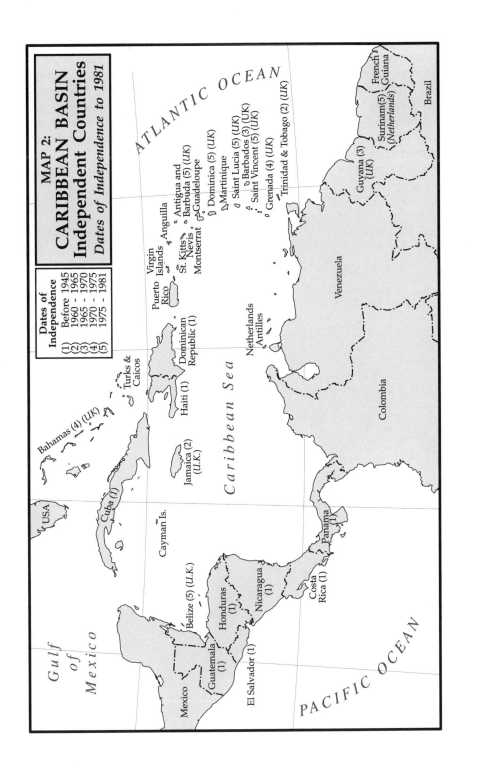

MAP 2:
**CARIBBEAN BASIN
Independent Countries**
Dates of Independence to 1981

**Dates of
Independence**
(1) Before 1945
(2) 1960 - 1965
(3) 1965 - 1970
(4) 1970 - 1975
(5) 1975 - 1981

ATLANTIC OCEAN

French
Guiana

Surinam (5)
(*Netherlands*)

Brazil

Guyana (3)
(*UK*)

Trinidad & Tobago (2) (*UK*)

Grenada (4) (*UK*)

Saint Vincent (5) (*UK*)

Barbados (3) (*UK*)

Saint Lucia (5) (*UK*)

Martinique

Dominica (5) (*UK*)

Guadeloupe

Barbuda (5) (*UK*)

Antigua and

Anguilla

Virgin
Islands

St. Kitts
Nevis
Montserrat

Puerto
Rico

Dominican
Republic (1)

Turks &
Caicos

Haiti (1)

Bahamas (4) (*UK*)

Jamaica (2)
(*U.K.*)

Caribbean Sea

Netherlands
Antilles

Venezuela

Colombia

Cuba (1)

USA

Cayman Is.

Panama
(1)

Costa
Rica (1)

Belize (5) (*U.K.*)

Honduras
(1)

Nicaragua
(1)

Guatemala (1)

Mexico

El Salvador (1)

*Gulf
of
Mexico*

PACIFIC OCEAN

of modernization and economic development. They have been drawn together by common needs into a variety of regional organizations: the Organization of American States (OAS), the Central American Common Market, the Caribbean Free Trade Area (CARIFTA) and subsequently the Caribbean Community and Common Market (CARICOM). The history of the Caribbean basin is a rich tapestry, in which the vitality of the culture, the challenges of economic development, and the problems of external dependency have been closely interwoven.

1

THE LEGACY OF EMPIRES

From the seventeenth through the nineteenth centuries, the Caribbean basin area was the arena in which most major and several minor European powers played out their imperial ambitions. Theories of empire – the role and value of colonies, the nature of wealth, and the dynamic of trade and investment – altered in the course of those centuries, ranging from statist mercantilist systems to a higher degree of free trade in the course of the nineteenth century. The nature of labour, patterns of settlement, and the relative importance of colonization by the metropolis evolved, with African slavery, which was predominant, indentured labour, and various forms of forced labour gradually giving way in the course of the nineteenth century to free labour systems and a higher degree of migration of peoples from the colonizing powers. Systems of governance also evolved, with a gradual movement away from centralized colonial rule involving little local participation to increased local autonomy and, in some instances, actual independence by the end of the nineteenth century, although most of the real independence was delayed well into the twentieth.

Although theories of empire and the relative value of colonies and of the Caribbean basin in general may have varied from one nation to another, few major powers, especially those seafaring nations with pretensions to international dominance, could avoid involvement in the region. From the seventeenth through the nineteenth centuries, the main players in the area were Great Britain, France, and Spain, with the Netherlands and Denmark playing comparatively less significant parts, although the Dutch had entered the region in force in the early seventeenth century. In the course of the nineteenth century, the United States also emerged as a more significant actor in the imperial drama, but the demise of the old empires and the rise of the new was not completed until the next century.

The motivation for empire rarely rose above the simple reality of naked power – economic, strategic, and political – although the perception of what constituted power might have changed over the course of the centuries. The initial attraction of the region, other than as a route to the Orient, was mineral wealth, primarily gold and silver, and, by the end of the colonial period, the islands and mainlands of the basin were dotted with major harbours for the transhipment of precious metals from Peru and Mexico and of fortresses for their protection against imperial rivals and privateers. The emergence of major plantation systems in the course of the seventeenth through the nineteenth centuries altered the role of the colonies and the social-labour dynamic in the region. An emphasis on sugar, tobacco, and coffee cultivation for export intensified demands for large numbers of comparatively inexpensive labourers, which were supplied in the main by the slave ships from Africa until the final end of the slave trade in the 1860s and the last vestiges of slavery itself in the 1880s.

Since the main objective of empire in the Caribbean was exploitation in the interest of the metropolitan core, it was not surprising that the region would be the source of frequent wars of imperial rivalry among the major powers. And, given the exploitative nature of the labour system that characterized the region, it was probable that there would be long-term racial and class conflict in the area as well. Admittedly, however, there were important differences in this regard between the large slave-labour sugar islands in the Caribbean and such mainland areas as Mexico, Central America, Colombia, and Venezuela, where the economies were more complex and the racial lines more blurred.

The main characteristics of Caribbean basin history through the nineteenth century, therefore, and the legacy of those centuries to subsequent generations, were imperial rivalry, war, forced and voluntary labour migration, slavery and indentured servitude, widespread racial conflict, class consciousness that was frequently tied to skin colour, a comparative absence of independent political experience, limited economic development and diversification, with economies generally monocultural in nature, and a widely shared sense of exploitation at the hands of the imperial powers. One could characterize this as a positive legacy only if one believes that such hardship built the character of the peoples in the Caribbean basin.

The Caribbean basin prior to the Spanish-American wars for independence

Christopher Columbus provided the first link between the Caribbean basin and overseas empire. Following Columbus's 1492 voyage in the service of Spain, Pope Alexander VI (a Spaniard) issued a Papal Bull which divided the non-Christian world between Spain and Portugal. By the terms of that Bull, Spain inherited the entire Caribbean basin. The Treaty of Tordesillas, concluded between Spain and Portugal in 1494, confirmed that arrangement.

Other European countries, however, gradually challenged the Spanish monopoly in the area. Protestant nations in particular were little impressed by papal authority to dictate global territorial division. King Francis I of France (1515–47), although himself a Roman Catholic, thought that his country had rights in America. At the same time, and most significantly, in the game of international power politics, Spain lacked the military and economic capacity to enforce its monopoly, forcing it to concentrate its strength on the larger and more important islands and coastal areas. The larger islands within the Caribbean were also inhabited by the gentle Arawak Indians, who seemed easy prey to the Spaniards in contrast to the fierce Caribs of the Eastern Caribbean. Spain's decision to concentrate its strength left other areas free to satisfy the ambitions of other Europeans – explorers, adventurers, and settlers from England, France, the Netherlands, and Denmark. As well, in 1655, when Puritan Oliver Cromwell headed the English government, English sailors also seized Jamaica, which despite its size, economic potential, and Arawak population had been largely neglected by Spain. Of more importance to the European balance of power than to the Caribbean, the wars of Louis XIV of France in the late seventeenth century, again altered the territorial balance in the area; among other provisions, the Treaty of Ryswick (Netherlands) in 1797 divided Hispaniola between France and Spain, thus establishing the basis for modern Haiti and the Dominican Republic. The Treaty of Utrecht (1713), which ended the War of the Spanish Succession (1702–13), had little direct territorial impact on the Caribbean, but it did serve to provide a greater degree of balance among England, France, and Spain in world affairs, and it also furthered the English ambition to advance its commercial position in the Americas and block French merchants from gaining access to Spanish American markets.

Between the 1750s and the 1820s, the region underwent a significant transformation. There was a series of major colonial wars, dominated by the shifting alliances and enmities among the British, French, and Spanish culminating in the Seven Years War (1756–63). By 1783, most British colonies on the mainland succeeded in gaining their independence from Great Britain, and this development had major short- and long-term implications for the area. Many of the major Spanish-American colonies – primarily on the mainland – successfully took advantage of the wars of the French Revolution and the Napoleonic era to realize their own independence from Spain, as did Saint Dominique (Haiti), considered the world's most valuable colony at the time of its rupture from France in the 1790s.[1]

The eighteenth century witnessed a series of colonial wars among the three major powers in the Americas: Britain, France, and Spain. Conflict was for territorial control and the defence of mercantilistic trade – or conversely the effort to break down trade monopolies. Throughout the century, and before, British merchants attempted to ignore Spanish trading laws in the region and conducted a lively trade at the expense of the Spanish treasury, and from the 1730s France and Spain allied against British efforts to expand activities and holdings in the area. Following the War of the Spanish Succession in 1714, Spain sought to tighten its controls over illegal trade. This involved the commissioning of *guarda-costas*, privateering vessels whose profits were to be shared with the Spanish crown, and the tightening of maritime court actions against illegal foreign traders. Tensions between the two powers led to war in 1739, the War of Jenkins's Ear. In the same year British forces seized Portobello on the isthmus of Panama and, as the war widened into the War of the Austrian Succession

(1740–8), the English navy unsuccessfully sought to capture both Cartagena on the coast and Havana (La Habana), two of the major fortified harbours in the region. Failure though these British initiatives may have been, they made it evident that there would be continued imperial confrontation in the area.

Less than a decade later, the conflict resumed in the form of the Seven Years War (1756–63), predominantly a war between French and British imperial ambitions but which by 1762 also involved Spain. The main theatre of action, as well as the main objectives of the Anglo-French conflict during the Seven Years War, was North America, and even the Indian subcontinent was part of the war; but the Caribbean figured prominently in the conflict. Since the primary British objective under William Pitt was to destroy France as an imperial power, it was not surprising that the valuable trade and sugar plantations of the Caribbean region should have been among the prizes sought by British policy makers. In the course of the war, British forces managed to occupy for various periods of time all the major French island colonies except for the most significant – Saint Dominigue. With the British declaration of war in 1761 against Spain as well, British forces turned their guns on the most important of Spanish possessions in the region – the harbour and treasury at Havana – taking the city in mid-1762 following a difficult and lengthy siege.

The Treaty of Paris (1763), which ended the Seven Years War, resulted in some territorial change in the Caribbean, although it was apparent that British military victories in the area over both the French and Spanish were designed to provide leverage elsewhere in the empires. Hence, the British relinquished Martinique and Saint Lucia, while retaining the Grenadines, Dominica, Saint Vincent, Tobago, and Grenada. Havana, perhaps the major prize of the war, was returned to Spain in exchange for British control over Florida. The small and highly vulnerable islands of the eastern Caribbean proved to be easy targets in the imperial struggles, some changing hands many times and often only briefly over the centuries. Their size and proximity to one another made them both easy prey and highly tempting.

The fortunes of empire can shift swiftly; for the British, the last quarter of the eighteenth century following the triumphs of the Seven Years War brought a dramatic reversal, as Britain lost its American colonies in a long and costly war – in human, material, and psychological terms. For the Caribbean basin, British preoccupation with the Thirteen Colonies provided France and ultimately Spain with an opportunity to recoup on their losses of the Seven Years War. The Caribbean was the main theatre of action for the French navy for most of the Anglo-American conflict until it played a critical role in 1781 at the Battle of Yorktown, which brought the war to an end. British diversion from the West Indies left its island possessions highly vulnerable, with the result that many of the small English islands were at one time or another taken by foreign assault. By the end of 1782, the French had captured St. Kitts, Monserrat, and Nevis and held all of the Leeward Islands except Antigua and most of the Windward Islands. The Spanish, who also coveted Jamaica, managed in the course of the year to gain control of New Providence in the Bahamas. Although they were not captured, the French navy blockaded both Jamaica and Barbados, in the process depriving the islanders of imported foodstuffs and other supplies and causing massive numbers of deaths among the population, especially of Jamaican slaves.

In one area, Britain did make inroads in the region during its conflict with the American colonies. In 1780, it declared war on the Netherlands and in the course of battle gained control over a number of Dutch islands, including Saint Barthélemy, Saint Maarten, Saba, and Statia, none of which held the economic importance of British Jamaica or French Saint Dominique.

The Treaty of Versailles (1783) that ended the American War of Independence had substantial implications for the major empires. The psychological and material loss to Great Britain was in itself immeasurable, and it also placed the metropolitan centres on notice that wars for independence among their more powerful colonies would be a major force with which they would have to contend in the coming decades. In the short term, the 1783 treaty had little impact on actual territorial holdings in the Caribbean, with Britain regaining what had been captured by France, with Spain gaining Florida, and with France retaining Tobago and Saint Lucia. More cataclysmic events would not be long in coming to the empires and their colonies in the Caribbean basin.

The onset of the French Revolution in 1789 and the Wars of the French Revolution in the 1790s, followed shortly by the emergence of Napoleon Bonaparte and the establishment of the first French Empire, heralded a transformation of monumental proportions for Europe and its overseas world. The Revolution and its international wars not only brought military and political change but also stimulated new ideas or provided a vehicle for older ideas to gain momentum. Along with the rationalism of the Enlightenment with the increased questioning of established values and institutions came the more revolutionary concepts in France of liberty, equality, and fraternity that became the rallying cry of revolution and of international war.

Such ideas seemed highly threatening for imperial powers with colonies, where forced labour was the norm; yet, it is doubtful that when revolution came – as it did in Saint Domingue in the 1790s – slaves and their leaders were driven by abstract notions of liberty rather than the brutality of the slave system itself and the racial hatred it engendered. Most importantly, especially for the French and Spanish colonies of the Caribbean area, the European wars of the French Revolution and Napoleonic period created a vacuum of power in the colonies that made possible colonial movements of independence.

Saint Domingue was the first and the most significant – economically, racially and psychologically – revolution of the late eighteenth and early nineteenth centuries, on one level symbolically more important even than that of the revolt of the American Thirteen Colonies against Britain. The imperial and white colonial fear of slave rebellion was a given throughout the colonial era, and the Caribbean, far more than the United States before or after independence, experienced frequent revolts of varying magnitude throughout these years.[2] Colonies of runaway slaves known as *maroons* were a significant phenomenon in the Caribbean region in the eighteenth and nineteenth centuries, and, depending on the nature of the imperial rivalries at any given time, slaves were often able to take advantage of those conflicts to seek refuge in another colony. So powerful were the *maroons* in Jamaica in the mid-eighteenth century, that British authorities imported Mosquito Indians from Central America in an ultimately unsuccessful effort to destroy the power of the renegade colonies. Failing in their effort at destruction, the British reached an agreement in 1738 establishing two homelands in Jamaica, an arrangement that remained in force until Jamaica achieved full independence in 1962.[3] At times, Spanish Puerto Rico provided refuge for slaves from British, Dutch, and Danish possessions. Spanish Santo Domingo, which shared the island with Saint Domingue, provided freedom to runaway slaves reaching its territory in the late eighteenth century; Cuba was also an important destination for runaway Jamaican slaves.

Saint Domingue's quest in the 1790s for emancipation of slaves through rebellion and the elimination of white rulers was of immense importance to the potential course of events throughout the region in the years that followed. Not only did the successful slave revolt strike terror in the hearts of slaveholders throughout the region, but the migration of former slaveholders to British and Spanish colonies in the region exerted a highly conservative influence on their new societies. Saint Domingue was overwhelmingly the richest colonial possession in the region when the French Revolution began, indeed of all contemporary colonies. The fact that its economy was monocultural was of little concern to French authorities. Its more than 7,000 plantations (mostly sugar but also coffee) produced an export trade that represented 40 percent of French foreign trade in 1789. Remarkably, it produced more sugar than all of the British possessions combined, and half the coffee consumed in the world came from the highland plantations.[4]

The political and social balance in Saint Domingue was fragile, however, with almost half a million slaves against only 40,000 whites and 26,000 free people of colour. With the uncertainty that followed revolution in France, and in spite of the fact that the French National Convention in 1790 invited colonial delegates, authorized colonies to establish legislatures and identified the colonies as integral parts of the mother country, revolt on the island came swiftly in 1789. It began with conflicting factions of whites, those opposed and those in favour of developments in France, with white slaveholders opposed to the abolitionist-leanings of French metropolitan leaders facing off against Royalist forces. The failure of white French leaders to move beyond support for a traditional slave and racist society led to a slave uprising fomented by free coloured leaders left out of the political and cultural transformation that was taking place around them. In 1791, the French Assembly extended full political rights to the small, free coloured population of Saint Domingue, but the refusal of the white French elite to accept such a concession meant civil and racial warfare, with much of the slave revolt concentrated in the North Province, where slaves massacred their former masters and destroyed once valuable plantations. Revolt quickly spread throughout Saint Domingue, spurred on by the French government's decision to abolish the slave trade in 1793 and slavery itself throughout its colonies in 1794, the first abolitionist act in the modern world.

White resistance intensified, although by this stage most of the whites had been slaughtered or had fled to France, the United States or neighbouring islands. In an effort to regain the momentum in 1793, white leaders in the southern province appealed to the British, then at war with France, to send an invasion force to assist them in restoring order in the colony. Vigorously endorsed by British slaveholders in the region, British forces from Jamaica invaded in September 1793, quickly taking the port cities from the French, at the same time attacking French interests throughout the Caribbean, rapidly gaining control of Saint Lucia, Martinique, and Guadeloupe.

The Anglo-French struggles over control of the islands continued through the decade, with territory constantly changing hands, especially as French power expanded in Europe. By the end of the decade, Britain controlled many of the French islands. It captured Trinidad in 1797, when the Spanish government allied itself with revolutionary France, and the Dutch islands when France overran the Netherlands and Spain. Yet, what was most significant about the developments in that period was the frequency of slave revolts on many of the islands and the transition of the Saint Domingue revolution into a slave-led and dominated political and military movement that successfully resisted the efforts of local white and metropolitan leaders to restore order. By the end of the century, the Haitian revolution was led by free blacks and former slaves, the most important of whom were the educated, property-holding freedman Toussaint L'Ouverture and his main military lieutenant Jean-Jacques Dessalines, an African-born slave. By 1804, Dessalines had gained control not only of French Saint Domingue but also, briefly, of Spanish Santo Domingo and had, with the aid of tropical disease, defeated a major French expeditionary force led by Napoleonic General Charles Leclerc. Although the Haitian experience proved to be unique, the former colony was independent and slavery was permanently abolished, a vivid reminder to the other slaveholding colonies of the Caribbean basin and the United States of what the future held, but, tragically, for the next two centuries the fledgling country slipped into economic backwardness, political turmoil, and widespread poverty.[5]

Napoleon and the Spanish-American wars for independence

The American and Haitian revolutions were the pinnacle of revolutionary success in the Americas prior to Napoleon's invasion of Portugal and Spain in 1807–8, invasions which radically transformed the colonial landscape in the Americas. There had nonetheless been significant transfers of territory during the Wars of the French Revolution. In 1800, Napoleon pressured Spain into ceding the massive Louisiana territories, then sold it three years later to the United States. The 1802 Treaty of Amiens among Britain, France, and Spain confirmed British rights to Trinidad, which had superior harbour facilities and close proximity to South America for trade – both legal and illegal. Nonetheless, the Spanish Empire in the region was relatively intact as the nineteenth century began.

Less than two decades later, Spanish fortunes had turned full circle, however, as a result of the Napoleonic invasion as well as indigenous dissatisfaction with Spanish rule in the Americas. Spain's empire in the Americas had been largely stripped away, leaving only Cuba and Puerto Rico firmly in Spanish hands, where they remained for the balance of the century.

Of the two forces – Napoleon and Creole desires for independence – the impact of Napoleon was by far the more weighty. Clearly there was dissatisfaction in the colonies with such issues as taxation, trade policies, and local political power, but when the flag of revolt had been raised, as by Francisco de Miranda with British support in Venezuela there was little popular echo, and such revolts were easily crushed. Once Napoleon invaded Spain and in 1808 placed his brother Joseph on the Spanish throne the international dynamic was substantially transformed. Joseph's hold on Spain did not last long. For several years he faced sustained Spanish resistance, bolstered by British forces; but it was this diversion and uncertainty of the locus of Spanish authority which meant disaster in the colonies. In Spain and its colonies, there were persistent conflicts between those who sought a restoration of a legitimate monarch and liberals who saw an opportunity to achieve substantial reform of governance, which they appeared to achieve in the 1812 Spanish Constitution.

For Spanish colonists without significant participation in the Spanish conflict or domestic political debate such developments seemed remote, and years of neglect of the colonies took their toll in building opposition to a restoration of meaningful Spanish authority in the colonies. That effort came with the return of Ferdinand VII to the Spanish throne in 1814. Ferdinand quickly sought to restore imperial power over the colonies and, beginning in 1815 with major expeditions to Venezuela and New Grenada, he fought unsuccessfully to regain what had already been largely lost as power shifted from Spanish-born colonists known as Peninsulares to American-born Creoles, who had gained their wealth and power in such areas as agriculture, trade and mining. Conservative Creoles, like their peninsular counterparts, were not social revolutionaries; indeed they frequently allied in resisting radical social change, such as that which had turned Haiti to flames. In 1810–11, Mexican Creoles opposed Father Miguel Hidalgo y Castilla and José Maria Morelos and the largely Indian and mestizo rebels they inspired. Although authorities crushed their rebellion and executed both leaders, Indian and mestizo resistance against both conservative Creoles and Spaniards was emblematic of a more radical independence movement than ultimately prevailed in most of the Caribbean rim. Between 1822 and 1844, Haiti established military control over Santo Domingo.

Elsewhere, a number of former colonies moved toward total independence. By 1821, New Spain (Mexico) attained its independence, but it was a conservative independence that rejected Spanish liberals; Panama, until 1821 part of the Vice-royalty of New Grenada, joined the independent Republic of New Grenada; the Captaincy-General of Guatemala, as much as a result of the developments that were occurring on its northern and southern frontiers, declared independence in 1821; by constitutional agreement between Venezuela and New Grenada the two nations joined as independent nations, while Spanish resistance held on until 1826 in Peru. By that time, the entire Caribbean rim, from Florida through Mexico, Central and the Caribbean coast of South America had changed hands, with few exceptions. The United States held all of Florida and Louisiana from the previous decade. In Central America, the region was independent of Europe except for the British presence in Belize and on the Mosquito coast of Nicaragua; on the South American coast, the Dutch retained part of Guyana, with the British receiving the territory that became British Guiana. The French also held control of a segment of that coastline. The borders between these states and, in particular, between British Guiana and Venezuela proved problematic, involving frequent diplomatic wrangling, sabre rattling among the parties, and international boundary commissions to resolve in the course of the next century. Although Spain retained Cuba and Puerto Rico, the islands represented only a shadow of the former empire.

Slavery and emancipation

Throughout the region, the nineteenth century witnessed growing disquiet about the institution of slavery and an important interplay among the major powers as well as among metropolitan political forces, colonial officials, slaveholders, and slaves themselves. As was so often the case in the history of the Caribbean basin, it was the interaction between local and foreign forces that determined local developments. In the case of slavery, it was this larger dynamic which brought about the demise first of the slave trade beginning with the British and Americans in 1807 and 1808 respectively, and then of the institution itself by the late 1880s, with Cuba the final Caribbean holdout.

On the former Spanish mainland, slavery was already an anachronism by the 1820s when the colonies gained their independence. For those colonies, emancipation came early and with little conflict. Necessity combined with ideology to end the institution in those areas. Creole leaders resisting Spain required manpower and provided freedom in return for military service; equally important was the fact that slavery was of less economic significance in Mexico, Central America, Colombia, and Venezuela than it was on the Caribbean sugar islands. Those practical considerations were of more importance than any ideological opposition to slavery, although one cannot entirely discount the impact of Enlightenment thought on revolutionary leaders in the former Spanish colonies. Formal abolition in Central America came in 1824, in Mexico in 1828, and in the remainder of independent Spanish America by 1858. Yet elsewhere in the Caribbean basin, as well as in the United States, slavery continued and in some instances demonstrated remarkable growth in the first half of the nineteenth century despite its critics.

In terms of both government policy and popular will, Britain provided much of the international leadership and requisite naval enforcement capability to bring the international traffic in human beings to an end well before there was any popular consensus on the desirability of slavery itself. Throughout the colonial era, the Caribbean basin had been the main recipient of the traffic in human cargo from Africa, primarily to work the sugar cane fields. Although Brazil was the single largest importer of slaves, more than 60 percent of the traffic went to the Caribbean in the eighteenth century. The Caribbean region imported more than 4 million Africans in that period in contrast to the approximately 2 million who reached all of the Americas in the course of the nineteenth century and another 1 million to the Caribbean in the last century of slavery. In the eighteenth century, the English and French Caribbean colonies dominated the trade, although the Dutch provided most of the shipping; the Spanish Caribbean accounted for only 10 percent of the traffic. In the nineteenth century, the Americans, British, and French were removed from the trade, but Spain continued to import large numbers of new slaves to fuel the dynamic sugar plantations of Cuba and, to a much lesser extent, Puerto Rico. The movement of slaves from Africa to the Americas was, especially given the difficulty of shipping in the pre-steam era, one of the greatest migrations, forced or free, in the history of humankind.[6]

Whatever the sentiments in the colonies, and there is no doubt that the opposition especially of slaves themselves and of free blacks was significant, it was decisions in the metropolitan centres that determined the fate of the slave trade and then slavery. The British and then U.S. termination of their involvement in the slave trade was significant for symbolic reasons, but also because the decision led to an increasingly intensive British pressure on other European governments to follow suit. The Dutch complied in 1814 at the end of the Napoleonic period. Spain, which never shared the widespread public revulsion against slavery, agreed by treaty in 1817 to end its involvement in slave trading by 1820, but in fact took no concrete action until the 1850s and even then virtually ignored another decade of illegal trafficking. During the years that Spain officially opposed slave trafficking, some half a million slaves entered Cuba, its most important plantation economy, and another 55,000 were transported to Puerto Rico. Spain was the last of the European nations to abolish slavery in its Caribbean possessions, and it did so only after a costly war in the 1870s. In 1880, Spanish authorities enacted non-compensated emancipation for slaves in Cuba and Puerto Rico, but as a concession to slaveholders provided an eight-year period of forced free labour – or *patronato* – for former masters. France adopted an equally hypocritical approach, agreeing by treaty with Britain in 1814 to end its participation in the slave trade after 1818, only to stand by while another 80,000 forced black labourers found their way onto the plantations of

Guadeloupe and Martinique prior to the 1830s. The curtailment of the trade derived as much from the strength and commitment of the British navy as any Spanish and French commitment to abolitionism, and even then Britain took little action until after it ended slavery in its territories in 1833.

The decision of the British Parliament in 1807 followed more than a decade of rising domestic political and popular opposition to the slave trade within the country. The Society for the Abolition of the Slave Trade was established in 1787, with William Wilberforce its main leader. Employing the same petition campaigns and clerical lobbying among parishioners – underlining the brutality, inhumanity, and evil of the trafficking – that characterized the main abolitionist onslaught a generation later, Parliament passed first in 1806 a Foreign Slave Bill which prohibited the shipping of slaves to Britain's newly acquired territories resulting from the Anglo-French–Spanish conflicts of the early Napoleonic wars; the same legislation was designed to stop British participation in slave traffic to the colonies of other nations. The following year, Parliament went the full distance, effectively ending the import of slaves into any British territories after March 1808. Additional treaties between 1808 and 1814 with Sweden and the Netherlands ended the carrying trade to their colonies as well.

With the accomplishment of the first goal – ending the slave trade – Wilberforce and his supporters turned their sights directly on the institution of slavery itself. Outright abolition was a more complex and difficult issue economically, politically, and psychologically for both the metropolitan governments and their colonies. For the colonial powers, it was always simpler to address the problem of slavery from a distance of several thousand miles than when the institution was interwoven into the fabric of one's social, political and economic existence. In the United States, abolition became the major source of sectional conflict between north and south, free and slave. Britain had only a few decades earlier lost much of its first empire through ill-conceived metropolitan policies and was loath to take actions that would alienate and cause possible rebellion in its Caribbean territories. Britain consequently adopted a gradualist and at least initially non-confrontational approach in the British Caribbean, beginning with legislation in 1815 requiring that all slaves be registered in an effort to control trafficking but also as part of a longer term preparation for emancipation itself. Britain followed the registration initiative with efforts in the 1820s to ameliorate the condition and treatment of slaves, much to the chagrin of colonial planters, who frequently ignored such restrictions on their autonomy. Throughout this period, abolitionist sentiment gained powerful adherents in Britain, and it was no oversight that an abolitionist, Sir James Stephen, administered Caribbean affairs in the Colonial Office.

If there was not open resistance from planters and slaveholders in general there was considerable lethargy in responding to metropolitan legislation until it served the economic and political self-interest of the slaveholders to move in that direction. Not until 1831, for instance, did Jamaica's colonial legislature pass a Bill adhering to the spirit of the Amelioration Acts of the previous decade; and then it did so in part in response to the massive slave rebellion that swept through the northwest section of the island. There, some 60,000 slaves, in part inspired by Baptist fire-and-brimstone lay preacher Sam Sharpe, destroyed several hundred plantations in the region, though killing barely a dozen whites.[7] Although this, like other slave revolts, was ultimately ruthlessly suppressed by troops, the constant fear of revolt and its frequent occurrence even in colonies such as Barbados which had few large-scale plantations, led slaveholders to reconsider the long-term viability of the institution.

Equally important, the Jamaican revolt aroused the passions of British abolitionists and their supporters in Britain, especially among the evangelical churches, which in turn escalated their petition campaigns against the institution. Confronted by their own convictions and those of several million of their constituents, British parliamentarians in 1833 passed an Abolition Act which ended slavery throughout the British Empire. The legislation provided for compensated emancipation – a paltry £25 sterling per slave – but sweetened that somewhat by requiring a period of indenture in several colonies (not Antigua or Barbados), during which slaves had to continue to labour without wage for their previous masters. For field hands, the indenture was six years, for domestic slaves only four. For later Trinidadian Prime Minister and historian Eric Williams, the ultimate hypocrisy was compensation for the slave owners but not the slaves.[8]

At the time of British emancipation there were more than 300,000 slaves in Jamaica, but only 22,000 in Trinidad, 15,000 in British Guiana (now Guyana), another 80,000 in Barbados, and a relatively insignificant slave population in British Honduras (now Belize).[9] It is important, as historians such as Franklin Knight have eloquently demonstrated, to understand the impact of emancipation on the Caribbean basin not solely in terms of the sugar economy but also in terms of the transition experienced by the former slaves.

Nonetheless, for imperial and colonial authorities, emancipation and the internal migration of former slaves meant substantially increased responsibilities for a variety of social and police services that were provided by slave owners prior to emancipation. Emancipation and political change in the Caribbean also meant the need to revise the structure of governance between colony and metropolitan centre. Spain's governance over Cuba and Puerto Rico was highly centralized in the nineteenth century, although that structure contributed to several sustained and major revolts on Cuba led by Creoles seeking more autonomy, the most important of which was the Ten Years War that erupted in 1868. Britain also experienced difficulties establishing a governance arrangement that met the needs of both mother country and colonies in the Caribbean. Barbados and the Bahamas were the most stable politically within the British realm and hence enjoyed a substantial degree of legislative autonomy; the remainder of the British territories, however, following years of racial conflict and other civil disorders, especially in Jamaica, were, after 1865, ruled directly from London with no local legislature. That structure remained in place until the end of World War II.

In purely economic terms, the end of slavery contributed to a substantial decline in sugar production in Jamaica. Trinidad, by contrast, enjoyed considerable expansion at the same time. The dilemma that confronted Jamaican planters went beyond emancipation; world production of sugar cane underwent considerable expansion in the years after 1840, notably in Malaya, the East Indies, the Philippines, Cuba, Puerto Rico, and Brazil, and European production of beet sugar also increased after the 1850s. The result was a sharp decline in world prices precisely at the time Jamaican planters in particular were attempting to restructure their economy. Jamaica held little attraction for European immigrant workers. Only a few thousand northern Europeans went to the island in the nineteenth century, at least prior to the 1860s, although more than 30,000 Chinese and East Indians made the commitment. Trinidadian planters were especially successful in the use of indentured East Indian labour, attracting more than 140,000 between emancipation and World War I. Smaller colonies such as St. Kitts, Saint Vincent and Grenada imported Asian workers as well, and East Indians also found their way to Dutch Guiana (Surinam), but nowhere did they have the long-term impact they did in Trinidad and British Guiana. The indenture system lasted until 1917; by that time East Indians and their descendants constituted one-third of Trinidad's population, and in many instances migration continued well after the end of the indenture system. Those Asian labourers rapidly became well established in agriculture in British Guiana and Trinidad, with subsequent cultural and political tensions between Asian and African-American segments of the population.

The Caribbean basin simply did not attract its share of the massive nineteenth- and early-twentieth-century European migration to the Americas. Except for Spanish-held Cuba, where Spanish immigrants continued to be attracted by the expansion of the sugar economy, of the approximately 4 million immigrants who reached Latin American nations between the 1820s and the 1880s, approximately 75 percent went to three countries in South America: Argentina, Brazil, and Uruguay, with smaller numbers to Chile, Puerto Rico, Costa Rica, and Cuba.

For the former slaves, as Franklin Knight and other historians have demonstrated, the destruction of considerable numbers of plantations in the last years of slavery and during the initial post-emancipation downturn provided an unmatched opportunity for formerly landless slaves to become a small landholding peasantry and to continue to fashion in freedom the social, economic, and political institutions which had been only embryonic in servitude. Specifically, Knight indicates that in Jamaica the number of black freeholders increased from 2,000 in 1838 to more than 20,000 twenty years later; in Antigua, freedmen and women brought thousands of new acres into cultivation after emancipation; and in British Guiana freed slaves between the end of the 1830s and 1848 purchased more than 400 estates with an estimated value of $100,000.[10]

For more than two centuries, slavery and the slave trade were dominant features of the domestic and international history of the Caribbean basin. They affected the economic, cultural, social, psychological, political, and military history of the region throughout its colonial history. Given the extent to which slavery was woven into the historical fabric of the Caribbean area, it was predictable that the institution would cast a very long shadow into the post-emancipation years, well after its last legal vestige ended in Cuba in the late 1880s. The history of slavery and the slave trade illustrates effectively the ways in which national and international history intertwine, indeed are so often inseparable.

The United States in the Caribbean basin in the nineteenth century

The United States has been a factor in shaping the international and domestic history of the Caribbean basin since it attained its own independence in 1783, but for most of the nineteenth century it was a relatively minor player overshadowed by the major imperial powers in the age of European expansionism. A variety of factors increasingly drew the United States into the region. As U.S. trade, overseas investments, and national security interests developed as the country grew from fledgling nation in the early nineteenth century to major power status by 1900, it proved impossible for the United States to avoid involvement in the Caribbean. Geographic proximity alone determined the future involvement of the United States. As U.S. power expanded in the course of the century, events in the region increasingly posed both challenge and threat to its interests. These included the continued presence of European powers in the area, or local turmoil in the Caribbean that threatened U.S. trade, investments, or national security.

Like the Caribbean basin societies themselves, the United States' situation in the region was strongly influenced by the wars of the French Revolution, the Napoleonic wars and the Latin American wars for independence. The United States had a clear interest in both regional stability and, paradoxically, a break-down of European colonial controls, especially in the area of trade. Traditional mercantilist-protectionist policies had made it difficult for U.S. merchants and other economic interest groups to gain the entrée desired into the markets of the area and to acquire the raw materials which became increasingly important to an emerging industrial nation in the late nineteenth century.

To the extent that there was any consistency of U.S. policy toward the Caribbean basin in the course of the century, the main premises were opposition to any further European expansion, the gradual removal of the European powers, and the openness of the region to American trade and investment. The Monroe Doctrine of the 1820s was the clearest expression of that policy, and it emerged as the Latin American wars for independence drew to a close and there seemed some danger of reassertion of Spanish imperialism if the Holy Alliance, which had restored Ferdinand VII to the Spanish throne, supported Spanish ambitions. At the same time, Russia was showing interest in the Pacific northwest of North America, and Congressmen in Washington actually spoke of the possibility of Russian troops in Havana. President James Monroe and his Secretary of State John Quincy Adams were determined to prevent any expansion of the European presence as the American nation itself gradually moved west to occupy the continent, and fortunately for the relatively weak United States, its policy objectives happened to coincide with those of Great Britain, which had the naval presence and diplomatic power to discourage any effort to recolonize the recently independent nations in the western hemisphere.

In the course of the century, the United States' position gradually moved from a defensive posture – holding the line against further European encroachment in the area – to a more active, expansionist approach. Several factors fuelled that transition. One was ideological. As much as one may be skeptical of ideology in shaping a nation's foreign policy, one cannot ignore the force of such notions as Manifest Destiny, mission, a sense of uniqueness of the American experiment, the desire to spread the values and institutions of capitalism and democracy. Such ideas also contained an element of racial superiority, and Americans shared such values with European Anglo-Saxons, who also doubted the abilities of blacks, Indians, and mestizos. Indeed, these factors played an important part in the way that Americans and U.S. policy makers acted in and toward the Caribbean region.[11]

Important as ideology was in shaping the expansionist orientation, there were also practical considerations of national interest, including trade, foreign investment, access to and control over commercial and military transportation arteries. Such issues became increasingly important to the United States in the course of the nineteenth century as it expanded to the Pacific. From war with Mexico in the 1840s, the United States incorporated what became modern Arizona, Texas, New Mexico, and California. Acquisition of California and of the Pacific northwest accelerated U.S. involvement in Asia. In 1854, Commodore Matthew Perry compelled Japan to open its ports to American trade. The Asian interest made a rapid route to the Pacific from the American eastern seaboard more urgent. In 1848, the U.S. Senate approved the Bidlack Treaty with Colombia, which obligated the United States to maintain freedom of transit and to maintain Colombian sovereignty on the isthmus of Panama (the first U.S. military commitment to any foreign power). In 1850, the United States and Great Britain concluded the Clayton-Bulwer Treaty, in which both nations pledged not to monopolize or to fortify against one another any transportation artery across the isthmus. Such developments greatly expanded the strategic and economic significance of the Caribbean basin.[12]

The British seemed increasingly alarmed by the growing power of the United States in the region at mid-century; but they were also realistic. In 1848, the British took control over the Caribbean mouth of the San Juan River in Nicaragua, renaming the port Greytown. The British Foreign Secretary, Lord Palmerston, insisted that Greytown, British Honduras (Belize), and the Mosquito coast were not included in the terms of the Clayton-Bulwer Treaty. Not until he became Prime Minister in 1859 did Palmerston return the Mosquito Coast to Nicaragua and the Bay Islands to Honduras, both a symbolic gesture designed for American not Central American consumption. Palmerston was astute when he observed that the reality in the region favoured United States over British domination. As he suggested, the Americans are "on the spot, strong, deeply interested in the matter, totally unscrupulous and dishonest and determined somehow or other to carry their Point."[13] Whatever the accuracy of Palmerston's assessment, by the outbreak of the American Civil War, Britain was no longer a significant player on the Caribbean coast of Central America, although it clung to major island possessions in the Caribbean and to British Guiana on the northeast South American coast.

The conclusion of the 1848 agreement combined with the California gold rush in that year to increase the urgency of a transportation route across the isthmus, with the result that U.S. capital interests promptly obtained a concession and began construction of the Panama railroad, which was completed in 1855. Like the long-delayed and troubled canal construction a generation later, the railroad construction brought thousands of labourers from the Caribbean region to work in the malaria-infested lowland jungles. The completion of the railroad was a milestone for the American presence in the area; the railroad transported thousands of Americans and other foreign nationals to the Pacific coast of North America and for the next two decades was the single most important contributor to the Colombian treasury. At the same time, the presence of American capital interests and large numbers of American and other foreign travellers proved to be a source of conflict between local Panamanians, many of whom were black, and white Americans. Riots and the difficulties Colombian authorities in Panama had in maintaining order led the United States on a number of occasions over the next decades to invoke the Mallarino-Bidlack Treaty and land troops on the isthmus.

The isthmus continued to gain strategic and commercial importance for the United States, but there was also considerable official and private attention to Cuba at mid-century and considerable American activity in other parts of Central America. Except for trade, the British, French, and Dutch territories at the time held little attraction for U.S. policy makers and little significance in the American popular imagination. Cuba was on the opposite end of the spectrum. Several factors stimulated that interest. One was the fact that the United States by mid-century was Cuba's most important trading partner, in spite of Spanish imperial efforts to restrain the contacts. A second was the fact that Cuba was the main slaveholding economy in the Caribbean in the nineteenth century at a time that slavery was under increasing attack in the United States. For southerners, their representatives in Congress, and the Democratic administrations of the pre-Civil War years, linkages with other slaveholding areas held out the promise of perpetuating the institution. Abolitionists, on the other hand, sought to topple slavery both in the United States and in the Caribbean. A third factor, although equally difficult to measure, was the traditional American hostility toward Roman Catholic Spain and its continued presence in the Caribbean. Most important, however, then as in the twentieth century, was the geographic proximity of Cuba to the United States – only ninety miles off the Florida coast.

Almost touching American shores was this prosperous outpost of decadent Spanish imperialism, a symbol of the former European empires.

What particularly concerned American policy makers about the Cuban situation, however, besides the Spanish presence, was Spain's weakness and its inability to maintain order on the island, thus increasing the risk of other European intervention in the region. Further European intervention would violate the American principle of non-transfer that had been articulated by Secretary of State John Quincy Adams in 1823.[14]

In mid-century, on the eve of civil war in the United States, sectional tensions fuelled an expansionist rhetoric along with individual acts of international irresponsibility. In the filibustering, annexationist forays of the 1850s in the Caribbean and Central America, Americans from the slave states took the lead, and they were explicit in their linking of expansion into the Caribbean region with the contradictory notions of Manifest Destiny and the extension of slavery. The rhetoric of southern expansionism was bellicose. *De Bow's Review*, one of the South's leading journals of opinion, referred to the Gulf of Mexico as a "Southern sea," and southern Congressmen claimed that the peoples of the Caribbean region would welcome Americans with enthusiasm.[15]

There were three main extra-legal filibustering expeditions from the United States into the Caribbean basin from 1849 through the 1850s, all initiated in the slave states. All were ill fated and all left an unfortunate legacy of American interventionism in the region. The first was an aborted invasion of Cuba in 1849 by several hundred mercenaries led by a Venezuelan-born Cuban and former Spanish military officer, Narciso López. Happily for Spain, the Cubans, and likely the mercenaries, the U.S. Navy prevented the expedition from leaving its base on an island off the coast of Louisiana. Yet, López's vision of a slaveholding Cuba liberated from Spain but annexed to the United States held widespread popular support in the United States, and he tried again the following year with more substantial southern backing. This time his force made a beachhead at Cárdenas only to be beaten back by Spanish troops and arrested by the U.S. Navy. Undaunted by failure, he landed another several hundred men in Cuba in 1851. On this occasion he and his compatriots were captured and executed, among them William Crittenden, who was the nephew of the U.S. Attorney-General.[16]

For several years one of López's major supporters, Mississippi Governor John A. Quitman, sought to rally another filibustering expedition. However, he faced the same obstacles that confronted others – lack of interest among Cubans and Washington's official opposition – with the result that by 1855 Quitman relinquished his ambitions.

More serious and more sustained initiatives in Central America were those inspired and led by Tennessee-born physician and lawyer, William Walker, whose motives were less transparent than those of López and Quitman in spite of considerable talk of Manifest Destiny. Following an aborted invasion of lower California – Mexican territory – Walker turned his sights on Central

27

America, specifically Nicaragua. Receiving a sympathetic response from the slaveholding southerner who was American Minister in Managua, Walker captured the country, assumed the title of President, and restored slavery in 1855. Remarkably, the Franklin Pierce administration recognized the short-lived Walker government in 1856. Walker fared less well with Nicaragua's neighbours as well as the leading American capitalist with transportation interests in the area, Cornelius Vanderbilt, who sided with Honduras, Guatemala, El Salvador and Costa Rica to send the American privateer packing. Not easily discouraged, Walker attempted to retake Nicaragua in 1857, 1858 and finally in 1860, when he was captured and executed in Honduras. He inspired considerable fascination in the United States, yet the reality of his exploits, from the extension of slavery to the brutality with which he treated Central Americans bore little relationship to the notion of expanding the values of American civilization. Unfortunately, it is one of the "American" legacies that survives in Central America to this day.[17]

What American filibusters failed to take by force of arms, American officials sought to acquire by diplomacy. Cuba remained the main target. Prior to the López expedition, in 1848 President James K. Polk (1845–9) made overtures to Spain to purchase Cuba for $100 million, but Spain was not interested and Spanish reticence was reinforced by both Britain and France, who were concerned about U.S. ambitions and any alteration of the balance of power in the Caribbean. The Polk initiative thus foundered on the reefs of international reality.

In the early 1850s, the Millard Fillmore administration in Washington rebuffed a more formal Anglo-French overture to pledge themselves not to seek Cuban annexation. On the one hand, the administration thought such a pledge would arouse considerable domestic political anger; at the same time, there was no desire to limit future options. Secretary of State Edward Everett assured European diplomats of American good faith while he lent credibility to fears of American expansionism in the Caribbean by claiming that the future status of Cuba was an American issue.[18]

The new Democratic administration of Franklin Pierce confirmed the European concerns by once again seeking to obtain Spanish consent to sell their valuable Caribbean possession. Working through the southern expansionist, pro-slavery minister in Madrid, Pierre Soulé, and two leading expansionist democrats who held the ministerial appointments in London and Paris, Secretary of State William Marcy instructed Soulé to purchase Cuba and failing Spanish agreement to seek active means of separating the colony from Spanish control. Working closely with his counterparts in Europe, Soulé followed instructions with enthusiasm, issuing a manifesto, the so-called Ostend Manifesto, claiming divine and earthly right to the island in the event Spain refused to part willingly with Cuba. Such a public display of chicanery was too much even for the administration that had encouraged him, and Soulé was recalled from Madrid; but one of his co-authors and fellow expansionist James Buchanan within two years was inaugurated President of the United States. In his first annual message to Congress, President Buchanan urged Congress to appropriate sufficient funds to purchase Cuba because of its commercial and strategic value to the United States. For the moment sectional divisions within Congress and the nation precluded such an eventuality, but expansionist visions and appetites were not so easily quelled.

The American Civil War and major diplomatic tensions between the United States and Great Britain arising from the international implications of the war partially diverted U.S. energies and attention from the Caribbean basin. Yet, even during the American Civil War and Reconstruction several developments of importance occurred.

The most serious threat to the United States emerged in 1861 when Britain, France, and Spain collaborated in an effort to collect outstanding debts from Benito Juarez's Mexico. When it became evident to the British and Spanish that Napoleon III intended to occupy Mexican territory they withdrew, leaving French troops to engage Mexican forces. By 1863, French troops had driven Juarez from Mexico City and Archduke Maximilian was installed as Emperor of Mexico. The U.S. Congress condemned the French invasion and occupation, but the Lincoln administration was too preoccupied with the Civil War to do more than express concern. The situation resolved itself without American action, however. By 1867, the last of Napoleon's French forces were withdrawn and the hapless Maximilian was left to be captured and executed. Yet, the French intervention underlined the vulnerability of the region to major European actions if politics so dictated.

An equally important factor driving American policy in the region during the Civil War and its immediate aftermath was the continued growth of American involvement in the Pacific and the obvious role of the Caribbean and Central America as a link between the seas. Secretary of State William Seward under Presidents Lincoln, Andrew Johnson, and Ulysses S. Grant held a vision of a more global commercial empire than had most of his predecessors, and the Caribbean basin was an important feature in that vision. The major Caribbean islands occupied important strategic positions as the United States sought to consolidate its influence in the region. At the end of the Civil War in 1866, Seward toured the Caribbean, making visits to Haiti, the Dominican Republic, Cuba, and St. Thomas. Seward made it evident that he believed the region of strategic and commercial importance and intended to act on those assumptions. In the midst of Civil War, the United States recognized the government of Haiti in 1862 for the first time since its revolution and three years later signed a commercial treaty. Clearly, Seward was impressed by the naval base potential of the region. Following his trip, the U.S. government offered to purchase from Denmark St. Thomas (with its fine harbour), along with St. John and St. Croix. The U.S. Senate, however, failed to act on the treaty, at the expense of positive Danish–American relations and the political career of the Danish Foreign Minister. The time simply was not right; a half-century later, in the midst of world war, it would be more propitious.[19]

Failure to bring the agreement with Denmark to ratification in the United States paralleled difficulties for the Grant administration over the small Swedish island of Saint Barthélemy, which Sweden offered to the United States on several occasions in the nineteenth century before it transferred the island to France, which had originally held the territory. American interest in the Dominican Republic also proved problematic. The U.S. government extended diplomatic recognition to the Dominican Republic in 1866. Against U.S. protests that the action violated the Monroe Doctrine, Spain had occupied the Dominican Republic from 1861 to 1865, and its departure cleared the way both for diplomatic recognition as well as a commercial treaty. This also provided Seward with an opportunity to revive the notion of acquiring Samaná Bay as an American naval base, for which an agreement had been negotiated in 1854, over, significantly, the protests of France and Britain. In the course of the Grant administration, negotiations with Dominican representatives led to conclusion of a treaty providing for annexation of the country to the United States, an agreement that the U.S. Senate rejected.

In the immediate aftermath of the American Civil War, Cuba also degenerated into a lengthy civil conflict – the Ten Years' War. That conflict disrupted trade and underlined the Spanish incapacity to bring meaningful reforms to the island at the same time that it maintained order. The high levels of financial losses born by the Creole plantation elite also served to increase the level of American investment in the island, further intensifying the likelihood that the island's future would be linked to the United States. In the 1890s, these issues and concerns crystallized with the stalemated Cuban–Spanish war and the rapid American defeat of Spain in Cuba and in the Pacific when it declared war in 1898. The U.S. military occupation of Cuba (1898–1902) inaugurated an American protectorate over the island that continued until 1934.

Thus, although the United States through the 1870s and 1880s demonstrated concern over any expansion of European interest in the Caribbean region, and certainly opposed the acquisition of territory or European participation in such projects as the construction of an isthmian canal, on the whole, the executive during the 1860s through the 1880s seems to have been well in advance of American public and congressional opinion. At the same time that the United States did not acquire territory in the region in this period, either for naval bases or as annexations, U.S. interests continued to make substantial advances in trade and investment in the area, most notably in Cuba. By the 1890s, as the general international situation shifted and the place of the United States within that system altered, a very new direction for American policy and international relations in the Caribbean emerged.

2

HEGEMONY IN TRANSITION

The emergence of the United States, 1890–1917

Against a background of declining European empires in the Caribbean basin, the United States emerged as a major presence in the area. On the eve of the Spanish-American war in 1898, Spain's hold was already tenuous. French interests were still involved in a failing effort to complete an isthmian canal through Colombian-held Panama. British policy makers were increasingly preoccupied with South Africa and the growing strength of Germany on the continent. Germany itself at the turn of the century did have what one historian has referred to as "dreams of empire;" its warships cruised the Caribbean basin reporting on economic, political and military developments, with a particular eye on opportunities for German developments, and its merchants and citizens were active in establishing business interests in the region, especially Venezuela.[1]

American interest in the region was not new, but its power to influence developments in the area had increased significantly in the previous fifty years. Since the middle of the nineteenth century, proponents of Manifest Destiny had identified Cuba as a legitimate possession of the United States, while others envisaged even greater expansion southwards. These hopes gained substance in the wake of the 1898 Spanish-American War, the settlement of which placed not only Cuba but also Puerto Rico, Guam and the Philippines under American control (Map 3). As Bonham C. Richardson observed, after this war "The United States stood alone as the supreme imperial power in the Caribbean region, the presence of a number of small European colonies there notwithstanding."[2]

A series of events symbolized the emergence of the United States as a hegemonic power in the region. One was the bombastic rhetorical 1895 intervention of the United States in the longstanding boundary dispute between Venezuela and British Guiana. A second was the Spanish-American War with the resulting U.S. acquisition of its first formal colonies as well as *de facto* protectorates in the Caribbean. A third was the construction of a U.S.-controlled isthmian canal through Panama by World War I. At the same time, especially in the era of Theodore Roosevelt, American officials clearly articulated a foreign policy that extended the Monroe Doctrine to the internal affairs of the nations of the Caribbean basin. As a consequence, by World War I, although there continued

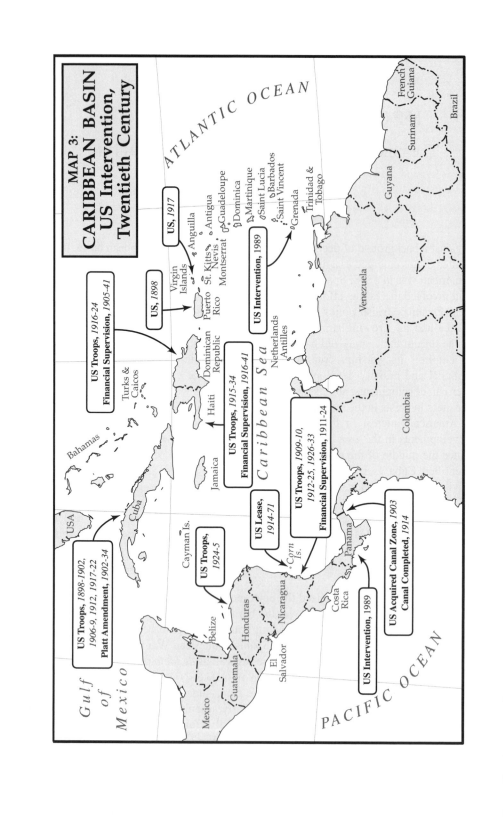

MAP 3:
CARIBBEAN BASIN
US Intervention,
Twentieth Century

ATLANTIC OCEAN

PACIFIC OCEAN

Gulf
of
Mexico

Caribbean Sea

US, 1917

US, 1898

Anguilla
Virgin
Islands
Puerto
Rico
St. Kitts
Nevis
Montserrat
Antigua
Guadeloupe
Dominica
Martinique
Saint Lucia
Barbados
Saint Vincent
Grenada
Trinidad &
Tobago

US Intervention, 1989

Netherlands
Antilles

US Troops, 1916-24
Financial Supervision, 1905-41

Turks &
Caicos

Dominican
Republic

Haiti

Bahamas

Jamaica

Cuba

USA

US Troops, 1915-34
Financial Supervision, 1916-41

US Troops, 1909-10,
1912-25, 1926-33
Financial Supervision, 1911-24

US Lease,
1914-71

Corn
Is.

Cayman Is.

US Troops,
1924-5

US Troops, 1898-1902,
1906-9, 1912, 1917-22
Platt Amendment, 1902-34

Panama

US Acquired Canal Zone, 1903
Canal Completed, 1914

US Intervention, 1989

Belize

Honduras

Nicaragua

Costa
Rica

Guatemala

El
Salvador

Mexico

Venezuela

Colombia

Guyana

Surinam

French
Guiana

Brazil

to be European colonial and economic involvement in the region, there was no doubt either in international circles or in the region that the United States was the metropolitan centre for the Caribbean.

Venezuelan boundary dispute

When Britain acquired British Guiana from the Netherlands following the Napoleonic wars, there was no clearly defined western boundary. Throughout the nineteenth century, Venezuela complained that Britain was exercising sovereignty over Venezuelan territory. In 1895, U.S. President Grover Cleveland and his Secretary of State, Richard Olney, ordered the British government of Lord Salisbury to submit the dispute to arbitration. As pressure intensified, the Salisbury government agreed to do so for the sake of peaceful relations with the United States. Great Britain and Venezuela established a five-member arbitration tribunal which consisted of two Americans (to represent Venezuelan interests), two Britons, and a Russian chairman, who was supposed to be neutral. In 1899, the tribunal rendered its decision and awarded most of the disputed territory to Britain.

Unfortunately, this did not end the problem. Fifty years later, in 1949, by which time the participants in the events were deceased, the private papers of Severo Mallet-Prevost, one of the American lawyers who had argued Venezuela's case, were published. His papers charged that the Russian chairman was guilty of collusion with the British, in anticipation that support for Britain in South America might win favours for Russia in Central Asia north of India. In 1962, citing the Mallet-Prevost papers as its justification, Venezuela renounced the 1899 decision and declared it null and void. Venezuelan maps began to show the disputed territory as Venezuela's *Zona en Reclamación*, and diplomatic and military action followed.

The ongoing dispute affected Guyana in a number of ways. First, for some years Venezuela excluded Guyana (post-independence British Guiana) from the Organization of American States and prevented it from signing a nuclear prohibition treaty for Latin America. Exclusion from the OAS meant that Guyana was not eligible for development funds from the Inter-American Development Bank.

Second, Venezuela launched armed attacks against the disputed territory, encouraged insubordination to Guyanese authority by residents of the areas in question, and alarmed Guyanese with a claim to the territorial sea. In 1966, the year Guyana became independent, Venezuelan forces seized the Guyanese portion of Ankoko on the boundary between Venezuela and the disputed territory. They remained there until after the conclusion of a *modus vivendi*, the Port of Spain Protocol, in 1970.

The Spanish-American–Cuban War

The apparent resolution of the Venezuelan–British Guiana boundary dispute – at least to the satisfaction of Britain and the United States – paved the way for a more general Anglo-American rapprochement in the next decade. The U.S. intervention in 1898 in the Cuban war against Spain, however, had more dramatic and immediate effects upon the level of U.S. involvement in the Caribbean basin. The Spanish-American–Cuban War was both catalyst and symbol of the transformation of international power that occurred in the course of the 1890s and first decade of the twentieth century in the Caribbean region. Spain's retention of the fragments of its empire in the area – Cuba and Puerto Rico – was an anachronism by the late nineteenth century. Liberal reformers in Cuba had made it evident during the Ten Years War (1868–78) that they would accept nothing less than a liberalization of trade and investment as well as political participation.

Many strands ran through Cuban reform thought prior to the mid-1880s: emancipationists opposed to slavery, slaves seeking freedom, liberals wanting trade and political freedom from Spanish dominance, restraints and inefficiency, those who sought total independence from Spain, those who sought annexation with the United States and those equally opposed to the U.S. connection. Embodied in the debate over Cuba's future were the seeds of Cuban nationalism, of *Cubanidad*. Although slavery and emancipation were no longer factors in the equation after emancipation in the 1880s, a variety of the other forces came together during the U.S.-tariff induced recession in Cuba after 1895 to produce a sustained rebellion against Spanish authority and a *Cuba libre*.

Inspired by Cuban intellectual-in-exile José Martí and led by Máximo Gómez in the field, within two years Cuban rebels controlled most of the interior of the island, leaving Spain in command of the coastal cities and shipping routes. It was not so much the rebellion itself but Spain's incapacity to contain and then crush the rebellion which led to U.S. intervention in April 1898. The rebellion resulted in the destruction of Cuban railroads, sugar plantations and processing plants, many of them owned by American investors who had acquired extensive properties as a result of the Ten Years War. The apparently stalemated rebellion, Spanish inability to respond effectively to the demands for change, American commercial and strategic interests in Cuba and the region, combined with a media-manipulated public outrage against the atrocities of Spanish authorities to lead President William McKinley to request a declaration of war against Spain. The intervention of U.S. naval and ground forces in the war led to a decisive victory within six weeks – the "Splendid Little War." That conflict quickly reduced Spanish military and political power not only in the Caribbean but also in the Pacific, as Cuba, Puerto Rico and the Philippines came under various forms of U.S. tutelage.[3]

The Spanish-American–Cuban War combined with other events in the region to alter the balance of international power in the Caribbean basin by the early twentieth century. The 1890s began and ended with Britain the main power in the region; but a major naval building programme in the United States in the 1890s, especially during the Spanish-American War, altered that situation, with the result that by 1899 the British navy viewed the American fleet in the Caribbean as already considerably superior to its own West Indian squadron.[4]

United States military forces occupied Cuba until 1902 and returned again from 1906 through 1909 in an effort to resolve domestic political strife. The United States was prohibited by the Teller Amendment, passed by the U.S. Congress prior to U.S. intervention in the war, from annexing Cuba. Senator Henry M. Teller introduced his amendment ostensibly to demonstrate to the world the idealism that prompted the U.S. declaration of war; he may also have been influenced by the fact that his state had an important sugar beet industry which had much to fear from imported Cuban cane sugar. Teller's initiative was, however, compromised by the Platt Amendment of 1901, an amendment to the Army Appropriation Bill of that year and later imposed by treaty on Cuban authorities. The Platt Amendment, introduced by Senator Orville M. Platt in conjunction with Secretary of State Elihu Root, provided for the U.S. right of intervention in the event Cuban authorities failed to protect "life, property and individual liberty." The amendment further stipulated that Cuban governments could not enter into agreements with foreign countries that might weaken its independence. To facilitate the implementation of this U.S. protectorate, Cuba ceded coaling stations and naval bases to the United States, in particular Guantánamo, which it retains to the present day.[5]

Puerto Rico

As a result of the Spanish-American War, the United States annexed Puerto Rico outright, an act made possible by the fact that the Teller Amendment made no reference to the less important island. The island's strategic importance in the region, especially with the possibility of an inter-oceanic canal, nonetheless quickly attracted the U.S. Navy, which established bases there.

Under U.S. direct rule, Puerto Rico ironically enjoyed less democracy than it had at the end of Spanish colonialism. Stripped of their Spanish citizenship, unless they specifically opted to retain it, Puerto Ricans lost their representation in the *cortes* at Madrid. Instead of the deputies who had been full members of the Spanish parliament, Puerto Ricans could elect one resident commissioner to represent their interests in Washington. That resident commissioner could speak on the floor of the House of Representatives, but he could not vote. Although Luís Muñoz Rivera and his associates achieved internal self-government for Puerto Rico in 1897, executive authority after the change of sovereignty would until 1948 rest with a governor appointed by the President of the United States. There would be an elected Puerto Rican Congress, whose proposed acts the governor could veto, and not until 1946 would a Puerto Rican become governor.

The Foraker Act of 1900, which established this form of government, failed to bestow United States citizenship upon Puerto Ricans. Senator Henry Teller of

Colorado, for one, judged Puerto Ricans unworthy of United States citizenship because they had acquiesced too easily to Spanish misrule over the centuries and had not demonstrated sufficient rebellious virility.[6] Not until the Jones Act replaced the Foraker Act 2 March 1917 would Puerto Ricans gain United States citizenship.[7] When one month later the United States declared war on Imperial Germany, young Puerto Ricans – as United States citizens – were eligible for the draft.

Puerto Rican status was a morass of contradictions. On the one hand there was the debate over citizenship, and there was the further illogic of treating the Puerto Rican economy for purposes of trade as almost a foreign entity, although this lasted only a few years. The Foraker Act placed a tariff upon Puerto Rican goods sold in the United States, albeit a tariff only 15 percent of the prevailing Dingley Tariff in force against foreign imports. At the same time, Puerto Ricans could not conclude trade agreements with foreign countries nor vote in Congress for protective tariffs for Puerto Rican commodities. Because Americans drank coffee from elsewhere and saw no need to protect Puerto Rican coffee, and because Puerto Rico's pre-1898 customers looked elsewhere for their coffee supplies, the island coffee industry never did recover from the 1899 hurricane. On the other hand, Puerto Rico adopted the U.S. legal system, with the jury system and the burden of proof which rested with the prosecutor rather than the defendant.

The Puerto Rican economy was left largely to languish in the first several decades of U.S. colonialism. The will and the funds were not there. Despite improvements in health – for instance in the treatment of anemia – such American observers as Governor Rexford Tugwell and journalist John Gunther registered shock at Puerto Rico's ubiquitous poverty as late as World War II.[8]

The Panama Canal

While the United States defeated Spanish forces, occupied Cuba, established a protectorate and annexed Puerto Rico early in the twentieth century, it also consolidated its position in Panama, ending more than half a century of uncertainty over the location and construction of an isthmian canal. As the century began, the United Kingdom had residual rights, and French commercial interests were still attempting to complete a canal. With its control of the Panama Railroad and dominance of commerce which passed through Panama, which was still one of nine Colombian departments, however, the United States had already become the pre-eminent force on the isthmus. Other European powers continued to demonstrate their concern over the area. Britain retained treaty rights at the turn of the century. German ships visited Panama and their commanding officers kept Berlin informed about secessionist movements as well as about German commercial interests.[9] German consular officials in Colón provided similar information.[10] Relations among the expatriates were reasonably friendly. In the autumn of 1900, the American director of the Panama Railroad invited the commander of the German warship *Vineta* to travel as a distinguished guest from

Colón to Panama City, and Captain Wollheim accepted.[11] Officers of the U.S., German, French, and British navies fraternized at Colón in December 1901.[12]

The United States quickly became the dominant power, but its hegemony was not without challenges. By the Hay-Pauncefote Treaty of 1901, the United Kingdom acknowledged U.S. authority on the isthmus, and private French business interests sold their canal rights to the United States in 1903. One historian has written, "French acquiescence in a Panama Canal settlement was a necessary prerequisite to French concurrence in the new American Caribbean."[13]

The Spanish-American War convinced prominent Americans that an interoceanic canal was a military necessity. In the spring of 1898, the battleship *Oregon* was operating off the Pacific coast of the United States when strategists decided that she was needed in the Caribbean war zone. By the time the *Oregon* had sailed down to the south of Chile and up to the Caribbean, the naval war had ended. Yet, the *Oregon*'s experience appeared to many as a warning that a faster and more direct naval route between the oceans was a strategic necessity. If commercial factors by themselves did not justify an expenditure of $2 billion on a canal, then military factors would.

First the administration of President William McKinley had to neutralize the British treaty rights. The Anglo-American Clayton-Bulwer Treaty of 1850 provided that neither the United States nor the United Kingdom would unilaterally build or fortify against the other a canal across the isthmus. After the Spanish-American–Cuban War, that restriction seemed at best anachronistic, at worst a liability. Although Secretary of State John Hay felt a moral obligation to honour treaty commitments, some Congressmen disagreed and supported the Hepburn Bill, which called for a canal built and operated exclusively under the auspices of the United States. Lord Salisbury's government did not want a confrontation. Already it faced a naval arms race with Imperial Germany, and the Anglo-French Entente of 1904 lay in the future. The United Kingdom could not afford too many adversaries at one time. If United States authorities defied the Clayton-Bulwer Treaty, the British would suffer a diplomatic humiliation. As it was, the British army was engaged in a prolonged and controversial war in South Africa. Moreover, since the opening of the Suez Canal in 1869, a canal across the American isthmus was less important to British interests than it had been in 1850.

For the sake of Anglo-American harmony, the Salisbury government agreed to abrogate the Clayton-Bulwer Treaty – for a price. Aware, however, that it was negotiating from a position of weakness, that price could not be very high. Salisbury rejected the Canadian suggestion of U.S. territorial concessions on the Alaska panhandle as a *quid pro quo* for the death of Clayton-Bulwer. Lord Pauncefote, the British Ambassador in Washington, negotiated with Secretary Hay a draft treaty which provided for the permanent neutrality and demilitarization of the Panama Canal, but the U.S. Senate failed to give the first Hay-Pauncefote Treaty the necessary two-thirds vote of approval. U.S. naval strategist Alfred Thayer Mahan warned that such a canal would enhance the effectiveness of Germany's navy. The Germans, he warned, would be in a position to sail back and forth, bombarding the Atlantic coastline of the United States one week, and the Pacific coastline only a few days later. The United States must fortify any forthcoming canal. The Salisbury government conceded the point, and the only benefit left to the British as a result of the second Hay-Pauncefote Treaty, approved by the Senate, was economic. Once the canal became operational, its toll structure would be identical for ships of all nations.

German ambitions in the isthmus were less critical than the British but not to be totally discounted. After Kaiser Wilhelm II's coronation in 1888, with the lead of such expansionists as Admiral Alfred von Tirpitz, and pressed by the lobbying of such groups as the Navy League, Pan-German League and Colonial League, Germany took a far more aggressive stance in the Caribbean than did Britain. Unlike the British, Germany continued to reject, emphatically, the application of the Monroe Doctrine to international law. Von Tirpitz was exercised by the U.S. victory over Spain in 1898 and its acquisition of former Spanish territory and recommended that German warships show the flag in the Caribbean to emphasize the German interest. Von Tirpitz was himself desirous of acquiring naval stations in the Caribbean, including Saint Thomas and Curaçao, although nothing was to come of these desires. Von Tirpitz's interpretation of the strategic significance of the Caribbean seem to have been similar to those of U.S. officials, who recognized the significance of the Caribbean as a link to the Pacific rim as well as in its own right. Hence Saint Thomas, for instance, could be used as part of the transmission system for a proposed German inter-oceanic telegraph cable designed to free Germany from communications dependence on British cables. Tirpitz's perception of the importance of an isthmian canal was equally direct. He stressed a potential canal's strategic importance to Germany and the threat it posed to German interests in the Americas and the Pacific if the United States were in a position to deny Germany access to the waterway.[14]

German ambitions notwithstanding, it was the British who posed the only real obstacle to the realization of U.S. ambitions at the turn of the century. With the Hay-Pauncefote Treaty resolving the British relationship, the government of President Theodore Roosevelt – who had succeeded the assassinated McKinley in September 1903 – had to select a site. A commission headed by Admiral John Walker of the U.S. Navy recommended the so-called "Nicaragua" route – up the San Juan River which separates Nicaragua from Costa Rica, across Lake Nicaragua, and onward to the Pacific Ocean. Nature herself had already provided many of the facilities. The San Juan River would require dredging, and engineers would have to dig through the height of land, but the U.S. Navy could keep ships in Lake Nicaragua. The Nicaragua route was geographically closer to the United States than the Panama route, and Americans were less likely than in Panama to contract lethal diseases when in the area. The Nicaragua route enjoyed a psychological advantage over the Panama one in that any canal there would be an all-American one, built and financed by United States citizens. By contrast, French consortia had been endeavouring without success for more than a quarter-century to build a canal across Panama. If the U.S. Congress were to choose the Panama route, it would have to purchase the French rights and assets and, presumably, share the glory. The Walker Commission initially recommended the Nicaragua route.

Nevertheless, Congress endorsed the Panama route. The French slashed their selling price from $102 million to $40 million, and President Roosevelt reconvened the Walker Commission to consider the implications. This time it thought that Panama was too good a deal to reject. From a diplomatic perspective, it would be easier to deal with one foreign government (that of Colombia, of which Panama was a department) than with two (Nicaragua and Costa Rica). Moreover, Nicaraguan President José Santos Zelaya was a nationalist who was unlikely to alienate his country's territory without extracting some significant concession. The Costa Rican constitution indicated that that country's sovereignty over its own territory was non-negotiable. Under the circumstances, Senator John Spooner of Wisconsin introduced legislation which authorized the administration to negotiate a canal treaty with the government of Colombia. Only in the event that agreement with Colombia proved impossible would there be talks with Nicaragua. Finally, the eruption of Mont Pelée in Martinique early in May 1902, when the Spooner Bill was before the Senate, strengthened the case for Panama. French lobbyist Philippe Bunau-Varilla – motivated by personal and national pride as well as a desire for compensation for the French assets – reminded the senators that Nicaragua too lay in a volcanic zone.

Congress approved the Spooner Bill, and President Roosevelt signed it into law. Secretary Hay then negotiated a canal treaty with Tomas Herran, Colombia's minister in Washington. Aware of the political turbulence of the past half-century in the area, it was an American *sine qua non* that any canal, expensive as it was bound to be, must be on U.S.-controlled territory, isolated from regional conflicts. The Hay-Herran Treaty provided for a U.S.-leased canal zone across the isthmus ten kilometres in width, five kilometres either side of the centre of the canal. The lease would last for ninety-nine years, subject to indefinite renewal at the pleasure of either incumbent Colombian or U.S. government. For this the U.S. would pay $10 million immediately and $250,000 per annum in rent.

For Colombian senators entrusted with ratification of the treaty as well as for other political groups in the capital of primary concern was the *de facto* loss of Colombian territory. The Hay-Herran Treaty meant, several warned, that Colombia was selling a strip of land to the United States for less money than the Americans were paying the French for their assets. Such an action would be dishonourable and a dangerous precedent. On 13 August 1902, in the absence of two Senators from Panama, the Colombian Senate rejected the Hay-Herran Treaty by a margin of twenty-four to zero.[15]

People in Washington responded at once. Although it had been acceptable for the United States Senate to reject the first Hay-Pauncefote Treaty, the rejection of Hay-Herran was quite another matter. Myopic politicians in Bogotá, thought President Roosevelt and Secretary Hay, were standing in the way of progress. Bunau-Varilla met both Francis Loomis at the State Department and President Roosevelt at the White House, and with appropriate words and body language, each learned what the others would do and were planning to do. Armed with that knowledge, Bunau-Varilla met Panamanian separatist leader Manuel Amador in New York. Provided that Amador and his friends would stage a "revolution" and proclaim Panamanian independence no later than 3 November 1903, Bunau-Varilla would pay the costs. Bunau-Varilla also insisted that in exchange for his largesse, he must become Panama's first Foreign Minister, with full power to negotiate a canal treaty with the United States. Anxious as he was that Panama secede from Colombia, Amador reluctantly agreed and then returned to Panama City to arrange the "revolution."

On 3 November, Amador and his colleagues proclaimed Panama's independence. Bribed with Bunau-Varilla's money, Colombian troops in the Panamanian capital remained in their barracks. When Colombian reinforcements arrived at Colón on the Caribbean coast, the U.S.-owned Panama Railroad refused to provide transportation across the isthmus, and ships of the U.S. Navy in the area guaranteed that no further Colombian troops would arrive. On 5 November, President Roosevelt's government extended diplomatic recognition to an independent Panama, and on 18 November, Hay and Bunau-Varilla concluded yet another canal treaty. In his memoirs,[16] Bunau-Varilla indicated that his intention was to negotiate a treaty too generous for the U.S. Senate to refuse. As the Republicans lacked a two-thirds majority, the Hay-Bunau-Varilla Treaty would have to be even better, from a U.S. perspective, than Hay-Herran. This time the Canal Zone would be ten miles, not ten kilometres, in width, and the U.S. lease would be "in perpetuity," not for a mere ninety-nine years. Hay and Bunau-Varilla were signing the accord as Amador and his associates arrived by ship at New York, and when the Panamanians reached Washington, Bunau-Varilla announced a *fait accompli*. He then threatened that unless they ratified the treaty by the end of the month, the United States would withdraw its recognition and leave the separatists vulnerable to punishment by Colombian authorities. Amador and the other Panamanians returned to the isthmus and the separatist junta gave its approval. Then on 30 November, it deposited the instrument of ratification with a U.S. Navy warship in the harbour of Panama City.

For the next eleven years, American engineers directed construction of the mammoth canal project. Unlike the Suez Canal, which by comparison was simply a ditch through a desert, the Panama Canal required locks and passed through some of the fastest growing and most dense jungle in the world. The Panama Canal represented modern technology, whose delicate mechanism required constant and reliable maintenance by skilled people. Otherwise, the jungle could have claimed it in no time.

The construction of the Panama Canal quickly confirmed, indeed symbolized, the hegemonic status of the United States. Pointedly, where the French had failed in the 1880s, the United States succeeded with great aplomb and amid greater publicity in the years 1904–14. In addition to its geopolitical and strategic significance, the canal's construction also "marked a quantum leap in Caribbean migration, and it established patterns followed by the next generation of immigrants." In providing employment plus new collective experience for thousands of West Indian workers, the Panama Canal also stands as an important event in the evolution of the Caribbean labour movement. Officially, canal authorities brought over just 31,000 men and women from the West Indies. Many more came on their own initiative, and Jamaica and Barbados alone each supplied 20,000 workers. Allowing for a high rate of turnover plus a number of dependants not included within the official calculation, one historian estimates that the actual number of men and women who migrated during the construction period is probably closer to 150,000–200,000.[17]

The choice of West Indian labour for the construction of the Panama Canal reflected contemporary white Euro-American perceptions and prejudices concerning black workers. These beliefs had their origins in the slave era and would last well into the late twentieth century. At first, contractors had pushed for the importation of Chinese workers, but Secretary of War William Howard Taft opposed this on the grounds that it smacked too much of slavery. Southern Europe offered a second source of labour, and between 1906 and 1908 some 12,000 workers were recruited from the continent. The trouble with Europeans, however, was that they cost at least twice as much in wages as West Indian labour, tended to drift off in search of better employment, and included unionists and anarchists who stirred up trouble on a number of occasions. These characteristics also applied to the U.S. workers recruited for the canal. In addition, American work crews soon divided along lines of colour, with whites securing all the senior and supervisory positions, while blacks did the bulk of the dirty, heavy, disagreeable work. Trade unions barred blacks from membership and so prevented them from promotion, even when clearly more proficient than their white supervisors. West Indian labourers therefore presented themselves as the least worst solution. Despite earlier reservations regarding the alleged work-shyness of Caribbean workers, contractors now hired them for their relative cheapness, physical strength and potential docility. With respect to the last point, canal authorities enforced an intimidating police presence in the Canal Zone, and whether because of or despite this there were no reported incidents of organized labour unrest throughout the years of construction.

West Indian migrant labourers left a permanent mark on Panama. Colón, Panama's second largest city and the Caribbean gateway to the canal, acquired a substantial English-speaking population. Yet, they were not well received by the Spanish-speaking majority, and authorities did not encourage further migration from the British West Indies after World War I. Racial tensions were exacerbated by the fact that the West Indians seemed to constitute a source of labour radicalism, being attracted to Garveyism and other West Indian movements in the interwar years. Those prejudices persisted for many years, reflected in a 1941 constitutional amendment which barred immigrants of "the negro race, whose native language is not Spanish."[18]

The canal and the Canal Zone around it became symbols for Panamanians and other Latin Americans of United States imperialism in the region. They were also a source of tension and conflict with local authorities and civilians during the course of the twentieth century. Its completion in August 1914 coincided with the outbreak of war in Europe that month, with the result that the canal assumed even larger commercial and strategic significance. Under the circumstances, American officials were not prepared to tolerate political unrest in Panama. Over the next few years, the Wilson administration sent the army and Marine Corps into Panama on various pretexts, and in 1918–19, it encouraged the reorganization of Panama's police force. This was an attempt to promote stability and avoid the controversy and financial costs inevitably associated by any intervention by United States Marines.[19] The reorganization was also an attempt to resolve a problem which had led to an official protest in October 1915 by the U.S. Minister in Panama. According to the minister, Panamanian police in Panama City and Colón, the terminal cities contiguous to the Canal Zone, were trigger-happy, and their carelessness and bravado were endangering U.S. soldiers and civilians.[20]

American interventionism and the European threat

Elsewhere in the Caribbean basin European–U.S. tensions continued in the first decade of the century. In 1902, a German-led blockade of Venezuela, some of whose citizens owed money to European creditors, caused concern to President Theodore Roosevelt. German warships were active in the Caribbean at the turn of the century, protecting German commercial and strategic interests in the region and collecting intelligence on local and regional developments, from the Panamanian secessionist movements to debt collection problems in such countries as Venezuela and the Dominican Republic. Indeed, German naval officers appear to have been among the strongest advocates of a German imperial policy. In late 1901 a Vice-Admiral of the German navy in Berlin, von Diederichs, itemized for the Head of the Admiralty the location of German naval vessels in the waters around La Guayra (Venezuela) and the availability of ships in other parts of the Caribbean to participate in a blockade of Venezuela. In mid-November 1901 there were four small German warships in the harbour at La Guayra.[21]

German interests in Venezuela at the time were not inconsequential. They included the German-owned Greater Venezuela Railway Company, the Disconto Bank, Norddeutsche Bank, Berlin Beton-und Monierbau, German-Venezuelan Sulphur Company, and the Orinoco Asphalt Company.[22] Nor were German and American concerns about Venezuelan stability ill placed. Some local German interests indicated disgust with the level of political corruption and mismanagement under President Cipriano Castro, the consequences of the ongoing civil war and the poor quality of health in the country, especially the prevalence of yellow fever and typhus and high levels of infant mortality.

As much as American officials may have shared German criticisms of the Venezuelan government early in the century, the Roosevelt administration did not want to witness any expansion of the German presence in the Caribbean. At the same time, President Roosevelt concurred with the Europeans that Venezuela and other Caribbean basin nations had a basic responsibility to meet their international financial obligations.

It was the Dominican rather than the Venezuelan situation that ultimately provoked the Roosevelt administration to action. Chaos plagued the Dominican Republic following the 1899 assassination of its dictator of twelve years, Ulises Heureaux. By 1904, the Dominican debt was more than the Dominican Republic could pay – $32 million, and creditors from European nations (principally Belgium, France, Germany, Great Britain, Italy, and Spain) as well as the United States wanted their money. In 1903, the Dominican Foreign Minister thought that he might settle some accounts by leasing coaling stations at Samaná and Manzanillo Bays to Germany, but German authorities expressed no interest. Between 1903 and 1905, French, German, and Italian warships visited (and threatened to visit) Dominican waters. Roosevelt did not want an international free-for-all; he did want political and economic stability in the region to minimize the need for European powers to intervene to collect debts or protect their other interests. Following his electoral victory in November 1904, the President announced his solution to the dilemma in his annual message to Congress. Best known as the Roosevelt Corollary to the Monroe Doctrine, the Corollary asserted a wide latitude for the United States to exercise an international police power in the event of "chronic wrongdoing" or a "loosening of the ties of civilized society."[23]

Indicative of the transformation that had occurred in the previous decade in the relative strength of the United States and Great Britain in the Caribbean, even prior to Roosevelt's assertion of an American right to exercise police power in the area, British Prime Minister Arthur Balfour renounced any intention of acquiring additional territory in the Americas and explicitly accepted the Monroe Doctrine as a part of international law.

The Dominican Republic soon felt the impact of Rooseveltian principles. Prodded by the United States Minister in the Dominican Republic while U.S. warships made appearances off the coast, President Carlos F. Morales (1904–6) "invited" the United States to administer Dominican customs posts, a principal source of government revenue. In effect, the Dominican government would be transferring its financial responsibilities to the United States. Both U.S. and Dominican governments concluded a treaty to that effect, and when the United States Senate failed to give the necessary vote of approval, President Roosevelt implemented it anyway. The arrangement was formalized by a new treaty in 1907, this time duly approved, and by 1911 the Dominican Republic was financially solvent.[24]

What amounted to a customs receivership under Presidents Roosevelt and Taft became military intervention under their Democratic successor, but after the outbreak of war in Europe in 1914 the general strategic situation had altered. Officials of the Woodrow Wilson administration sought neutrality in the world war between 1914 and the declaration of war in early 1917, but true isolation from Europe proved illusory. The Mexican revolution on its southern border considerably increased U.S. feelings of vulnerability, as warring factions vied for the upper hand between 1911 and 1920. It was not surprising, given this concern over stability, that the Wilson administration proved to be both trigger-happy and overly sensitive with their southern neighbours. Neither the Taft nor Wilson administrations recognized the government of Victoriano Huerta when the latter overthrew and had murdered President Francisco Madero. The British, faced with war in Europe and holding major oil properties in Mexico, had to balance American and Mexican ill-will. Reliant on U.S. war materiel, they sided with Wilson.

Twice in the next several years, U.S. troops invaded Mexican territory, raising memories among Mexicans of the war between the two nations a half-century earlier that had cost Mexico half its national territory. At Tampico in April 1914 Huerta's local commander arrested American sailors who had ventured too near the military installation. Mexican authorities quickly released the sailors and apologized to the American squadron commander, to no avail. Wilson used the incident as an excuse to obtain congressional approval to use military force to settle this affair of honour, and incidentally to attempt to drive Huerta from power and to seize a shipment of German weapons. U.S. sailors and Marines landed in force at Veracruz in late April 1914, and before the exchange was over several hundred Mexican troops and nineteen Americans were killed. The affair was costly in human life and had little impact on Huerta's fortunes.

In 1916, Francisco "Pancho" Villa's border raids into New Mexico, killing a number of Americans, provoked Wilson to action once again. He immediately dispatched General John J. Pershing with a punitive expedition of almost 7,000 troops, who pursued the retreating Villa more than 300 miles deep into Mexican territory. There they remained until relations moved toward war with Germany in 1917.[25]

Haiti also presented the Wilson administration with a strategic dilemma. Although the U.S. Navy did not believe that it required a base in Haiti, with those it already possessed in Cuba, Puerto Rico and near the Panama Canal, Môle St. Nicolas in Haiti was an excellent harbour, which would provide Germany with strategic advantages should it fall into German control. With the outbreak of war in Europe and the increasing danger of U.S. involvement, the Wilson administration found continuing political instability in Haiti unacceptable. The collapse of the government of Guillaume Sam with no end in sight to political chaos led Wilson to send in troops in mid-1915. For the next nineteen years, the U.S. military ruled the Haitian half of the island as the real power behind a series of inept but docile puppet governments.[26]

During the Roosevelt, Taft and Wilson administrations, Nicaragua proved to be equally unstable, faced with internal political factionalism and financial chaos as well as conflict with its neighbours and vulnerability to European influence. With harbours on both Caribbean and Pacific coasts, and proximity to the Panama Canal after 1915, Nicaragua posed another strategic problem for the United States. On several occasions during the pre-1920s, U.S. forces occupied Nicaraguan territory, fought against competing Nicaraguan factions, and trained Nicaraguan troops in anticipation of ultimate autonomy. American officials also held control of the Nicaraguan customs service in an effort to bring financial stability. During the Wilson presidency, Secretary of State William Jennings Bryan concluded the Bryan-Chamorro Treaty, which granted the United States the right to construct a canal through Nicaragua in return for a payment of several million dollars. Bryan was unable, however, to gain Senate approval for a provision in the Treaty allowing for the right of military intervention similar to the Platt Amendment for Cuba. Equally important, nonetheless, was the prohibition against the leasing of any naval bases to European powers in the Gulf of Fonseca, and to ensure that the Nicaraguan coasts were not left vulnerable to European ambitions, Wilson ordered U.S. warships to patrol during the 1916 Nicaraguan elections. Hence, in Nicaragua as in Haiti and Mexico, the U.S. sought to balance its global strategic and economic goals with regional responsibilities. The legacy of U.S. intervention in Nicaragua as elsewhere was a mixed one. There was excessive reliance then as in subsequent years on military and police force and too little energy devoted to the establishment of pluralistic political institutions and a sense of civic responsibility; but one can hardly hold the United States entirely at fault for problems that were endemic in the region in the first half of this century.

U.S. Marines also occupied the Dominican Republic in 1916, one year after their occupation of Haiti, and two years after landing in the Mexican port of Veracruz. Since May 1914, President Wilson's government had been threatening intervention to end political instability, and when civil war broke out between forces loyal to President Isidro Jiménez (1914–16) and partisans of General Desiderio Arias, the moment of truth was at hand. Arias occupied the capital city, Santo Domingo, and at his bidding the Dominican Congress impeached President Jiménez. Jiménez then prepared to retake the capital. Anticipating violence, the U.S. Navy landed Marines to protect the U.S. legation, but no violence materialized. It was obvious that Jiménez lacked the strength to invade Santo Domingo, and preferring retirement to American military support, he resigned, leaving a vacuum of power.

The objective of U.S. officials here as elsewhere was economic stability and the elimination of strategic vulnerability. More American forces landed and occupied the capital. When the Dominican Congress met in mid-summer and elected another president unacceptable to the United States, Dr. Francisco Henriquez y Carbajal, the Wilson administration withheld recognition. As the Marines controlled the customs posts, the Henriquez government lacked the funds it needed for financial viability. Finally, in November 1916, the invaders proclaimed a U.S. military government to be in control of the Dominican

Republic. Captain Harry Knapp, the military governor, dismissed all Dominican cabinet ministers and replaced them with officers of the United States Navy and Marines. These men and their military successors, most of whom did not speak Spanish, remained in control until 1922, when they began to share power with a provisional Dominican government. The Marines did not withdraw from the Dominican Republic until 1924.

Despite President Wilson's good intentions, the occupation weakened the cause of democracy in the Dominican Republic. Congress did not meet, and violators of any of the military governor's 821 decrees faced trial before a military court. Many of those decrees were severe, curtailing freedom of speech and imposing rigid press censorship.[27] Officers administering what passed for justice often resorted to brutality. Too often they considered discipline and obedience higher priorities than the due process of law. There was ongoing guerrilla warfare between the Marines and Dominican nationalists in the mountainous eastern provinces of Seibo and San Pedro de Macoris.

The Marines' legacy appears overwhelmingly negative. Apologists for the Corps have stressed the American impact on Dominican health, education, policing, and infrastructure.[28]

The same authors argue that in imposing order on the Dominican Republic, "the Marines learned valuable lessons in counter-insurgency."[29] As well, the American presence had its cultural implications. Baseball became a major Dominican sport after 1916, and the Dominican Republic's boy scout movement traces its origins to the U.S. occupation. By contrast, historian Bruce Calder admits to modest progress in education, health, and sanitation, but he judged the occupation "basically unproductive for all concerned."[30] Improvements in the infrastructure reinforced the economic status quo, says Calder. Those living in poverty remained poor. The deeply entrenched racism of the Marines replaced the milder variant of the Dominican elite against the black and mestizo majority.

There is less disagreement that the occupation damaged the U.S. image in the Dominican Republic and elsewhere. John Bartlow Martin, U.S. Ambassador to the Dominican Republic in 1962–3, found that some towns continued to celebrate the date of the Marines' withdrawal. Martin also met politicians who proudly announced that they had begun their political careers as opponents of the Marines.[31] On the international stage, Dominicans orchestrated such controversy for the United States that the Harding and Coolidge administrations (1921–3 and 1924–9 respectively) found the occupation more trouble than it was worth. Indeed, Calder thinks the damage to the U.S. reputation more significant than the guerrilla warfare in persuading the U.S. government to withdraw the Marines.[32]

The British Caribbean

If the British were prepared to yield hegemony to the United States over Panama and much of the rest of the Caribbean, they continued in the early twentieth century to adhere to a strong imperial policy toward their major island possessions in the Caribbean. Among the key architects of colonial policy was Joseph Chamberlain, Colonial Secretary in the Conservative government which assumed office in 1895. A believer in Imperial Unity, Chamberlain sought a revitalized and unified British Empire which, together, would be more than a match for any foreign challenger. A Royal Commission which went to the West Indies in 1897 confirmed that the mother country's adoption of free trade more than half a century earlier and the subsequent development of cane sugar had ruined the islands. As a direct result of the Commission's findings, the British government banned the importation of subsidized foreign sugar, and this rendered insular sugar more competitive. In 1898 the British government established an Imperial Department of Agriculture in Trinidad, which found ways to combat pests, diversify crops, and increase output. An Act of 1899 provided low interest loans for the development of transportation facilities. Jamaica's share was £110,000, which permitted the rail system, which in turn made feasible banana production in the mountainous interior. Henceforth, coffee and bananas could reach markets along the coastal plains and abroad. Nevertheless, the number of sugar estates continued to drop – from 513 in 1848 to 211 in 1887 to 77 in 1911.

In 1900 all members of the Legislative Council came from the tiny but influential European or mulatto minorities. A few men of purely African extraction – the preponderant group in Jamaica – won seats before World War I, and by the 1920s blacks constituted a majority. Before World War II, most councillors were black. At the same time, blacks entered the Civil Service in similar proportions. One individual who helped black Jamaicans take pride in themselves was Marcus Garvey, a trade unionist from Jamaica who spent some years in the United States. With the new constitution of 20 November 1944, every Jamaican adult, regardless of colour or sex, gained the right to vote for members of a fully elected House of Representatives. Women had gained the right to vote in 1919, the year women gained legal equality with men in the United Kingdom and one year before the 19th Amendment took effect in the United States. However, as late as 1938, property and literacy requirements limited balloting to one-twelfth of the adult population.

In the years after the Morant Bay rebellion, the Jamaican economy experienced a mixture of fortunes. On the one hand, sugar production continued to decline, with the number of estates falling from 513 in 1848 to 211 in 1887 and just 77 by 1911. The demand for plantation workers, however, dropped by only one-third, from 30,000 in 1860 to 20,000 in 1910, suggesting that the estates that remained in production were, on average, the larger operations. At the same time, smallholders had begun to make advances in the cultivation of bananas. As a result, by 1896 sugar represented only 18 percent of the island's total value of exports.

During the decades of British and Anglophile control, Jamaica also developed ties with the United States, Panama and Canada. In the middle of the nineteenth century, Jamaicans had helped to build the Panama Railroad across the isthmus of Panama. An estimated 20,000 additional Jamaican workers, accompanied by three or four times as many dependants, went to Panama after the United States gained control of the Canal Zone in 1903.[33] There they worked as labourers on the Panama Canal. Attracted by the higher standard of living, many stayed.

Trinidad

The black population increased throughout the nineteenth century, more by natural reproduction than through migration because the British withdrew from the African slave trade in 1807. As in British Guiana, East Indians arrived to maintain the supply of cheap labour on the sugar plantations, invariably owned by people of European extraction. An estimated 143,090 indentured labourers went to Trinidad from the Indian subcontinent, and while that may pale in comparison with the 238,909 who went to British Guiana, it is quadruple the number who went to Jamaica, which in turn attracted more than ten times the number who went to Grenada, the next largest recipient.[34] The flow of East Indians lasted from 1845 until 1917, and many of them remained in Trinidad once they were legally free to return to India.

Given the composition of the population, Trinidad had less self-government than most of the other British colonies. Most of the residents were people of colour, and most of the Europeans were Roman Catholics. What minimal representative government there was disappeared in 1898 as part of the "reforms" organized by Colonial Secretary Joseph Chamberlain. Chamberlain, who assumed office in 1895 as part of Lord Salisbury's Conservative cabinet, envisioned a centralized British Empire, a Greater Britain, which would be competitive with the other giants – the United States, the Russian Empire, the German Empire. Before 1898, Trinidad's Legislative Council, which advised the governor, was hardly representative, dominated as it was by wealthy planters, and business and professional people. Even that was too much for Chamberlain. As of 1898, appointees of the Colonial Office would outnumber Trinidadians of any description. At the same time, Chamberlain abolished the elective local council in Port of Spain, which had existed since 1853 and which offered elected politicians their only outlet. Despite a high property franchise, blacks as well as mulattos had served as councillors. Its abolition increased the perception of government tyranny on the eve of the water riot.

Other British colonies had fared less well. In British Guiana and Trinidad, where sugar accounted for three-quarters of total exports, planters had benefited from Cuba's embroilment in war in the years 1868–78. The Spanish colony soon recovered, however, to provide a serious source of competition (slavery remained in force in Cuba until 1886). At the same time, Europe had begun to exploit beet sugar as an alternative source and effectively drove colonial sugar supplies out of the market. Thus whereas Britain had imported 63 percent of its sugar from its Caribbean in 1861, by 1900 this figure had fallen to just 2.5 percent. Some assistance came in 1898, when Joseph Chamberlain, Britain's Secretary of State for the Colonies, founded the Imperial Department of

Agriculture for the West Indies, an institute designed to conduct teaching and research into better techniques and methods. In itself, however, this move represented a further signalling of Britain's intention of distancing itself from direct responsibility for the colonies.

Colonialism and trade unionism

The absence of any trade union activity on the Panama Canal was, broadly speaking, characteristic of the Caribbean as a whole in the years before World War I. Rarely did workers express or exhibit any sense of collective identity or voice their grievances and demands in an organized fashion. The region's first significant wave of union organization did not occur until after the war, but it was not totally without precedent. Despite the many obstacles in their paths, certain groups of workers did attempt to organize themselves in this earlier period.

The first recorded trade union in the Caribbean was the Trinidad Workingmen's Association (TWA), formed in 1890. The Association's name and structure programme derived from the English Workingmen's Associations formed earlier in the century, whose basic aims were to improve the living and working conditions of their members, to secure a cheap and fair press, and to educate workingmen and their families. Under the leadership of pharmacist Walter Mills, the TWA adopted a similar programme, which its first President, Walter Mills, presented to the 1897 Royal Commission of Inquiry into the present sugar depression and the question of relief. In this respect, the TWA was a forerunner of later Caribbean labour organizations as it combined the functions of a trade union proper with those of a political pressure group. Membership of the TWA was small, numbering perhaps fifty in the late 1890s and consisting mainly of carpenters, masons, tailors and other skilled workers. Its failure to influence the government of the day led to a temporary lapse in activity between 1898 and 1906, at which time it reorganized and resumed its petition of the authorities. Under the leadership of pharmacist Alfred Richards and tailor Adrien Hilton, the TWA increased its membership to 233. The organization continued to operate until 1914, when dissatisfaction over the programme of constitutional reform led to a split within the Association. Nevertheless, the TWA stands not simply as an abortive forerunner of future trade unions, but as an important link between the late nineteenth century and the post-war years.[35]

Another precursor of future developments occurred in British Guiana in the early 1900s. In 1900, the Reverend H. J. Shirley, a non-conformist minister from England, arrived in the country and soon began to criticize local labour conditions. He advocated the formation of an Owenite "big union" that would encompass all classes of worker and helped to establish a labour newspaper to promote the idea. Although Shirley was recalled in 1903, his influence lived. In 1905–6, rural and urban workers combined in the Labour Union Scheme, while in 1905 dockworkers and unemployed people joined forces in the country's first identifiable labour strike. One of the strike leaders in 1905 was Herbert Critchlow, a man who went on to form the British Guiana Labour Union in 1919.[36]

In Jamaica, too, there were examples of trade unions in the pre-war period. The island's skilled craftworkers, such as the Artisans' Union and the Printers' Union (which counted among its members one Marcus Garvey) predominated. There was also a Tobacco Workers' Union. While most of these organizations soon fizzled out and left no concrete legacy for post-war developments, one union at least signified the growing influence of the United States in all facets of Caribbean activity. The Jamaica Trades and Labour Union was officially affiliated with the American Federation of Labor, and thus brought at least a section of Caribbean workers within the ambit of American control and concern.[37]

Patterns of trade and investment

For the Spanish Caribbean the Cuban war for independence was the major watershed between an old empire and a new; but the emergence of the United States as the major investor and trading partner with Cuba in particular was evident before U.S. forces invaded the island. For the United States and its business community the Caribbean basin may have been a relatively minor component of national trade and investment prior to World War I, most of which remained linked to Europe, but the island colonies and nations of the region, trade and investment with the United States and other major powers was their life blood. The bulk of U.S. Direct Foreign Investment (DFI) between 1897 and 1914 was in Europe, followed by Canada and Newfoundland. Although less significant than those in Europe, investments in Cuba and the West Indies increased almost tenfold prior to World War I, involving a wide range of activities, from sugar and tobacco production to railroads, public utilities, and mining. As it was absorbed into the American orbit following the Spanish-American–Cuban war, Puerto Rico also became dominated economically by U.S. capital and trade. Mexico was also a significant recipient of investment as its oil industry emerged as a major international player. Central America, even with the construction of the Panama Canal, continued to lag well behind Cuba and Mexico. By 1914 the U.S. had displaced Britain as the main investor in the Caribbean region, although, with only $3.5 billion in total overseas investments, the United States remained well behind the British in world terms, with the latter's investments totalling more than $18 billion (see Table 1).

United States trade with the Caribbean region witnessed steady growth in the late nineteenth and early twentieth centuries. Even with a Spanish mercantilist policy in effect over its insular possessions, Cuba and the United States had substantial bilateral trade by the 1890s. In 1891, for instance, Cuba imported 22 million pesos worth of goods from Spain and 12 million from the United States, but it exported only 7.1 million pesos of commodities to Spain in contrast

Table 1 United States direct and portfolio investment, 1897 and 1914 (millions of U.S. dollars)

Area	1897	1914
Europe	151.0	691.8
Canada/Newfoundland	189.7	867.2
Cuba/West Indies	49.0	336.3
Mexico	200.2	853.5
Central America	21.2	93.2
South America	37.9	365.7
Africa	1.0	13.2
Asia	23.0	245.9
Oceania	1.5	17.0
Other	10.0	30.0
Total	684.5	3,513.8

Source: Cleona Lewis, *America's Stake in International Investments* (Washington, DC: Brookings Institution, 1938), p. 606.

to 62 million to the United States. By 1900, with the war over, Spain virtually disappeared from the economic scene, and U.S. exports to Cuba increased to 34 million pesos. However, Spanish nationals migrated to Cuba in unprecedented numbers, an estimated 200,000 between 1902 and 1910. In the first year of World War I, Cuba absorbed 69 million pesos of imports from the United States and exported 148 million pesos to the U.S. This was in marked contrast to Cuba's 28 million pesos of two-way trade with the United Kingdom and less than 7 million pesos with Germany in the same year.[38] Most trade was with the major industrial/colonial powers rather than within the region, consistent with a pattern of dependency on external markets.

Between 1900 and 1916, the region's main exports continued to be agricultural products and natural resources: sugar, tobacco, cotton, coffee, bananas, and lumber on the agricultural side; oil, lead, silver, copper and zinc on the mineral side. Cuban exports of sugar increased in value from 31 million pesos in 1902 to 73 million in 1905 and 133 million by 1914 with the outbreak of war in Europe. Tobacco exports in contrast remained relatively constant, from 15 million pesos in 1902 to 28 million pesos in value in 1914.[39] Mexico had the most diverse range of exports in this period, with exports of coffee, copper, cotton, lead, petroleum and petroleum products, silver and zinc. The Mexican example, however, was not the norm. Elsewhere there tended to be concentration on one or two major exports. Hence, the only major export of Trinidad and Tobago until 1912, when oil and oil products entered the export picture, was sugar. The Dominican Republic's exports were overwhelmingly cocoa and sugar, with coffee consistently a very distant third. Throughout these years Panama's only significant export was bananas; El Salvador, Haiti, Barbados, and Guatemala were single export economies. Nicaragua concentrated on bananas and coffee until cotton emerged as a very tertiary export in 1935. The Netherlands Antilles did not achieve significance as a processor of crude oil until 1929.[40]

Great Britain remained a major economic player in the region throughout the two decades leading to World War I. Even with the movement of Cuba, for instance, into the American orbit with the Spanish-American War, Britain's total trade with Cuba and Puerto Rico in 1900 was valued at over £2 million, with Haiti and Santo Domingo at more than £400,000, with Mexico at £2.5 million, and the Central American states at £1.5 million. Within its own colonial realm, British trade ranged from a low of less than £140,000 with Bermuda in total trade in 1900 to almost £4 million with the British West Indies.[41] By 1916 British exports to Cuba were valued at more than £2 million, followed in importance by Colombia and Venezuela.[42] In 1913 British imports from the British West Indies were worth over £2 million, followed at a distant second by British Guiana, whose exports were only £648,000, out a total value of imported merchandise from British countries in excess of £191 million. By contrast in the same year Britain imported from Cuba, Central America, and Colombia respectively more than £3.6 million, £2 million, and £1 million in goods.[43]

Germany remained a distant third in comparison with U.S. and British trade and investment in the area. Although both trade and investment increased in the decades prior to World War I, in 1913 German trade with all of South America represented only 7.6 percent of German trade in contrast to the U.S. with 28 percent and the British with 22 percent. The contrast was even more marked in investments, with German holdings calculated at only $600 million in contrast to the British with $5 billion and the Americans with $1.5 billion. Most German investments were in Argentina, followed by Chile and Venezuela.[44]

On the eve of World War I, the balance of power in the Caribbean basin had definitively shifted to the United States, although the legacy of European empires remained strong in the region's cultural, economic and political institutions and traditions. World War I would serve to further consolidate the American position by weakening the European powers economically and militarily.

3

THE CONSOLIDATION OF AMERICAN POWER, 1917–45

Between World War I and the end of World War II the expansion of the U.S. presence in the Caribbean basin was dramatic. That transition derived from many factors and had many faces. U.S. policy makers were driven in large part by the desire to maintain stability in a region that was viewed as strategically important to the nation. Proximity to the United States intensified strategic concerns. The now operational Panama Canal (since 1914) made the access routes and strategic locations along those routes in the Caribbean of extreme importance to American military and commercial interests. Trade and investment flows increased significantly in these years as well, with Cuba remaining of particular significance.

The consolidation of U.S. hegemony parallelled the decline of Europe. The comparative weakness of Britain and France in the aftermath of World War I and their limited capacity to maintain a strong presence in the region also increased the need for American vigilance with the increased presence of communism in the area in the 1920s and the rise of Nazi Germany in the 1930s. The end of World War I coincided with the Bolshevik phase of the Russian Revolution, which in its international dimensions after 1919 raised the constant spectre of Bolshevism wherever nationalism, anti-colonialism and radical labour organizations and activities emerged in the Caribbean region, although there is little doubt that U.S. officials in the interwar years (and later) tended to exaggerate the real threat from the left to U.S. security. Internal political and economic instability throughout the Caribbean basin combined with the rise of Nazi Germany and its broad imperial ambitions to intensify U.S. sensitivities to those who seemed unable to maintain stability in their own houses; that situation was especially acute as the world moved toward and then into the maelstrom of World War II in 1939. Such strategic and geopolitical considerations melded with pre- and post-Wilsonian notions of American mission and the progressive ideals of what U.S. historian Emily Smith Rosenberg appropriately refers to as "spreading the American dream." As much as the United States eschewed formal internationalism in the 1920s and 1930s by failing to join the League of Nations, its increasingly global reach and commitments to its main areas of strategic importance continued to produce an outward looking vision of foreign involvement that fundamentally belied the isolationism which has been attributed to the period.

European nations as well, specifically Britain and France, were distracted by other issues and priorities in the interwar years. The post-Versailles decades were not happy ones for either nation as they fought to cope with inflation, war debts, reparations, diminished trade with the protectionist United States, the rise of Japan in the Far East, and the re-emergence and rearmament of a bellicose, expansionist Germany and Italy. For all of these European powers, issues closer to home appeared more urgently in need of attention than the seemingly insignificant colonial questions that characterized the Caribbean. It was not until much of continental Europe fell to the Nazi onslaught after 1939 that the Caribbean colonies assumed enhanced importance, especially those which belonged to the conquered nations and where the danger existed that they would come into German hands. The French surrender to Germany in June 1940 was a major blow to both France and Britain. The rapid and humiliating French defeat left Britain alone against Germany, and French colonies in the Caribbean were highly vulnerable, especially when the unoccupied section of France established a largely collaborationist regime at Vichy under Marshal Pétain. Under these circumstances, it was not surprising that the United States would assume almost total control of the Caribbean, extending the role it had played during World War I and the interwar years.

Before the outbreak of war in Europe, a heightened nationalism among Caribbean nations also presented a challenge to the United States and the other imperial powers. Such nationalist anti-colonialism was manifest in literary, political and labour movements, many of which had strong transnational ties and inspiration. Such nationalism derived from many factors and predated World War I, as the 1909 publication by Venezuelan nationalist and anti-American César Zumeta of "The Sick Continent" attests. Like his contemporaries José Marti and Enrique Rodó, Zumeta's anxieties over the political, cultural, and economic threat to the Caribbean basin posed by American power intensified with the U.S. defeat of Spain and the occupation of Cuba and Puerto Rico. Unlike the more romantic revolutionary Marti, Zumeta increasingly viewed a more autocratic, strong Latin American state and leader as an important bulwark against the United States, fearing that without the capacity to set their own houses in order, the weaker nations of the region would be vulnerable to foreign intervention. Hence, Zumeta became a lifelong supporter of Venezuelan strongman Juan Vicente Gómez, who ruled Venezuela from 1908 through 1935.[1]

During World War I, there were mixed messages from Washington on the nation's colonial ambitions. On the one hand, the Wilson administration tightened its grip on the region for economic and national security reasons during the war. On the other, Wilson and his officials inspired decolonization impulses when they spoke of national self-determination, especially at the Versailles peace settlement. That Wilson had central Europe rather than the Caribbean in mind was of little import to colonial residents in the Caribbean region. Improved communications, especially with the advent of radio and telephone linkages, significantly shortened distances among peoples in the area and served to spread political and cultural ideas beyond colonial elites. For many residents of the Caribbean basin the years through the end of World War II were ones of continued poverty, political repression, and frustration; for others, these years were ones of rising expectations for economic development and political autonomy. It was the interplay among the forces of domestic transformation in the Caribbean and great power rivalries that provided the essential historical tension of the period.

The stirring of nationalism and antagonism toward imperial domination and occupation were not limited to the U.S. experience. Throughout the Caribbean during and after World War I resentments intensified, in part because of treatment received by the colonial powers during the war. Only reluctantly did Britain accept troops from the West Indies for World War I service, for instance, and those recruited had to operate in segregated conditions at lower rates of pay than those of their white peers. People "not of unmixed European blood" could not become officers, and black soldiers had to dig trenches and clean latrines rather than engage in combat duty. After the war, the Trinidadian newspaper *Argos* and Marcus Garvey's *Negro World* encouraged black pride. The war also saw the end of Indian migration to Trinidad and Tobago. The nationalist movement in India was so influential at a time when British authorities needed their co-operation that it became impossible to ignore complaints that the indenture system was degrading to Indians.

From intervention to the good neighbour

The transformation of the Caribbean into an American lake assumed many forms – economic, military, and cultural – but it was the military occupations of the years from World War I on of Haiti, Cuba, the Dominican Republic and Nicaragua which seemed to set the tone of the period.[2] Of the four the occupation of Cuba was the briefest, lasting only during World War I, although the economic, political and cultural linkages that developed between the United States and Cuba were likely far closer than those with the other countries which the United States occupied. The Haitian occupation was the longest, enduring from 1915 to 1934. Regardless of duration, they were all controversial at home and abroad. In each instance they contributed to emergent nationalist sentiments and for the long term solved little either for the countries occupied or to advance U.S. strategic and geopolitical objectives.

The United States faced increasing opposition to its interventionist approach in the interwar years, notably at the major inter-American conferences of the period: Havana in 1928, Montevideo in 1933 and Buenos Aires in 1936. U.S. officials gradually made concessions to Latin America as a whole. At the Havana conference in 1928 Secretary of State Charles Evans Hughes still spoke vigorously in defence of the U.S. right of intervention; in the same period President Calvin Coolidge's officials warned against the threat of Bolshevism in Mexico and Central America. In 1929 the State Department strongly protested against a Cuban legislative initiative that might have compromised the terms of the Platt Amendment embedded in the Cuban constitution, providing for U.S. intervention to preserve Cuban independence.[3]

Yet, there was a gradual shift in U.S. policy away from this intransigence. The shift derived less from a change in policy objectives than from the clear realization that the use of the Marines as a constant instrument of policy in the Caribbean basin had become anachronistic and counter-productive. Such military interventionism was not a factor in the South American rim of the basin, specifically in Colombia and Venezuela, although there was increasing nationalism in the 1920s and 1930s which seemed to pose a threat to the security of foreign investment, especially in the oil industry. In Venezuela, Juan Vicente Gómez provided a comparatively stable investment climate for the foreign oil industry. By 1929, U.S. investment in the South American oil industry was 34 percent of total American overseas investment in oil development. The largest producer in Venezuela was the Anglo-Dutch interest Royal Dutch Shell, followed by three U.S. firms: Standard Oil of Indiana (El Lago) and Standard Oil of New Jersey, which in 1928 gained control of the Creole Syndicate. There were only minor labour problems and no threat of nationalization until World War II following the 1938 nationalization in Mexico. The anti-Americanism that existed tended to be popular and intellectual in its origin and orientation. It was especially strong in the Lake Maracaibo area of oil production because of the characteristically discriminatory policies the foreign companies followed toward their Venezuelan workers. The more intellectual critique tended to focus on such issues as the negative images of Latin Americans that American films tended to project in the 1920s and 1930s as well as the rampant American materialism projected in the films. There was even concern about the environmental degradation of the Lake Maracaibo region by the oil industry. Nonetheless, Gómez did implement legislation for the development of the oil industry in the 1920s that prohibited monopolies, required companies to maintain active development on their concessions, and provided for shorter concession periods than the companies could obtain in parts of the Middle East. As in Colombia, Gómez also encouraged non-American interests. In general, he sought to maintain a pluralistic foreign policy that would keep the United States guessing about his intentions. The United States did not join the League of Nations; Venezuela did. Although he relied primarily on U.S. weapons and military training, he also contracted a French aviation mission to train Venezuelan pilots.[4]

Following Gómez's death in 1935 and the inauguration of the moderate populist Eleazar López Contreras, Venezuelan politics became more open but also more volatile. López established a series of reform measures know as the February Program in 1935–6, including a more nationalistic approach to the oil industry, only to revert to more repressive tactics in 1937 when confronted with popular protests, labour activity and a strengthened political opposition. López's successor in 1944, Isaias Medina Angarita, kept Venezuela solidly within the U.S. orbit during World War II, permitting U.S. forces to enter the country in

1942 to assist with training and military installations and ultimately maintaining a moderate approach toward the oil companies.[5]

Colombian politics and society were more complex and sophisticated than Venezuela's and there was a higher degree of economic nationalism in the interwar years, although in the final analysis the country followed a foreign policy orientation not dissimilar to that of their neighbour and long-time rival. By the end of World War I, Colombia had already begun to pursue a mildly nationalistic policy toward foreign investment in subsoil mineral development. In Colombia, the dominant force in the oil industry was Standard Oil of New Jersey, which held the major DeMares oil concession through its Tropical oil subsidiary. Gulf Oil held the important Barco concession in northeast Colombia on the Venezuelan border and adjacent to the Venezuelan developments at Lake Maracaibo. By the late 1920s, the conservative government of Pedro Nel Ospina revoked Gulf Oil's concession and set about drafting far more nationalistic oil legislation. Between the conciliatory work of Ospina's successor, Enrique Olaya Herrera, a more moderate approach by Gulf Oil officials, who were concerned by potential political instability in Venezuela, and the persistent work of U.S. State Department officials, the Colombian government moderated its oil legislation and reached agreement by 1931 with Gulf Oil on the Barco concession. Yet, anti-Americanism still ran high in the country, especially after the bitter and protracted 1938 strike against the United Fruit Company in Magdalena. Tension between Colombia and the United States revolved largely around the degree of American influence in the Colombian economy. Not only did United Fruit dominate the banana industry against the self-identified interests of Colombian growers, but also Americans controlled the oil industry, pipeline development, and ultimately in the course of the interwar period Colombian aviation with the outbreak of World War II. In the course of the 1920s, the U.S. State Department also played an important facilitating role in providing American expertise in such areas as the restructuring of Colombian central banking. Also like Venezuelans and other residents of the Caribbean basin, Colombians were concerned about the potential and real impact of Yankee culture, although the indigenous culture was sufficiently vibrant and well-established that in the pre-television age, the main cultural impact from external sources came in the areas of industry, technology, and foreign investment.[6]

Although direct U.S. military intervention on the continent was not a real threat in the interwar years, American interventionism remained a source of inter-American conflict, with the result that in the late 1920s and early 1930s, the United States was under considerable pressure from its neighbours to make a conciliatory commitment. The Japanese invasion of Manchuria in 1931 and the strong denunciation of the act from the world community underlined the need for the United States to find alternative tools to achieve similar objectives. The result was increasing reliance on economic and political instruments of policy and a rhetorical shift to Franklin Roosevelt's notion of "giving them a share."

Calvin Coolidge's Republican successor and former Secretary of Commerce Herbert Hoover undertook a tour of Latin America as President-elect, the first such tour by a U.S. President. He worked effectively to withdraw U.S. troops from the region in the course of his presidency, and spoke, well before Franklin D. Roosevelt, of the idea of a good neighbour approach to relations with Latin America. As well, the planning for the 1933 conference of inter-American states at Montevideo, at which there was further movement toward commitment to non-intervention, took place during Hoover's presidency. The Hoover administration also released in 1930, not with much enthusiasm one might add, however, the State Department's Clark Memorandum on the Monroe Doctrine (Under-Secretary of State J. Reuben Clark). Prepared during the Coolidge administration when Frank Kellogg was Secretary of State, the Clark Memorandum separated Theodore Roosevelt's Corollary asserting the right of the U.S. to exercise a police power in the region from the original principles of the Monroe Doctrine articulated by President Monroe a century earlier.[7] More importantly, however, the Clark Memorandum was silent on whether or not the U.S. claimed the right to intervene or would refrain from doing so. As well, U.S. policy makers in word and deed always made clear that the Caribbean basin was considered distinct from the rest of Latin America. What the United States could not or would not attempt in Argentina, Brazil or even the larger Caribbean basin nations such as Venezuela and Colombia might be warranted in Cuba, Nicaragua, Haiti or the Dominican Republic, for instance.

At the Seventh Pan-American Conference at Montevideo in 1933 Secretary of State Cordell Hull moved the United States further along the road toward accommodation of Latin American demands with his signature of the Convention on the Rights and Duties of States, renouncing intervention as a tool of policy, with the important caveat that nations retained their rights under international law and their existing treaty obligations. Three years later at the Buenos Aires conference, the participating states, including the United States, reaffirmed that pledge; but, again American officials soured the moment by indicating that it was only military intervention that was being prohibited. The fact that by 1936 there were no U.S. occupation troops in a Latin American or Caribbean nation (except for the Canal Zone) was consistent with the U.S. position at Buenos Aires, but the leaders of the region were not fully reassured.[8]

The military occupation that the Wilson administration established in Haiti during World War I ended in 1934 when Franklin Roosevelt, who had, as assistant secretary of the navy under Wilson, helped to draft the Haitian constitution. It seemed only fitting that the withdrawal of troops from the impoverished nation should have taken place under Roosevelt, with his freshly asserted commitments to a good neighbour approach to hemispheric relations.

Yet, the historical record of the almost two decades of occupation remains, and by all accounts it was less than a success. Haiti remained in the economic basement of the hemisphere, and American tutelage failed to create the political and economic institutions that might have contributed to the later maturity of Haitian political culture. The Marines enforced their control through the Gendarmerie d'Haiti, whose officers, at first, were all Americans. Indeed, as late as 1921, years after the war against Germany had ended, there were only nine Haitian officers out of 117. The Marines controlled communications, health, and road building, the last of which they did by reintroducing the French practice of forced labour. Major Smedley Butler, who took charge of Haiti's Gendarmerie, shared the prevailing contempt for Haiti's elite.[9]

The Marines also imposed press censorship, although in a country with a 95 percent illiteracy rate this hardly mattered. When some provisions of the U.S.–Haitian treaty proved unconstitutional, Haitians changed their constitution. Henceforth, foreigners would, for the first time, be allowed to own land in Haiti, and the Haitian President would be the one to decide when elections would take place. Because he was too nationalistic, President Dartiguenave had to vacate office in 1922, and his successor – Louis Borno – did not permit elections until 1930, following a series of strikes in 1929. In the turbulence following the strikes, Marines shot and killed ten Haitians at Aux Cayes. American authorities imposed martial law and sent additional Marines, but President Herbert Hoover – never enthusiastic about foreign interventions – appointed a commission to investigate the situation. Meanwhile, Hoover's top representative in Haiti, U.S. Minister Dana G. Munro, opposed a French loan which might have strengthened the Haitian economy, for fear that it might also strengthen French influence in the country. If there were outside influence, thought Munro, that influence ought to be American.[10]

The occupation left behind a mixed legacy in Haitian consciousness, and Haitian literature reflected that ambiguity. U.S. troops moved into a cultural environment in Haiti that was highly sensitive to issues of race, and Haiti's elite was well aware of the white supremacist values of many Marines and the collective tyranny of the military occupiers. Yet, the review of Americans in Haiti varied. At one end of the continuum was Frédéric Burr-Reynaud's *Anathèmes*, written in 1930, a poem in which "Marines" rhymed with "latrines" and in which the Marines appeared as conceited hypocritical bullies. At the other was J. B. Cineas' *L'Héritage Sacré*, a novel written in 1936–7. Its hero was a kindly scientist, Dr. Philip Benfield, who greatly admired and learned from the Haitian people among whom he worked.[11]

Nevertheless, some have seen a positive side to the Marine occupation. Historian Hans Schmidt stressed the American contribution to the fields of sanitation and public health, improvements to infrastructure (notably telephone communication, roads, harbours and airport facilities) garbage and sewage disposal and to hospitals, especially rural health clinics. He also suggested that Haitian women enjoyed an improved socio-economic status with a growing number of women moving into the professions and political movements as well as lower status secretarial positions. Such gains were ephemeral, however. Once the Marines left, the telephone system collapsed and the roads and ports became unusable. Haiti's literacy rate remained the worst in the western hemisphere.[12]

One historian, Brenda Gayle Plummer, argues that in many respects, the Marine occupation had a negative impact on the economy. In 1933, President Stenio Vincent and the State Department agreed that the National Bank of the Republic of Haiti would remain under U.S. supervision until 1947, by which time Haiti would have repaid a loan acquired in 1922. A U.S. citizen, Sidney De la Rue, took charge and made certain that the non-Haitian creditors received moneys owing to them from the impoverished country. During the occupation, France's commercial ties with Haiti lessened. Haiti had commitments which prevented it from importing French goods at the levels demanded by Paris, and whatever Haiti produced was readily available in France's tropical colonies, where France had a greater degree of control.[13]

The experience of the Dominican Republic with U.S. military occupation from World War I into the 1920s paralleled that of Haiti. The positive contributions tended to be to infrastructure rather than to the establishment of democratic institutions, although clearly endogenous factors in the Dominican Republic were also responsible for the continuation of caudillism in politics and the fragility of democratic political institutions in subsequent decades.

As noted in Chapter 2, the U.S. military occupation of Haiti came at a time of increasing nationalism throughout the Caribbean and Latin America, with the result that American officials increasingly sought alternative means to maintain a similar level of control without direct military involvement. Haiti proved an especially difficult challenge, however, because of the persistent poverty, lack of substantial economic development and massive levels of political corruption in coming decades. Military occupation in itself appears to have done little to alleviate either the inadequate level of development or to infuse a commitment to democratization on the part of Haiti's leaders. On the contrary, the occupation fuelled additional anti-Americanism.[14] That anti-American sentiment continued to plague U.S. governments in the course of the 1920s and long after the final withdrawal of U.S. forces.[15]

U.S. State Department official, Sumner Welles, negotiated with Dominican politicians for elections and a subsequent Marine withdrawal in 1924,[16] but in the short run, little changed. The political elite consisted of the very people who had governed until 1916, and the winner of the 1924 presidential election, Horacio Vásquez, extended the four-year term to which he had been elected by a constitutional amendment. In 1930 there was a change for the worse. During the occupation, the Marines had trained an internal security force, the Guardia Nacional Dominicana, which could maintain domestic tranquillity within the Dominican Republic after the Marines' departure. One of the star students of the Marine academy at Haina was a thug named Rafael Leonidas Trujillo Molina, recruited into the National Guard in 1918. In 1930, Trujillo – by then head of the National Guard – forced President Vasquez to resign, and Trujillo remained in charge – either as President or through a puppet President – until his assassination thirty- one years later.[17]

Even the stability of the Trujillo years did not guarantee that the U.S. would be content with the trading relationship between the two countries. Like other countries in the Caribbean basin in the depression years, the Dominican Republic found attractive alternative trade connections with European countries and Japan. Imports from the United States declined in value from $8.5 million in 1930 to $4.7 million in 1934, although exports to the U.S. – comprised mostly of sugar, molasses and cane syrup, fruit, cacao, and coffee – remained constant in the same period at slightly more than $4 million. The decline in U.S. exports resulted directly from increased Japanese, German and Dutch competition, especially for cotton textiles, cement, chemicals, lard and some iron and steel products. Although Japanese purchases from the Dominican Republic were seen as token, France had a formal agreement with the nation providing for duty free entry of specified French brand name products, and France was an important traditional market for Haitian coffee.[18] As well Trujillo's government protested the 1934 U.S.–Cuban Reciprocity Treaty as discriminatory against Dominican trade.[19]

On the political side, Trujillo brought limited benefits to his nation. He did provide the stability of authoritarianism, and he presided over a period of unprecedented growth.[20] It was during his era that the island's military balance of power tilted in favour of the Dominican Republic, despite Haiti's larger population, thus reducing Dominican fear of a Haitian invasion. In the late 1930s he also offered asylum to Jewish refugees from Hitler's Germany. At a time when other nations were less hospitable, Trujillo offered them 26,000 acres at Sosua, where they could use their energy and their knowledge to improve Dominican agriculture, although fewer than 700 accepted the opportunity over the next several years.[21] Trujillo biographer Robert D. Crassweller has suggested that they owe their admission to the Dominican massacre of Haitians in 1937, an event which made Trujillo anxious for some positive international press. It was good public relations for a Dominican diplomat to announce to the Evian conference of 1938 that his country would admit 100,000 Jews. In 1940, the Dominican government formalized the terms of entry.[22]

German sources, however, indicate that the Dominican government was thinking along these lines even before the 1937 massacre of several thousand Haitian labourers who had migrated into the Dominican Republic in search of work on the plantations.[23] Early in 1937, the German legation in Ciudad Trujillo indicated to Berlin that Dominican newspapers were reporting a willingness to accept 2,000 Jewish families. According to the Interior Minister, Trujillo's brother-in-law General Garcia, authorities wanted competent farmers, and a major reason for delay was the possibility that the Jewish farmers would leave the land and go into business. The German legation further suggested that Trujillo wanted to make a name for himself on the international stage.[24] If Trujillo was concerned about his image *before* the Haitian massacre, as the German legation was speculating, he certainly had good reason to perform some good deeds in its aftermath. Sosua's Jews, it would appear, were the beneficiaries.

However, these gains cost the Dominican people dearly, particularly in Trujillo's later years. A lack of protection for basic civil liberties, torture of political prisoners, corruption, and widespread economic disparities characterized the Dominican Republic under Trujillo, but he was able in the post-World War II years to play successfully on American anxieties about communism to retain U.S. support.

Like Haiti and the Dominican Republic, Nicaragua was under U.S. military occupation at the end of World War I. The Taft administration had sent in American forces in 1912 to maintain the Conservative Party in power, but by the mid-1920s the country seemed comparatively stable and the rationale for a continued U.S. military presence equally thin. The Coolidge administration did not use U.S. forces to supervise the 1924 presidential elections and withdrew those forces the following year. Then, the situation once again unravelled. The coalition government which took office in the wake of the elections was unable to withstand a challenge from the main losing candidate, Emiliano Chamorro. The deposed but legitimately elected government, led by Vice-President Juan Sacasa, turned to Mexico for assistance against Chamorro's forces. This proved to be an imprudent decision, raising the spectre in Washington of radical, revolutionary, Mexico carrying its revolutionary politics into Central America. Although there was no basis for such claims, the Sacasa–Chamorro conflict provided the Coolidge administration with its rationale to return 5,000 U.S. forces to Nicaragua, this time under a more insightful political veteran, Henry Stimson.

Stimson rejected both of the main pretenders to the presidency, opting instead for former President Adolfo Diaz as acting president, thus neutralizing Sacasa's military support in the country, with the major exception of César Augusto Sandino. For the next five years, until he was betrayed and murdered, this young son of a wealthy family and former employee of the United Fruit Company led a successful, nationalistic, almost messianic, opposition to the U.S. Marines and their Nicaraguan collaborators. Sandino's capacity to elude, taunt and humiliate U.S. Marines over those years gave him the mythical proportions that would inspire the Sandinista revolution against the Somoza government in the 1970s.

Other than the martyred Sandino, the United States left one other major legacy when it withdrew the Marines in 1931: the U.S.-established National Guard. In Nicaragua, as in other areas of the Caribbean basin that the U.S. occupied in the early twentieth century, the training of indigenous military forces as an institution of stability was a high priority. Such an approach was both politically more palatable in the United States and economically more satisfactory to the U.S. Congress as the depression deepened late in the Hoover administration. Neither the National Guard nor the United States, however, ever managed to resolve the problems associated with its own creation: it was difficult for it to shake off its identification as a despised American creation; and the U.S. found it difficult if not impossible to restrain the National Guard and mold it into an instrument that defended democratic institutions rather than repressing legitimate political opposition to a succession of authoritarian regimes. In 1936, one of its main leaders, General Anastasio Somoza, seized political power, and, using the National Guard as his personalist army, maintained one of the tightest dictatorships and family regimes in Latin America until overthrown by the Sandinistas in 1979.[25] It had to be more than coincidence that the three most ruthless and dictatorial regimes in the Caribbean basin – Trujillo in the Dominican Republic, Somoza in Nicaragua, and the Duvaliers in Haiti – all emerged in the countries that had been most closely controlled by U.S. military forces during and after World War I.

Cuba

Although Cuba escaped the formal U.S. military occupation of Haiti and the Dominican Republic in the 1920s and early 1930s, the more complex and sophisticated nation remained a protectorate of the United States until the Platt Amendment was abrogated in 1934. Even the end of the Platt Amendment was not without ties, however, since the Reciprocity Treaty of that year was intended to preserve and enhance the U.S.–Cuban trade linkage against European and Asian competition. Throughout the century the U.S. retained its naval station at Guantánamo and used the presence of U.S. troops in eastern Cuba to subdue labour action in 1917.[26] In the immediate aftermath of World War I, in an effort to promote political stability, the U.S. supervised, indeed controlled, national elections. On other fronts, from World War I through the 1930s, American economic and cultural influence in Cuba continued to grow apace. Baseball became one of the nation's pastimes, passions, and sources of talent for the major leagues in the United States. Mah Jong caught the same faddish interest as a game in Cuban circles that it did in the United States; American films, architecture, consumer goods and technology were visible manifestations of U.S. dominance; U.S. capital continued to flow into the island's agricultural, industrial and ultimately tourist industries at a level that was unmatched elsewhere in the Caribbean basin, rising from $220 million on the eve of World War I to $1.5 billion prior to the 1929 crash. Sugar continued to be the main engine of economic development, but in addition to the traditional landed elites both a substantial bourgeoisie and a significant and increasingly influential industrial labour movement also emerged, both of which were to be essential elements in the subsequent political transformation of the nation. Yet, along with U.S. cultural and economic dominance came an emergent Cuban nationalism, which bridled at the lack of Cuban autonomy in every sphere and which paved the way to the revolution of 1959.[27]

During and after the protectorate, the U.S. sought to contain the stirring of Cuban nationalism and the perceived dangers of a labour movement, a danger to both American capital and U.S. control over Cuban political agendas. Such concerns were strong in the early 1920s when there were frequent labour disputes and reached a crescendo in the late 1920s and early 1930s when the lengthy and increasingly repressive administration of Gerardo Machado

(1925–33) unravelled and in its wake left several years of political uncertainty as contending forces of the right, left and centre manoeuvred for pre-eminence. That uncertain environment of course provided an opening for more radical labour and political elements, with the result that Washington greeted with relief in 1933 the emergence of a conservative, military-backed regime under Sergeant Fulgencio Batista as a replacement for the more liberal but ineffectual government of Grau San Martin. Without the political intrigues of Franklin Roosevelt's representative in Havana, Sumner Welles, Cuba might well have taken a more liberal turn in the mid-1930s.

The transformation of Caribbean labour

Amidst the diplomatic and military confrontations that occurred in the region in the interwar years, there were also important changes taking place in the composition and organization of labour in the area, changes that had significant implications for the later domestic and international history of the Caribbean. The migration of Haitian workers into the Dominican Republic in the 1930s, for instance, as well as the violence with which they were greeted, underlined one of the important characteristics of the human history of the area: the high level of mobility of its peoples and the severe unemployment and underemployment that workers faced for most of the twentieth century. Many of the labour conflicts that took place in the interwar years had international ramifications, if only because of the foreign sources of much of the investment capital, the dependency relationship of the countries and colonies relative to Europe and North America, and the foreign sources of labour organization. While the riots and labour disturbances that swept the region in 1919–24, 1928 (Colombia) and 1935–8 involved local grievances and were of local inspiration, just as importantly they indicated the enduring influence of both the Caribbean's colonial heritage and the changing international power relationships in the region in the twentieth century. Such influences were reflected in several ways. First, the structure of colonial trade, within which the role of the Caribbean was to cultivate raw materials for export, continued to restrict economic diversification. Consequently, low wages, unemployment and underemployment remained characteristic of Caribbean society. Second, both imperial and national governments were slow to accept trade unions as a legitimate form of organization, as were the multinational corporations which employed much of the labour. Laws pertaining to collective action continued to be restrictive in nature and such restrictions contributed not so much to the outbreak of labour actions but to the confrontations into which those labour actions evolved. Third, the legal restrictions on trade unions caused many labour organizations to adopt political programmes designed to bring about changes in the law. This brought them into contact with political anti-colonial movements in the islands which also emerged in the interwar years, and the two struggles became intertwined. Nor could Caribbean residents have been oblivious to the events of the Mexican revolution throughout the 1910s, including the military intervention of the United States in 1914 and 1916. Although the Mexican revolution was not in itself a war of national liberation it had significant anti-colonial dimensions which stood as a symbol for Caribbean nationalists throughout the post-war era.

Cuba was not alone in the Caribbean basin in its stirring of nationalism and labour militancy. On a more general tableau, World War I aggravated long-standing tensions and hardships among workers in the region. Although the war caused a rise in the price of sugar and other commodities, drought conditions and the threat of German submarines to transatlantic shipping limited the degree to which producers benefited from increased demand and higher prices. For Caribbean workers equally significant were the rise in the cost of living and the slump in wage levels. In British Guiana, for instance, the cost of basic necessities rose by 118 percent between 1914 and 1920 and continued to rise in the 1920s: the cost of housing alone rose 50 percent. In Trinidad, the general increase was even greater, with prices rising by 145 percent between 1914 and 1920.[28]

Discontent over wage levels resulted in a few strikes during the war itself, as for instance oil and asphalt workers at Fyzabad and Point Fortin, Trinidad, in 1917; but in 1918–24 strikes and labour violence were far more widespread. Disturbances occurred in Jamaica in 1918 and 1924; in Trinidad in 1919 and 1920; in St. Lucia in 1920; in the Bahamas in 1922; in British Honduras in 1919 and again in 1920. The scale and distribution of unrest was unprecedented, and at least one historian argues that "such a pattern of disequilibrium matches that of 1935–8 in the British Caribbean."[29] In British Honduras in July 1919, the agitation was organized by a group of returned Jamaican soldiers with the support of local unemployed and underemployed workers. Riots followed in downtown Belize and were sufficient in scale to prompt local authorities to send an SOS. The response to that call for assistance symbolized the transition in international power that was taking place in the region, as a U.S. naval vessel arrived on the scene only shortly after a British cruiser landed troops to restore order.[30]

The United States was also important in the rising political challenge to British colonial rule after World War I in the British Caribbean. Marcus Garvey, whose experiences included a stint in the Panama Canal Zone in 1911, left Jamaica for New York in 1916. There he was instrumental in founding the short-lived but highly popular Universal Negro Improvement Association (UNIA), which raised the level of working-class blacks and stressed the importance of Africa as the original homeland. Branches of the UNIA were established throughout the British Caribbean, and Garvey himself returned to Jamaica following his deportation from the United States for conviction on fraud charges. In 1929 Garvey formed Jamaica's People's Political Party, an organization that claimed the support of the island's working class.[31]

The interwar years witnessed not only continuing labour tensions but also the formation of more established labour organizations. In Colombia, workers on the banana plantations of the Caribbean coast and oil workers in the interior led the way, largely under the aegis of socialist and anarchist organizations. There a number of strikes, directed primarily against the United Fruit Company or Tropical Oil, were highlighted by the bloody 1928 banana workers' strike which inspired Gabriel García Márquez in *One Hundred Years of Solitude*.

In Venezuela, President Juan Vicente Gómez was highly repressive of political dissent and organized labour throughout the 1920s and early 1930s, in part to appease the foreign oil companies that held exclusive control over the oil industry. Gómez's labour and immigration policies were not, however, entirely satisfactory to the oil companies. The latter tended to prefer imported English-speaking black West Indian workers, but Gómez barred them after the economic downturn of 1929 intensified competition for jobs. At the same time, Venezuela's labour legislation did not permit strikes, with the result that the labour environment for the oil companies in Venezuela was more favourable than elsewhere in the Caribbean. That situation altered after 1935 when Gómez's authoritarian regime gave way to the more tolerant if not liberal government of Eleazar López Contreras, who liberalized labour legislation, tolerated political opposition, and introduced a moderately progressive series of laws which provided both protection and greater freedom for working people.[32]

In British Guiana, Hubert Critchlow, a popular cricket champion, pioneered the labour movement among black dockworkers with the formation of the British Guiana Labour Union, which began largely as an eight-hour movement. By early 1920 the organization claimed 10,000 members, including not only the largely black dockworkers but also the East Indian workers on the sugar plantations. The organization had limited success in practice, however, losing most of its strikes in the early 1920s, and the subsequent shift of its leaders toward political action decimated its support among workers by the late 1930s.[33]

In Jamaica, trade union activity was restricted by the fact that, unlike in British Guiana, labour organizations enjoyed more limited legal rights. The Trade Union Ordinance of 1919, for instance, modelled on the British Trade Union Act of 1871, freed unions from the charge of criminal conspiracy to which they had been vulnerable until then but left them liable for damages resulting from strike action and failed to legalize legal picketing. The 1919 legislation, described by Zin Henry as "the first pillar of freedom, though indeed a weak column," reflected the view of Governor Probyn that Jamaican workers were not prepared for strong trade unions. Trade unionism failed to make much headway in Jamaica in the 1920s and was limited to the formation of two branches of the Longshoremen's Union in 1918, both of which survived only to mid-decade.

In Trinidad, where the TWA had already provided the basis of a labour move-ment, trade unions fared better in the post-war years. The return of dissatisfied former soldiers from Europe provided the movement with momentum at the end of the war. In particular, Captain Arthur Andrew Cipriani, a Corsican Creole who had led an earlier recruitment drive in Jamaica, played a critical role. A stalwart socialist and seemingly inexhaustible organizer, Cipriani persuaded workers and returned veterans to join the TWA and acted as the stevedores' representative during a November 1919 strike. Despite strong opposition from the port's shipping agents, who brought in strike-breakers and requested the support of the British army, the strikers eventually secured a 25 percent wage increase.[34]

The stevedores' success in 1919 led to a wave of strikes across Trinidad during the year, from city street cleaners and government-employed carpenters to sugar workers on the island's estates, also involving some of Tobago's workers. Trinidad's governor responded by ordering the arrest of many of the strike leaders and requesting the assistance of British troops and naval vessels. Although he also appointed a Wages Committee to investigate workers' claims, conditions worsened, with the result that the government resumed its repressive approach and in 1920 passed the Strikes and Lockouts Ordinance, forbidding strikes but providing for compulsory arbitration in disputes.

Similar to developments led by Critchlow in British Guiana, Cipriani broadened the TWA's activities to include political agitation and from 1925 to 1945 he secured election to the island's legislative council. The transformation of the TWA from a labour into a political organization was completed in 1932 following the enactment of a new and more restrictive Trinidad Trade Union Law, which effectively rendered trade unions powerless. On the advice of the British Trades and Labour Congress, in particular its secretary Walter Citrine, Cipriani converted the TWA into the Trinidad Labour Party in 1934.[35]

The 1930s were a watershed in the development of labour movements in the Caribbean. The worldwide depression hit all sectors of the region's economy and its labour force. In some countries, such as Colombia with the election of Liberal Alfonso López, or Mexico with the election of Lazaro Cárdenas, the depression brought to power governments more favourably disposed toward labour and prepared to act against foreign companies. In others, notably in Central America and Cuba, governments remained hostile and repressive. Riots and disturbances were frequent through the decade, and labour agitation in the British Caribbean especially parallelled and intersected with political nationalism as public issues.

The change of government in Britain with the 1929 election of the Labour Party put into power a party that was far more concerned about the conditions of colonial workers than had been its predecessor. The new Secretary of State was Lord Passfield, formerly known as Sidney Webb, the influential Fabian Socialist. Along with his Parliamentary Under-Secretary, Drummond Shiels, Passfield did much to rewrite and revise labour laws as they applied to the West Indies. In particular he urged colonial governors to work with the unions in their jurisdictions to improve wages and conditions and to establish minimum standards of health and safety. Passfield lent formal endorsement to the formation of colonial trade unions with the publication in 1930 of the so-called Passfield Memorandum, which urged colonial governments to supervise and register unions to prevent them from falling under the control of what he referred to as "disaffected persons." When colonial governors responded coolly to the initiative, the Labour government established the Colonial Labour Committee, whose task was to help draft legislation for the colonies, but the initiative was undercut by the electoral defeat of the party in mid-1931, even though the Conservative government retained the Committee within the Colonial Office and increased the role of the British Trades Union Congress (TUC) in formulating colonial labour policy and assisting trade union development in the Caribbean. Hence the British trade union movement provided much of the critical leadership needed by the local movement in the depression years.[36]

The contribution of the British labour movement to its Caribbean counterpart was most visible in the career of Walter Citrine, TUC secretary in the 1930s. Citrine was a frequent visitor to the islands in the decade; he served on the 1938–9 West India Royal Commission (Moyne Commission) inquiring into the labour riots. He was influential in convincing Cipriani to form the Trinidad Labour Party (TLP) and helped to secure fellowships for Caribbean trade unionists to attend Ruskin College in England and sending advisers to the West Indies to provide guidance on labour organization. Citrine and the TUC also undercut the influence of the left wing of the Caribbean labour movement.[37]

Jamaica was hit hardest by depressed economic conditions and was the scene of the Caribbean's most widespread and prolonged labour unrest.[38] The 1938 disturbances began when 700 workers on a sugar estate in Frome struck and subsequently clashed with police. Tension escalated when dockworkers went on strike in Kingston, and rioting spread to include public works employees, former soldiers, cane and banana workers. The strikes contributed to the formation of the Bustamante Industrial Trade Union (BITU), which continued to prosper through World War II, with 1944 membership estimated at 54,000, representing 80 percent of Jamaica's total union membership and making the BITU the Caribbean's largest labour organization.[39]

Simultaneous with the formation of the BITU, in 1938 Norman Manley, a lawyer and long-time advocate of working-class rights, organized a federation of a number of small craft unions into the Jamaican Trade Union Council (JTUC), which they affiliated to Manley's People's National Party (PNP), a nationalist party seeking Jamaican self-government. Manley's main rival for leadership of the nationalist and trade union movement was William Alexander Bustamente, who in 1944 formed the Jamaican Labour Party (JLP); the party won twenty-three seats – and political power – to the PNP's four in the first Jamaican elections to be held with universal suffrage. The JLP governed Jamaica for most of the next three decades.[40]

In Trinidad, labour disturbances hit the oil and sugar industries. In contrast to Jamaica, the unrest in Trinidad occurred within the context of a workforce that had already made significant advances in organization. In addition to Cipriani and the TWA/TLP, a number of other charismatic leaders emerged in the 1930s. Oil pipe-fitter Uriah Butler, for instance, established the British Empire Workers and Citizens Home Rule Party in 1936, a party whose stated aims included improved trade union legislation, the enactment of health insurance provisions, and assistance for the unemployed to secure work.

It was Butler who precipitated the rioting and subsequent general strike among the oil-field workers in 1937. Employers refused to meet workers' demands and once again British troops were dispatched to restore order. Under the presidency of Adrien Cola Rienzi, a young East Indian lawyer and Leninist activist, oil workers formed the Oilfield Workers' Trade Union in 1937, but it took another year and a half of labour stoppages before a collective agreement was reached in 1939.

The strikes and riots across the British Caribbean in the 1930s led the British government to conduct a series of Royal Commissions to inquire into the conditions and causes of conflict. Known for the names of their respective chairmen, the Moyne, Forster, and Orde Brown commissions produced a wealth of information on wages, working conditions, trade union organization and the lack of adequate social welfare in the Caribbean colonies. The commissions also made a series of recommendations which did much to shape the context and legal framework within which the new unions evolved during the war and post-war years.

The labour disturbances of the 1930s therefore mark a turning point in the history of the Caribbean labour movement. The unprecedented scale of direct action had won workers the right to organize and the promise of substantial social reforms. The commissions which recommended reforms also represented a late attempt by the British government to shore up its role as a colonial authority of real power and responsibility in the region. In fact, the outbreak of unrest had firmly demonstrated that the long- distance, hands-off approach to rule in the Caribbean was no longer viable. Developments during the war and post-war years would witness instead a more direct approach to controlling events in the Caribbean, but the lead would be taken not by Britain but by the United States.

Trade patterns

The growing importance of the United States was also evident in the patterns of trade. While Britain continued to be the leading destination for the exports of its own colonies, the United States had easily become the most important supplier of goods and services in the region. Figures for Kingston, Jamaica, in 1921, for example, show that 67.6 percent of total imports came from the United States compared with 18.1 percent for Britain. In technology and cultural industries, U.S. interests were even more dominant. By 1931 the United States supplied Jamaica with 95 percent of its automobiles and 99 percent of its cinema films. However, given the realities of global and regional military and economic power, the United States gradually absorbed Jamaica into its sphere of influence. The U.S. also gained a military base in Jamaica under the 1940 destroyers-for-bases deal.

Panama

At first, the United States government and U.S. citizens in the region took full advantage of Article III of the Hay-Bunau-Varilla Treaty. The article stated that the United States could govern the Canal Zone "as if it were sovereign." For more than three decades, Americans created their own industries in the Canal Zone, felt free to hire U.S. citizens for any type of work, and paid Panamanians less than they paid Americans with equivalent skills and responsibilities. When Panama's Minister in Washington, Ricardo J. Alfaro, complained to Secretary of State Charles Evans Hughes in 1923, Hughes was distinctly unsympathetic.[41] This was a situation certain to create problems. Panama City developed into the shape of a snake, several kilometres in length but only a few blocks wide, sandwiched between the Canal Zone and the water's edge. The Canal Zone surrounded Panama's second largest city, Colón, on three sides; on the fourth side there was water. To travel overland between Colón and its hinterland, one had to travel through the U.S.-occupied Canal Zone. Tensions between the Americans and Panamanians intensified during and after World War II.

World War II in the Caribbean

World War II significantly increased great power tensions in the region, especially in instances in which European nations fell to the Axis powers and control over their Caribbean colonies became an issue. Yet the impact of war went well beyond great power competition for colonial possessions. The war brought economic questions, heightened ideological tensions, spurred labour migration into high employment areas, and on balance served to strengthen the United States presence in the same way that the war accelerated tendencies toward economic and military integration among the United States, Canada, and Mexico. The war intensified interdependence between the island and mainland countries and colonies in the Caribbean basin and in particular between those countries and the United States.

The Caribbean occupied an important strategic location during the war, well before formal U.S. belligerency. American and European officials worried about well-established and highly placed German émigrés in the countries of the Caribbean basin, particularly in Venezuela, Colombia and Central America, where they were prominent in mercantile and aviation activities. U.S. policy makers sought, often against considerable local opposition, to neutralize the German presence, frequently failing to make effective distinction between real Nazi agents and good citizens of German heritage. Throughout the region Germans and those nationals accused of trading with the enemy were blacklisted by the U.S. and Britain, and in critical strategic areas such as aviation, the U.S. successfully achieved its objectives of removing German involvement entirely.[42]

There were several anxious moments in the Caribbean, at least from Hitler's *Blitzkrieg* in the spring of 1940 until U.S. forces launched "Operation Torch" and liberated French North Africa in November 1942.[43] When German forces over-ran the Low Countries and defeated France, the U.S. and British governments feared a German presence on Dutch and French islands in the Caribbean. During the warm months of 1940, there was no guarantee that the United Kingdom would withstand the Nazi onslaught, and even if it did, there was no guarantee that British forces – badly needed for the defence of the mother country – could hold the British West Indies against a determined German attack.

To prevent such possibilities, both the U.S. and Canadian governments took action. Secretary of State Cordell Hull and Congress reaffirmed the no-transfer principle of the Monroe Doctrine, first developed during the administration of President John Quincy Adams (1825–9) to prevent the transfer of Cuba or Puerto Rico from Spain to Great Britain or France. In other words, no colonial possession in the western hemisphere could be transferred to the jurisdiction of a different (presumably stronger) European power, which might then threaten the security of the United States. In July 1940, foreign ministers of the Latin American republics and the United States met in Havana and collectively applied the no-transfer principle to the British, French, and Dutch possessions. If a German takeover of any of those territories appeared imminent, one or more western hemisphere country could establish a trusteeship on behalf of the others. Canadian soldiers replaced British forces in Jamaica from 1940 to 1946, Bermuda and the Bahamas from 1942 to 1946, and British Guiana from 1942 to 1945.[44]

The canal made Panama of unique strategic importance to the United States. Given the shortage of warships as a result of the Washington (1922) and London (1930) naval disarmament agreements and the Japanese attack on Pearl Harbor (1941), the Panama Canal played a vital role in allowing the U.S. Navy to maximize its resources on both oceans during the conflict against both Germany and Japan. Well before the outbreak of war the Franklin Roosevelt administration, sensitive to the vulnerability of the U.S. position and the importance of the canal, acted to reduce Panamanian hostilities. While Nazi Germany would hardly have sympathized with polyglot Panamanians, most of them of non-European extraction, it might have exploited their grievances. Thanks to its legation in Panama City, Hitler's government was certainly aware of the grievances.[45] In 1936 Roosevelt agreed to increase the annual rent to $430,000 and to save certain types of jobs for Panamanians. Three years later, the U.S. Senate gave its advice and consent.

There were definite limits to Roosevelt's generosity and patience. On the eve of the conflict in Europe, his government thwarted – with full Panamanian co-operation – a German plan to purchase land at Pinos Bay, where aviators and submarine crews might have landed surreptitiously and replenished their supplies. To avoid costs, U.S.-based owners of ships engaged in international commerce often registered their ships in Panama instead of in the United States. During the undeclared naval war between the U.S. and German navies in the autumn of 1941, some of those owners wanted to arm their vessels. The nationalistic government of President Arnulfo Arias refused permission. There was reason for both American and Panamanian anxiety about German intentions in the country since Panama was a centre for Axis espionage in the region at least until the United States became a belligerent. Captured German documents later revealed that the head of Germany's spy agency, the *Abwehr*, Admiral Wilhelm Franz Canaris, maintained personal contact with Germany's chargé d'affaires in Panama. There were *Abwehr* agents in the Canal Zone, among them Hans Heinrich Schackow and Ernst Robert Kuhrig. Schackow pretended to work for the Hapag-Lloyd Steamship Company in Balboa, while Kuhrig pretended to earn his living repairing typewriters. Schackow and his subordinates reported to *Abwehr* headquarters through the German legation in Panama City and provided detailed information on the state of the locks, the Canal Zone's electrical supply, and the degree of U.S. military preparedness in the area. Less well-trained, lower-level Panamanians could – and did – report on the movement of ships through the canal.[46] There were Panamanians who wished their goverment to pursue a more pro-American policy early in the war. Some of them, including the President's brother, Harmodio Arias, approached the U.S. Embassy and asked what the response might be in the event of a *coup d'état*. Ambassador Edmund C. Wilson replied that any coup would be Panama's business, not that of the United States, and the conspirator regarded that as a green light.[47] On 16 October, the coup took place. Arnulfo Arias went into exile, Harmodio became President, and a few days later, U.S.-owned ships of Panamanian registry received permission to arm. Any Japanese threat to the Panama Canal vanished after the Battle of Midway in 1942, any German threat with Germany's 1943 defeat in the Battle of the Atlantic. Meanwhile, the British government had taken decisive action of another sort. The British economy and war effort depended heavily upon oil extracted from Venezuela and refined in the Dutch islands of Aruba and Curaçao. Trinidad was another source of supply. Oil from the Persian Gulf would be vulnerable to Axis submarine attacks in the Mediterranean, and Great Britain and Mexico were disputing the value of British oil investments expropriated by the administration of President Lazaro Cárdenas (1934–40). Given the neutrality legislation in the United States and the neutralist sentiment in that country, the governments of Prime Ministers Neville Chamberlain and Winston Churchill could not rely on the United States to fulfil its petroleum requirements.

In May 1940, as soon as Hitler's army overran the Netherlands and without waiting for permission from the Dutch government which was relocating to London, British forces from Jamaica and French forces from Martinique occupied Aruba and Curaçao. (It was to replace those British forces that the Canadian soldiers went to Jamaica.) At the outbreak of hostilities in September 1939, five German ships lingered off the Dutch islands, site of some of the world's largest refineries. Standard Oil's refinery in Aruba could process more than 250,000 barrels of crude each day; Royal Dutch Shell was another multinational active on the Dutch islands. In preparation for war, the Hitler regime had lessened Germany's dependence on Caribbean oil and come to rely upon Romanian and Soviet oil, which would, presumably, withstand British naval warfare. However, Hitler's navy could sink British oil tankers or destroy the refineries, and jeopardize the British supply. It was a British responsibility to guarantee that that did not happen.[48] The British occupation of Aruba and Curaçao, quickly approved by the Dutch government-in-exile, was a clear violation of the no-transfer principle of the Monroe Doctrine. The State Department offered a token protest, in part to satisfy Venezuelan authorities. However, official Washington was quietly relieved that Aruba and Curaçao had some protection and that U.S. forces did not need to provide that protection.[49]

The fall of France and the Havana Conference, 1940

The capitulation of France and the establishment of Field Marshal Philippe Pétain's Vichy regime seriously complicated the situation. Cordell Hull feared a violation of the long-established no-transfer principle should French colonies in the western hemisphere come under German control. German forces having occupied Paris, the first Pétain cabinet met in Bordeaux shortly before midnight 16 June 1940 and agreed to an armistice with Nazi Germany. At 12:30 the following afternoon (still early morning in Washington), Pétain broadcast a message to the French people: "I tell you today that it is necessary to stop the fighting." Not unreasonably, regular French forces abandoned their weapons and rejoiced that they had survived the war. Pétain had not waited to learn what Hitler's conditions were for an armistice which did not go into effect until 25 June.

If Pétain had only an academic interest in Hitler's intentions, Hull was not prepared to sit idly by. At 10 a.m. 17 June, moments after he would have received news of Pétain's broadcast, Hull's fears changed to alarm with concern focused on possible German designs on Martinique, Guadeloupe and French Guiana. Even if Hitler did not wish to assume administrative control over these colonies, it was reasonable to fear that he would demand the right to use their harbours for German submarines, which were already causing havoc in the shipping lanes of the Caribbean.

The German defeat of France also jeopardized the security of Dutch and British possessions in the Caribbean. When Hitler's forces overran the Netherlands in May 1940, the Dutch government fled to London and continued to govern Dutch overseas possessions from England. Yet, in 1940 the British Isles seemed highly vulnerable to the German onslaught, and should London fall then Washington would be confronted with a Germany that potentially controlled not only all of western Europe but the British, Dutch, and French colonies in the western hemisphere. Even without the total defeat of Great Britain, possible German control over part of the British and French fleets would seriously threaten U.S. security as well as that of the Caribbean basin and South America.

The broader military and political situation was complicated by the roles of local French officials in the colonies. Admiral Georges Robert, France's High Commissioner to Martinique, Guadeloupe, and French Guiana and commander-in-chief of French naval forces in the Caribbean, disliked General Charles de Gaulle and his followers. De Gaulle, with British support, disavowed Hitler's terms of capitulation which Pétain had accepted. Robert also disliked the British and the United States, which he regarded as a predator which sought to expand at the expense of France's West Indian possessions: Martinique, Guadeloupe, and French Guiana. His base of support was strongest in Martinique and weakest in French Guiana. In Martinique, the *beke* or European population had greater influence than in the other French Caribbean departments. Surrounded by people of colour, the *bekes* gave discipline and tradition a higher priority than liberty, equality, and fraternity. Robert also counted on the loyalty of the French navy, which had four cruisers anchored off Martinique – the *Esterel*, the *Barfleur*, the *Quercy*, and the *Emile Bertin*. The *Bearn*, an aircraft carrier with more than 100 aircraft of various descriptions, also lay at Martinique. Another cruiser, the *Jeanne d'Arc*, sat off Guadeloupe.

There was no naval presence in French Guiana, whose geographical position was relatively remote from Martinique and Guadeloupe. Gaullist Captain Claude Chandon went to British Guiana and conspired with Governor Sir Wilfred Jackson to establish a friendly administration in French Guiana. However, the plan failed for a number of reasons. Vichy sent two agents to the French Caribbean – Jules Carde and Pierre Revoil. They went first to French Guiana, where they tightened security, threatened the dismissal of dissenting bureaucrats, and warned that relatives still in France might pay some consequences if their colonial cousins were not entirely loyal to Vichy. British authorities should have interned them as they passed through Trinidad on their way to Martinique and Guadeloupe but, to Churchill's dismay, the governor was hospitable to them. Moreover, it quickly became U.S. policy to establish a *modus vivendi* with the Vichy regime in the hope that it would not become too intimate with Nazi Germany.[50] The United States government would not have sanctioned an Anglo-Gaullist assault on French Guiana. Protected as they were by the French Navy and under surveillance of the U.S. Navy, Martinique and Guadeloupe were even less accessible to the Anglo-Gaullists than was French Guiana.[51]

The Roosevelt administration sought to achieve the "neutrality" of the French West Indies as it tolerated Pétain's collaboration with Hitler. Rear-Admiral John W. Greenslade of the U.S. Navy and Robert agreed that those French ships and aircraft which were already in the Caribbean would stay there and that U.S. observers would maintain constant surveillance to guarantee that they would remain. A U.S. naval officer would live in the French West Indies and U.S. patrol aircraft could land in Martinique on a daily basis to make certain that Robert and his associates were fulfilling their part of the bargain. In return, the United States would send consumer goods to Martinique. Armed with this agreement, in September 1940 Robert sent the *Quercy* to French Guiana with 300 marines who were to fight any Gaullists and keep French Guiana clearly in Vichy's column.[52]

Hull wanted support – preferably unanimous support – from the Latin American republics, since he knew that with their endorsement the no-transfer principle would have more legitimacy than it could possibly have as a unilateral declaration by the United States. After the European war had begun in September 1939, hemispheric foreign ministers met in Panama, where they discussed their countries' interests as neutrals. In Panama they had agreed to call a consultative meeting of the American republics in the event there should be a change in the sovereignty of any American territory subject to the jurisdiction of a non-American state, with that change threatening the security of the "American continent." With the fall of France, Hull considered that situation had been realized. The foreign ministers were scheduled in any event to meet that October in Havana; Hull now suggested that the foreign ministers meet as soon as possible.[53]

Even under such desperate circumstances, it was no mean feat to establish a consensus on what should be done. First, there were the enthusiasts who wanted immediate action and a minimum of discussion. Haitian President Sténio Vincent reportedly preferred that the U.S. take direct action, either alone or in concert with other American republics, to assume control of the Dutch and French possessions, with the precise nature of the control to be subject to later discussion at Havana. Vincent was concerned that Germany might seize the French and Dutch islands before the delegates met in Cuba, and it would prove far more difficult to dislodge German forces once they were in place than it would be to take pre-emptive action.[54]

Venezuelan Foreign Minister Gil Borges also regarded the situation as urgent; he further feared that the Havana meeting would generate provocative language on the part of the delegates that might worsen the relationship with Germany in the region. For Venezuela the proximity of the Dutch islands of Aruba, Bonaire, and Curaçao made any change in their control a direct security threat. Given the importance of the Aruba and Curaçao refineries operated by the multinational oil companies with Venezuelan oil, Venezuela's economy was highly vulnerable. It was understandable, therefore, that Borges wanted the U.S. government to take prompt action. Hull was, however, unwilling to act prior to an agreement being reached at Havana, and it was impossible for several of the delegates to arrive in Cuba prior to mid-July.[55]

Cuba, Colombia, and Mexico – in spite of the latter's current dispute with the U.S.- based oil companies over the 1938 nationalization – were ready to co-operate with the United States. Outside the Caribbean area, Brazilian leaders were especially anxious to consolidate their relations with the United States in order to offset their problems with pro-Axis Argentina. President Getulio Vargas offered to host the conference if such action would facilitate a hemispheric agreement, an offer that Hull politely declined on grounds that a change in venue would offend Cuban authorities.[56]

A variety of competing territorial claims brought additional complications to an already difficult situation. Venezuela had not forgotten its earlier claims to much of British Guiana. It also wanted control over the Dutch islands should the Netherlands' sovereignty lapse.[57] Guatemala wanted assurance that whatever happened at Havana would not affect its claims to British Honduras.[58] Argentina sought similar assurances about the Falkland (Malvinas) Islands, to which it continued to lay claim and which Britain had annexed in 1833.[59]

Indeed, the interests among the southern cone countries of South America as well as several of the Andean countries had little in common with those of the Caribbean basin at this stage. One large body of opinion in Uruguay, for instance, regarded the Havana conference as a charade to increase U.S. economic and military power in the British, French and Dutch possessions. U.S. goals, thought members of Uruguay's Herrerista Party, were to gain bases and to sell obsolete weapons at high prices. The Uruguayan government itself feared antagonizing Germany at a time that German forces seemed on the verge of total victory in the European theatre.[60] Considerations other than relations with Germany also conditioned the Latin American response to Hull's pressures. Peru's Foreign Minister wondered why he should have to travel all the way to Havana rather than communicate by telegraph.[61] The Bolivian Foreign Minister refused to attend because the United States would not promise assistance to the tin industry nor commit itself to construction of a railway between Bolivia and the Brazilian port of Santos.[62] In the end, the foreign ministers of Argentina, Brazil, Chile, Peru, and Uruguay did not attend the Havana conference.[63]

While he worked to draw together the American republics into a common front, Hull also sought to maintain friendly relations with Pétain's government in the hope that he might help to detach it from the embrace of Hitler's Germany.[64] However, the Havana conference itself threatened any harmony between the United States and post-Armistice France. Pétain and his ministers questioned the validity of placing French colonies on the Havana agenda when German authorities had not, they insisted, made representations about their disposition.[65]

In spite of the obstacles, the delegates to the Havana conference reached agreement within ten days of the beginning of the conference in late July. The joint communiqué asserted that the British, French, and Dutch possessions in the hemisphere would not be allowed to fall under the control of either Germany or Italy. Should a change in sovereignty appear imminent, the republics of the hemisphere would have to consider their own security interests and the wishes of the inhabitants of the colonies. The republics should then install provisional governments which would retain control until the colonies achieved independence or were restored to their previous status, "whichever shall appear the more practicable and just."[66] Hull had triumphed. The no-transfer principle had achieved multilateral standing.

Happily, there was no need to test the Act of Havana. Britain withstood the German onslaught in the Battle of Britain. Moreover, on 2 September 1940,

Roosevelt and Churchill implemented their destroyers-for-bases agreement. Even before the war had started, Britain had agreed to lease sites for bases in Bermuda, St. Lucia, and Trinidad to the U.S. Navy so that it might patrol the Caribbean during any war against Hitler's Germany. The political climate inside the United States discouraged implementation of that secret agreement until Hitler's 1940 *Blitzkrieg* and seizure of the European coastline from Norway in the north to the border between France and Spain in the south. When Churchill begged for support to prevent a German invasion of the United Kingdom in the summer of 1940, President Roosevelt provided fifty aged destroyers. However, he needed some sort of payment to justify that unneutral gift, and the bases served that purpose. The U.S. Navy would receive not only lands in Bermuda, St. Lucia, and Trinidad, but additional ones in Jamaica, Newfoundland, and British Guiana. In the course of the war the Dutch islands also remained loyal to the London-based government-in-exile, beyond Hitler's grasp. In November 1942, when Hitler's forces did invade that part of France controlled by Marshal Pétain, France's Caribbean possessions recognized the authority of the new anti-Pétain, anti-Hitler French government in Algiers.

One of the British bases acquired by the United States as a result of the destroyers-for-bases agreement was at Georgetown, on the Bahamian island of Exuma, and it made a significant socio-economic impact. The Americans needed labour, and they hired black residents of Exuma at wages close to what American workers would have received – a real shot in the arm for the desperate local economy. In 1942, the U.S. presence extended to the Bahamian heartland, New Providence Island, site of Nassau, the capital. The contractor, the Pleasantville Company, sparked a riot when it indicated its willingness to hire 2,400 Bahamians at two dollars per day. The average rate for black Bahamians at the time was but two shillings (30 U.S. cents) per day. Fearful of losing their labour force to the Americans, Bahamian authorities limited the income unskilled Bahamians could receive to four shillings (60 U.S. cents) per day. The result was that black Bahamians drove trucks for one shilling per hour, while white Americans received $1.50 per hour for the same work. After riots to protest the discrepancy, the Bahamian government allowed a ceiling of five shillings per day. Legally the Newfoundland and Bermuda bases were not part of the payment for the destroyers but bonuses provided to the United States at the same time as the other base sites and for the same purposes.[67]

In U.S. strategic planning, there would be three subsections to Caribbean defence: the first centred in Puerto Rico, but including the U.S. Virgin Islands and Antigua; the second centred in Guantánamo Bay, but including Jamaica and the Bahamas; the third centred in Trinidad, but including St. Lucia and British Guiana.

Apart from the destroyers-for-bases arrangement, the first U.S. military intervention on behalf of the Allied cause was the occupation of Surinam. There the attraction was bauxite, which was vital to aircraft manufacture. There were several challenges in connection with Surinam's bauxite. German submarines might try to sink ships with cargoes of bauxite, as indeed they did beginning in February 1942. Most of the half-million tons produced annually at Mackenzie in British Guiana was the property of the Montreal-based Aluminum Company of Canada (Alcan) and went to markets in Canada and Britain. The United States imported an equivalent or greater quantity from the Surinamsche Bauxite Company's facilities at Moengo and Paranam. While inland and thus protected from submarine volleys, they were vulnerable to sabotage. Both the London-based Dutch government-in-exile, headed by Queen Wilhelmina, and the U.S. government took precautions. During the summer of 1940, Dutch authorities in Surinam arrested Germans and Dutch nationals suspected of Nazi sympathies. The U.S. Navy opened a base on Trinidad's Chaguaramas Peninsula, site of a bauxite transfer station. Nevertheless, given the friendliness of Pétain's Vichy government to Hitler's Germany, there remained the possibility of saboteurs who might launch an attack across the frontier from French Guiana.

On 1 September 1941, President Roosevelt asked Queen Wilhelmina for permission to send up to 3,000 infantry to protect the bauxite facilities in Surinam. On behalf of her government-in-exile, the Queen agreed, although Dutch authorities were not pleased that President Roosevelt wanted a Brazilian presence in Surinam as well. Given the length of the Surinamese–Brazilian border, President Roosevelt thought Brazilian co-operation indispensable, and the Dutch reluctantly acquiesced.

For similar reasons, Roosevelt came to regard a U.S. military presence as desirable at Aruba and Curaçao. The oil refineries – much closer to the ocean than the bauxite mines – were accordingly more vulnerable to Axis attack. Moreover, the presence of U.S. forces on the Dutch islands would free British forces for action elsewhere at a time when the United States was still formally neutral. However, in this instance, diplomacy moved slowly. As the Dutch feared, the presence of Brazilians in Surinam would serve as a precedent for a Venezuelan presence in Aruba and Curaçao, and relations between the Netherlands and Venezuela had not been as friendly as those between the Netherlands and Brazil. Anglo-Dutch talks faltered on this issue. Churchill and Roosevelt met in Washington between 22 December 1941 and 14 January 1942 and agreed that, notwithstanding the formal U.S. entry into the war on 7 December, U.S. forces should replace British ones on Aruba and Curaçao. On 2 January 1942, Roosevelt insisted that six U.S. aircraft go to Curaçao to protect the refineries from submarine attacks, and the Dutch agreed.[68]

Once the United States became a formal belligerent in December 1941, Rexford Tugwell – U.S. governor of Puerto Rico – faced a plethora of problems. A U-boat campaign in the Western Atlantic and the Caribbean began before the middle of January, 1942. There were heavy losses of ships with bauxite and oil in waters near Trinidad and the Guianas. German submarines threatened supply lines between the United States mainland and Puerto Rico, and many consumer goods became scarce or unavailable in Puerto Rico's stores.[69] San Juan, the capital, occupied a strategically vulnerable piece of real estate. Puerto Rico was vital if the U.S. Navy were to protect the approaches to the Caribbean, but the possibility existed that its impoverished people, at least some of whom wanted independence, might not willingly share the risks of U.S. occupation in order to keep the Germans at a distance. Some Puerto Ricans were sympathetic to Hitler's Falangist ally, Generalissimo Francisco Franco in Spain. False alarms of submarine sightings could be frightening, and there was genuine cause for fear. In the spring of 1942, German submarine attacks sank a minimum of six tankers and damaged property on the Dutch island of Aruba, and what they did in Aruba they might do in Puerto Rico. Senior U.S. military officers were often contemptuous of Puerto Ricans, and there was no guarantee that relations between service personnel and islanders would always be harmonious. In December 1941, President Roosevelt ordered the evacuation of military dependants from Puerto Rico – a move hardly likely to inspire confidence on that part of Puerto Ricans (who were U.S. citizens) in their government's ability to defend their homeland. Tugwell favoured construction of a Trans-Caribbean Highway across Cuba, Haiti, and the Dominican Republic, with strong naval protection for the ferries which would connect the islands, and in 1942 the U.S. army improved road connections between Port-au-Prince, Haiti, and San Pedro de Macoris in the Dominican Republic. Tugwell did try to co-operate with his British and Dutch allies in the distribution of consumer goods, and as of July 1942, there was an anti-submarine net to protect San Juan harbour.[70]

Meanwhile there remained the problem of the French Caribbean, led by Vichyite Admiral Georges Robert. Despite an agreement between Robert and Rear-Admiral John Greenslade of the U.S. Navy, supplies continued to leak from Martinique to Vichy-controlled North Africa. Robert purged the French Caribbean of possible Free French sympathizers and replaced them with loyal Vichyites. A rumour that the *Emile Bertin* had left Martinique for Africa proved false, but the search for the facts consumed precious time and money on the part of the U.S. Navy. Pétain's own behaviour cast doubt on any professions of neutrality and indicated an increased degree of collaboration with Nazi Germany. On 21 February 1942, a German submarine surfaced off Fort-de-France so that an officer with connections in Berlin might receive medical attention. The very idea that Martinique could assist and prolong the German U-boat campaign in the Caribbean was quite intolerable.

Nevertheless, the Roosevelt administration restrained itself. It was preparing for Operation Torch (the liberation of North Africa) and did not want a diversion. Besides, it felt confident that it could impose a fair degree of damage control on Robert. The U.S. government sent an observer to Martinique to monitor Robert's communications with Vichy and warned Robert not to forward any sensitive information. Nor, thanks to British penetration of the Vichyite Embassy in Washington and theft of Vichy's crypto system contained there, could Robert forward information which American authorities could not decipher. The U.S. Navy closely monitored French shipping.

Even the success of Operation Torch did not persuade Robert to switch sides as had his mentor in Algiers, Admiral Francois Darlan. He had support from *bekes* and the Roman Catholic Church. Vichyite laws stripped people of colour not born of a French father of their French citizenship and excluded them from public office. It was illegal for residents of the French Caribbean to listen to foreign radio broadcasts. Undoubtedly Robert thought his position fairly secure.

It was not. The U.S. government asked the French Caribbean's principal trading partners – the Dominican Republic, Venezuela, Brazil, Canada, Great Britain, and the Netherlands Antilles – not to trade with the French islands. Free French activists entered Guadeloupe and Martinique illegally from the neighbouring British islands of Dominica and St. Lucia.

The first part of the French Caribbean to defect to the Free French was French Guiana. It was farthest from Martinique, had strong local leaders, and would have joined the Free French in the autumn of 1940 had it not been for U.S. opposition to an Anglo-Gaullist invasion. The Roosevelt administration lost whatever hope it might have had in the Vichy government when Pétain ordered French soldiers in North Africa to resist the American landings in November 1942, and in March 1943, U.S. officials in French Guiana promised Vichyite Governor Rene Veber safe conduct from the French Caribbean if he would resign. Veber's successor, Yvan Vanegue, then invited a U.S. military mission into French Guiana. The U.S. acquired a strategic airfield, Le Gallion, in French Guiana, from which the U.S. Air Force might maintain links with Brazil and Africa.

Guadeloupe was next. Paul Valentino, a Gaullist active with the French resistance, seized control on 4 June 1943. Martinique remained the toughest nut to crack.

The U.S. had broken relations with Admiral Robert on 30 April 1943, but he continued to wield authority in Martinique. The *bekes* were stronger there than in Guadeloupe, the Resistance weaker. However, lack of support for Robert anywhere outside Martinique, the proximity of Dominica and St. Lucia, and the influence of Martinique's intellectuals – most notably Aimé Cesaire – led to his downfall. It also helped that French soldiers based in Martinique were not less committed to him than were French sailors. If Robert had used the navy to fight the army, the U.S. would probably have intervened, and before that could happen, Robert resigned. On 30 June 1943 Robert announced that he was leaving office in order to prevent the shedding of French blood.

Reluctant as he might have been to see French people killed, Robert was not as unwilling to destroy French property which might fall into the hands of Vichy's enemies. He destroyed eight aircraft and beached the *Bearn*. However, he did not, as feared, send France's gold reserves, which the *Emile Bertin* had carried to Martinique in 1940, to Spain, and U.S. authorities guaranteed him safe conduct to Puerto Rico, from where he could make his way to France.[71]

With the success of Operation Torch, the demise of the Vichyite governments in French Guiana, Guadeloupe, and Martinique, and Allied victories in the Battle of the Atlantic, the Caribbean became a safer sea. By mid-1943, the Allies had won on that front.

At the same time, Canadian soldiers went to Jamaica to relieve British forces required to do battle against the Axis. With France near collapse, Great Britain needed its army for the European theatre and home defence, yet Jamaica's governor thought it would "be risky to remove all white troops."[72] Few in Ottawa appear to have considered the possibility of racial conflict in Jamaica, with Canadians on the one side and Jamaicans of African descent on the other, and before the end of May 1940, the Winnipeg Grenadiers set sail. Four different Canadian battalions served in Jamaica in 1946, one of which faced possible redeployment in 1945 to patrol Belize airport in British Honduras and prevent a Guatemalan invasion. That redeployment, however, never materialized, because British colonial authorities dealt directly with the Canadian commander in Jamaica, and when the Department of National Defence in Ottawa learned what was happening, it ordered the troops to remain in Jamaica. Fortunately, the Guatemalan soldiers near the border of British Honduras were fighting forest fires, not mustering for an invasion.[73]

U.S. forces did go to Jamaica on 4 April 1941, albeit in very limited numbers. The Vernam Naval Air Station on Little Goat Island near Kingston initially had so few service personnel attached to it that the brigadier in charge of Canadian and British forces became their superior. To avoid tensions, the situation prevailed even after U.S. forces outnumbered Canadians in 1942. Nevertheless, an advertisement "for white workers only" did provoke outrage, and the City Council of Kingston protested directly to President Roosevelt.[74]

Trinidad also proved important. Mail from South America to Europe passed through Trinidad, where British counter-intelligence could intercept and read it. Canadian service personnel also went to wartime Trinidad.[75] As a result of the destroyers-for-bases deal of 1940, the United States leased land at Chaguaramas and elsewhere which gave the U.S. Navy a base close to the Panama Canal and to the oil fields of Trinidad and Venezuela in waters infested with German submarines. Although they received compensation, some residents had to leave their homes or change their locale for recreation. The high wages paid by the Americans lured rural people, including Indians, to Port of Spain and gave them a taste of urban living. The sight of white Americans engaged in manual labour or drunken white sailors shattered the image of white racial superiority.

Trinidadian novelist Ralph de Boissiere captured the flavour of the base in his 1956 novel *Rum and Coca-Cola*. According to de Boissiere, Trinidadians of Asian and African extraction were less than ecstatic about the British ruling class, whom they considered to have siphoned off too much of the island's wealth for themselves. There was ambivalence toward the Americans, often more racist and bossy than the British in the workplace but practitioners of free love off the base. Many residents of Chaguaramas whose homes were expropriated regarded the compensation which they received as less than adequate. As American suburbs mushroomed and the number of U.S. citizens became increasingly numerous, Trinidad seemed unfamiliar even to the native born. The influx of Americans produced inflation, and the building of the base created a labour shortage. The labour shortage, in turn, produced labour unrest for, given the need for a workforce at Chaguaramas and the Americans' desire for servants, workers could afford to go on strike against their civilian employers.[76]

Dominican historian Bernardo Vega has commented upon the apparent inconsistency in U.S. foreign policy from 1941 to 1945, a policy which opposed totalitarian dictatorships in Europe and Asia but collaborated with them in Latin America, as for instance in the Dominican Republic. Any Caribbean government which could maintain order at home and help in the struggle against the Axis necessarily became a friendly government. That Trujillo could control any compatriots sympathetic to the Axis was indisputable, said Vega. The German community in the Dominican Republic had shrunk to insignificance, and the Italian community had also diminished in size. The Spanish community was overwhelmingly favourable to Franco, most Republican exiles having relocated in Mexico, Cuba, or Venezuela, but as long as Franco remained more or less neutral, there was little problem there. Such Dominican exiles as Juan Bosch, who would be elected President in 1962, one year after Trujillo's assassination, said that a triumph for Hitler would be a setback for democracy everywhere: they urged Dominicans to support the war effort, and the Dominican Republic declared war on the Axis only a week after Pearl Harbor. Vega suggests that World War II was, in a sense, very much a "blessing" for Trujillo because it caused authorities in the U.S. to place greater emphasis upon current hemispheric defence needs than upon such issues as violations of human rights. Under the circumstances, Washington tended to ignore the authoritarian behaviour of its Caribbean client states.[77]

In neighbouring Haiti, Haitian leaders hoped that international tensions leading to World War II would provide additional leverage in gaining support from Washington. Haitian President Stenio Vincent desperately sought a U.S. air base at Gonaives, where the U.S. Navy already had every right to send ships whenever it pleased. Indeed, the U.S. Minister in Port-au-Prince, Ferdinand L. Mayer, referred to the "virtual naval base which we now have at Gonaives."[78] Vincent actually wrote a book entitled *Imposant les Jalons* (*Marking Out the Fundamentals*) in which he envisioned an inter-American military alliance whose charter members would be the United States, Cuba, Haiti, and the Dominican Republic. The alliance would be compatible with principles outlined at the Buenos Aires and Lima Inter-American conferences of 1936 and 1938.[79] When Germany invaded Poland, and Great Britain and France went to war, Vincent reaffirmed his offer. At the very least Vincent thought that the U.S. should "establish a small air base in Haiti which might be used as a stopover point for planes flying between the United States and Puerto Rico."[80]

However, the U.S. government was not inclined to provide significant levels of military support. As long as the U.S. Navy could go freely to Gonaive, the U.S. had all the facilities it needed in Haiti, said Hull. A U.S.–Haitian accord, he warned, might jeopardize U.S. relations with other Latin American countries.[81]

It was a longstanding U.S. tradition, Hull advised, to avoid formal military alliances.[82] The U.S. would, nonetheless, use its army and navy to prevent a German takeover of Haiti.

Failure to cement a U.S.–Haitian alliance in 1939 meant that when Hitler launched his successful *Blitzkrieg* in the spring of 1940, Vincent was not as co-operative as he might have been. He still wanted U.S. air bases and "secret agents" on his territory, but until they materialized, he would be somewhat tolerant of Axis activity in Haiti. In June 1940, Vincent bowed to German pressure and released a prominent Nazi who had been arrested for defrauding Haitian customs. He promised to cancel KLM's (Royal Dutch Airlines') landing rights but did not rush to fulfil that promise. He transferred Port-au-Prince's chief of police, more diligent than himself in the pursuit of Nazis, "to an insignificant provincial post."[83]

Vincent also sought an increase in U.S. financial assistance, especially given the fact that in the aftermath of the *Blitzkrieg*, Haiti had lost most of the European markets for its agricultural exports. Nor did he consider himself without bargaining clout. If the U.S. government wanted full Haitian co-operation at the forthcoming Havana conference to deal with Dutch and French colonies in the Caribbean, it should prepare to be generous.[84] Moreover, Vincent utilized Vichy France for his own benefit. Despite U.S. objections, he would not cancel a trade treaty between Haiti and France without financial compensation.[85] In January 1942, when foreign ministers of the western hemisphere's twenty-one republics met in Rio and recommended that their nations suspend diplomatic relations with the Axis powers, former Ambassador to the United States Elie Lescot had replaced Vincent as President. The Lescot government offered full co-operation to the U.S. war effort, and in April 1942, President Lescot paid a state visit to Washington. The State Department's communiqué noted an increase in financial assistance to Haiti and said that it was "the pledge of the two Governments to employ their full resources against the common enemy."[86]

The Haitian shift toward co-operation in the war effort parallelled the position of other Caribbean nations. In this respect the regional response to the Axis threat was more positive and concerted than had been the case during World War I. In contrast to Mexican neutrality in World War I, Mexico committed forces that served in the Asian war theatre in World War II. Unlike their stance in World War I, when there was reason to fear German penetration of Hispaniola and the Danish Virgin Islands, the U.S. had full support from its Caribbean neighbours after the Japanese attack on Pearl Harbor.

The period from World War I through the end of World War II were major transitional ones in the international system. The face of the world had been transformed by 1945, with two superpowers shortly confronting one another in the international arena, with the U.S. for a few years in the post-war era pre-eminent because of its nuclear monopoly. Neither Britain nor France enjoyed its pre-war importance internationally, and the movements for decolonization in the Caribbean gained more realistic momentum. After 1945 such movements were as much or more the concern of the United States than of the formal European imperial nations. The global reach of the United States on the one hand made the Caribbean basin of less significance than it had been in the era of traditional technology and warfare; on the other hand the emergence of the Cold War intensified the desire of American policy makers to ensure the stability of the region as a bulwark against international communism.

4

FROM WAR TO REVOLUTION, 1945–1959

Several themes dominated the international history of the Caribbean basin in the years between the end of World War II and the Cuban revolution: rising nationalism and the straining for decolonization; the continued migration and emigration of Caribbean peoples; and the preoccupation of the United States with a perceived threat of international communism in the region. There were as well other new developments in the region, one of the most significant of which was the gradual emergence of tourism as an important economic, cultural, and political phenomenon. Improved transportation connections, enhanced and larger-scale tourist facilities and active promotion by the U.S. and local tourist industry, increasingly made the Caribbean basin a tourist destination. Historian Jay Mandle indicates that Barbados was on the cutting edge of tourist development in the 1950s, passing a Hotel Act in 1956 and establishing a Tourist Board two years later. Within the British Caribbean, Jamaica lagged behind Barbados; British Guiana did not prove a popular destination, and Trinidad and Tobago did not encourage tourism. In the pre-1960s, with many individual exceptions, the majority of tourists were well-to-do, drawn to the gaming tables and nightlife of cities such as Havana or to the still unspoiled isolation of smaller villages, historic sites, and tranquil beaches prior to the onslaught of mass tourism in the subsequent decades. As Brenda Gayle Plummer has eloquently suggested in her treatment of Haiti, "among the North American cognoscenti, Haiti's appeal related to a general revolt against the perceived materialism and conformity of U.S. life in the 1940s and 1950s." Consistent with what would become a lamentable but predictable trend, regional governments in their efforts to induce tourist expenditures were torn between giving tourists whatever they desired and attempting to put a clean, positive face on their societies – such as the effort to require peasants coming to Port-au-Prince to wear shoes. In the coming decades tourism would have one of the most important cultural impacts of any other aspect of the foreign presence in the region. It is thus surprising that a volume on Caribbean culture published in 1955 would make no mention of tourism.[1]

On the whole, tourism in the pre-Cuban revolutionary years proved to be less significant in the regional dynamic than nationalism. Nationalism was also twinned with a desire on the part of Latin American leaders to move their nations into the industrial era, to transcend their often monocultural export-driven economies. Yet, given the private sector orientation of U.S. foreign economic policy in the 1940s and 1950s, the Latin American expectations of substantial U.S. assistance in attaining those goals in the early Cold War years were soon frustrated, giving rise to stronger expressions of economic nationalism and in some instances – notably the Cuban – revolution. Although at times it was difficult to distinguish between the force of Latin American nationalism and developments driven by the Cold War, of the two themes, the latter was the most significant factor in shaping U.S. policy before 1959, and events in Colombia, Guatemala, and Cuba among others proved to be highly volatile and divisive.

The role of the Caribbean within the Cold War bipolar conflict had been ensured by the 1940 wartime extension by Britain to the United States of ninety-nine-year leases on a number of British bases in the region: British Guiana, Jamaica, Trinidad, Antigua, the Bahamas and Saint Lucia. As historian Anthony Maingot notes, the construction of naval and air bases on these acquisitions made the United States "the undisputed military power in the whole Caribbean area and conferred the responsibilities that entailed." Any challenge – real or perceived – to this hegemony would have to be repelled.[2]

By the end of World War II, had there been any lingering doubt about the identity of the hegemonic power in the region the U.S. rapidly dispelled such doubts. World War II had further weakened British and especially French economic, military and political influence throughout their empires, including the Caribbean basin, and it was not until after the Castro revolution in Cuba that the Soviet Union became a real factor in the multinational dynamic of the area. Only the United States possessed the will and capacity to replace the declining empires of Europe. Thus, from 1945 through 1959 the United States was the unchallenged power in trade, investment, and military relations, and other U.S. institutions such as organized labour also played an increasingly important role in the region in the context of the struggle to contain communism.

The 1947 Rio Pact, pledging inter-American solidarity against external aggression, followed by the formation of the Organization of American States at the Bogotá conference in early 1948 provided the main institutional framework of the Cold War in the Americas. As early as 1948, there was a widespread perception in U.S. policy making circles that communism and the Soviet Union posed a real threat to the hemisphere. The political crisis in Colombia which coincided with the meeting of inter-American leaders there in 1948 – occasioned by the assassination of popular Liberal leader Jorge Eliecer Gaitán – seemed to confirm that perception. Following several days of rioting in Bogotá, Colombia broke diplomatic relations with the Soviet Union. The *Bogotazo*, as the riots became known, as well as the decade of bloody civil war that followed, had, in retrospect, little to do with communism and nothing to do with the Soviet Union, but in the context of the early Cold War such conflict heightened anxieties that Latin America was highly vulnerable to communist agitation.[3]

The Bogotá conference also contributed to the ongoing debate among the American states over the status of European colonies and territories in the Americas. In the 1940s and 1950s a number of the Latin American nations persistently lobbied through both the United Nations (UN) and the OAS for an end to European colonization in the Americas. In the Caribbean, Guatemala was the most active in this regard, focusing on the status of British Honduras, although Mexico also took a hard line on the European presence; Colombia, the Dominican Republic and Venezuela were more measured in their views, in spite of the latter's ongoing dispute over the border with British Guiana.[4]

At Bogotá in 1948, a number of delegations, notably those of Argentina, Chile, Guatemala and Venezuela, led an initiative to establish a Commission of Dependent Territories, a resolution that was finally signed by seventeen nations. The Commission was charged with the responsibility of studying the situation of the colonies and "occupied" American territories, whatever their status, and to seek peaceful means for the abolition of colonialism, especially by extra-continental countries.[5] For the Caribbean basin the main targets of concern were British Honduras, which Guatemala claimed, the British West Indies, and the Guianas. The U.S. delegation abstained on the creation of the Committee on Dependent Territories on the grounds that the conference was not a court of law and that action appearing to support the claims of one of the parties to a territorial dispute was inappropriate, especially since the major parties to the dispute were not present. Rather, it was suggested that mechanisms for the resolution of such disputes existed through the UN, although U.S. policy makers were also reticent to see the issue given prominence at the UN. Given the Cold War context the U.S. position was also consistent with its view that continued colonial rule appeared the best bulwark against the more significant threat of international communism. British governments in the post-war years encouraged the development of colonial self-government, partly as a practical means to reduce the costs of colonial administration in a region that had lost its strategic and economic value to Britain.[6]

U.S. policy toward the issue of decolonization in the area had already been articulated in 1947 when the United States accepted membership in the Caribbean Commission, established by agreement with the governments of France, the Netherlands, and the United Kingdom. The objective of the Commission was, as Secretary of State George C. Marshall informed Congress, "to encourage and strengthen international cooperation in promoting the economic and social welfare and enhancement of the non-self-governing territories in the Caribbean area," an objective that Marshall stressed was "vital" to the security interests of the United States.[7] Decolonization in the post-1945 era was thus an integral part of the larger debate over the Cold War, as was the case elsewhere in the Third World.

For European countries with dependencies in the Caribbean and for those dependencies, the relationships were far more complex than the simplistic polarization inherent in U.S. Cold War policies. France emerged from World

War II in political and economic tatters from its wartime occupation by Nazi Germany. As much as it may have desired a return to the pre-war days of colonial glory, such was not to be the case either in the Caribbean or Indo-China. Yet, the French approach differed significantly from that of Britain, with a firm commitment to the integration of its colonial peoples into French life. Thus, by plebiscite in 1945 French Guiana, Guadeloupe, and Martinique chose political union with France, becoming *départements* of the French republic.

The Netherlands moved in a similar direction; shortly after World War II, the Dutch government extended the rights of internal self-government and universal suffrage to its insular territories, Curaçao, Aruba, Bonaire and the three Leeward Islands of Sint Maartens, Sint Eustatius and Saba. A decade later they formed, with the Netherlands and Surinam, the Kingdom of the Netherlands. That arrangement remained the norm for the next forty years, with only Aruba pressing for the independence it ultimately attained in the 1990s. The Netherlands West Indies were of divergent significance in the region. Curaçao and Aruba became major refining sites for Venezuelan oil, providing them sporadically with the highest standards of living in the region. Surinam's economy was more mixed, depending as it traditionally had on agricultural resources as well as newly developed mineral resources significant for the Cold War years. The other four islands never transcended their economic disadvantages, with their ever dwindling populations depending on the prosperity of their sister colonies.[8]

U.S. officials in the post-war era viewed the Netherlands as an important actor in the region and to that end sought during the Truman and Eisenhower administrations to establish a formal agreement on U.S.–Dutch military co-operation in the Caribbean. When they finally reached agreement in the Eisenhower years, the arrangement provided for U.S. forces to be stationed in the Netherlands West Indies, but only with the consent of Dutch authorities. The Dutch preference was to be responsible not only for local defence but also for the defence of a sub-area of the Caribbean that included the sea approaches to the Netherlands Antilles and areas contiguous to Venezuela and Colombia. They also requested that U.S. troops stationed in the Netherlands West Indies be placed under the command of a Dutch officer, both positions of which were rejected by the United States, and the compromise solution was to have a U.S. commander in control of sea communications and a Dutch commander in control of domestic forces.[9]

Specific situations such as the Colombian drama after 1948 and the more generalized debate over decolonization made U.S. and European policy makers in the 1940s and 1950s more sensitive to political transformations in the region that seemed to advance the interests of international communism. Prior to the Cuban revolution in 1959, Guatemala was the main source of such concerns in the Caribbean basin, although it was not the only nation or colony that occasioned alarm. Cold War tensions spilled over into a wide range of institutions, not the least of which was the labour movement, where east–west conflict was embodied in the formation of rival labour organizations – the pro-communist

World Federation of Trade Unions and the anti-communist International Confederation of Free Trade Unions (ICFTU). Both organizations won adherents in the Caribbean. In addition, the U.S. government worked closely with the Inter-American Regional Organization of Workers (ORIT), the western hemisphere branch of the ICFTU. One of the main programmes was to operate workshops for prospective labour leaders, initially at the University of Puerto Rico and, when ORIT became sensitive to working with government, U.S. officials operated the programme in co-operation with U.S. organized labour organizations.[10]

The real history of organized labour in the region was far more complex and significant than the often simplistic Cold War dichotomy. In the post-war era, notably in the British Caribbean, colonial governments now recognized the value of trade unions to functional democracy and even incorporated them into the political decision-making process. The growing influence of labour became even more pronounced with the expansion of the suffrage in these years, with Jamaica achieving universal adult suffrage in 1944, Barbados and Trinidad in 1946, British Guiana in 1953, and British Honduras in 1954. This relatively slow progress toward full democracy defied the recommendations of the British Royal Commissions established to deal with the 1930's disturbances and fuelled the fires of anti-colonialism as a political force in the region in the post-war era.

The Guatemalan debate

Much has been written on the question of U.S. surrogate intervention in Guatemala in 1954 and the preceding opposition to a series of reformist Guatemalan governments which U.S. officials believed threatened U.S. strategic and economic interests in the country and the region. The Guatemalan debate in the Caribbean highlighted the difficulties of separating the implications of rising economic nationalism, decolonization and Cold War anti-communism in the international history of the region. U.S. officials were primarily concerned with the impact of Guatemalan nationalism on U.S. private sector investment and on national security should that economic nationalism, combined with U.S. policy actions, push Guatemala closer to the Soviet bloc.

Guatemalans elected two consecutive reformist administrations in the late 1940s – Juan José Arévalo, and in 1950 Jacobo Arbenz.[11] The latter's strong commitment to agrarian reform and economic development on one level seemed consistent with the foreign policy orientation of the Democratic administration of Harry Truman, but it ran hard against the grain of U.S. private and public interests when the Arbenz government expropriated several hundred thousand acres of idle lands to which the United Fruit Company held title. A commitment to compensation proved inadequate to salve the wounds of either the company or American opinion, and the arrival of the Republicans in power under Dwight D. Eisenhower, with John Foster Dulles as Secretary of State and Allen Dulles director of the CIA (Central Intelligence Agency), spelled doom for the Arbenz government. The United Fruit Company and its supporters inside and outside the administration (the Dulles law firm had long represented the company) mounted an expensive, vigorous and extensive public relations campaign in the United States to discredit Arbenz and to link his government with both domestic and international communism. Such views were not limited to either the Dulleses or the United Fruit Company, however. In its annual assessment of the state of affairs in Latin America in 1952–4, the State Department described the Guatemalan government as "pro-communist," and in Britain the London *Times* in 1954 portrayed both Peronism in Argentina and communism in Guatemala as "dangerous trends."[12]

Inaccurate and irresponsible as the United Fruit Company public relations campaign against Guatemala was, it was less disturbing than the decision of the Eisenhower administration in 1953 to authorize a CIA covert operation against Arbenz and in support of the ambitions of exiled and U.S.-military trained Colonel Carlos Castillo Armas. Castillo Armas and the CIA trained a force of insurrectionists at military bases in Nicaragua and Honduras with the explicit objective of overthrowing Arbenz.

In the course of 1953 Guatemala became increasingly isolated from the inter-American system at the same time that U.S. officials believed that communist elements in the country were engaged in subversive activities in other countries of Central America. In April the Arbenz government withdrew from the Organization of Central American States (ODECA), claiming that the other governments of the region had aggressive intent toward Guatemala. The Arbenz decision appears to have been in direct response to an initiative on the part of El Salvador to have the organization discuss measures to contain communism in Central America. U.S. officials viewed the Guatemalan decision to withdraw as a victory for communist political forces within Guatemala, who were opposed to ODECA, but the United States, determined that the Guatemalan withdrawal should not result in the collapse of ODECA, lent moral and military assistance to the other Central American countries.[13]

In 1954 U.S. officials escalated their pressures on Guatemala in an effort to isolate it from others in the region. In addition to curtailing any foreign assistance to Guatemala, Eisenhower officials took the larger issue of communism to the Tenth Inter-American Conference at Caracas in March 1954. The Caracas conference agenda was, as the London *Times* correspondent in Washington noted, "explosive," focusing not only on the threat of communism but also on the larger issues of colonialism and economic development.[14] The conference was further complicated by the unofficial presence of a spokesman for the recently deposed Cheddi Jagan People's Progressive Party government in British Guiana.

It was evident even before the conference opened that the Latin American countries did not view international communism with the same fervour as U.S. officials but were prepared to co-operate with the United States in return for economic development assistance, including price controls for raw materials and long-term investment. President Pérez of Venezuela set the tone of the conference in his opening remarks, a thinly veiled reference to U.S. policy objectives, when he appealed to the member states to approach one another with respect, not to impose one's views on others, or in the name of "doctrines" to intervene in the internal affairs of other nations.[15]

U.S. Secretary of State John Foster Dulles was not to be deterred. He informed the delegates that it "was time to make clear . . . that we see that alien despotism is hostile to our ideals; that we unitedly deny it the right to prey upon our hemisphere. . . . There is no place here for political institutions which serve alien masters." With the irony characteristic of inter-American relations, the authoritarian regimes of Cuba, the Dominican Republic and Peru quickly fell in line with the U.S. position, likely savouring the prospect of economic assistance. Among the Caribbean delegations Nicaragua and Honduras gave immediate support to Dulles's anti-communist resolution before the political committee and Venezuela shortly followed suit. The Guatemalan Foreign Minister on the other hand branded Dulles' position as an unfair attack on Guatemalan democracy under the guise of anti-communism, and the Mexican delegation advanced an amendment to the Dulles' resolution that would have required an actual invasion of the Americas by an extra-continental power as justification for collective military action by the American states. When the final vote was cast, the U.S.-sponsored resolution passed seventeen to one, with Guatemala the sole negative vote but with Mexico and Argentina in abstention. As he departed Caracas, Dulles ominously warned: "Now we still have the task of ensuring that the enemies of freedom do not move into the breach which has been disclosed within our ranks."[16] The administration shortly acted on that premise.

In the absence of economic and military aid from the United States and with clear evidence of military dissidence, Arbenz turned to the Communist bloc for the purchase of weapons; that action provided the political and international rationale for the CIA to unleash the forces of Castillo Armas. The rebel forces fared badly on the ground, but Arbenz's support rapidly disintegrated. His government's efforts to have the UN Security Council investigate allegations of U.S. intervention failed because of successful U.S. diplomacy with Britain and France, with the result that he was effectively isolated internationally. With U.S. planes bombing Guatemala City, U.S. Ambassador John Puerifoy collaborating with his opponents and demanding his resignation, and the official military turning against him, President Arbenz resigned and went into exile.

The first of the modern U.S. anti-communist covert operations had been successful, establishing both an unfortunate precedent in inter-American relations and provoking a strong anti-American backlash throughout the Americas as well as in some European circles. In Britain, although the government publicly co-operated with the Eisenhower administration, the more balanced, less messianic British approach to Cold War issues in the Third World ran against the ideological orientation of U.S. foreign policy.[17] The Guatemalan affair was a blatant violation of sovereignty and intervention in the internal politics of an

American state with no substantive evidence of a serious threat to the security of the hemisphere from the Soviet bloc. From the U.S. perspective, however, that fact was irrelevant. The overthrow of Arbenz provided the United States with stable though authoritarian regimes in Guatemala for the next several decades, and the Caracas resolution lent the credibility of inter-American endorsement.

Cuba

If Guatemala was the main focus of Cold War policies in the Caribbean in the post-war decade, Cuba appeared to be one of the regional success stories. It had one of the highest standards of living in Latin America as a whole, even if the economy remained overly dependent on the production and export of sugar and the gap between the rich and poor, between urban and rural Cuba, was disturbing evidence of potential explosiveness, what Ramon Eduardo Ruíz appropriately refers to as the "splintered society."[18] High levels of unemployment and under-employment (an estimated 30 percent), especially in the countryside, combined with adult illiteracy and malnutrition, contrasted sharply with the high living foreigners who flocked to the casinos and brothels of Havana and the Cuban elites who lived well on the backs of the poor. Such disparities were exacerbated by the tragic fact that Cuba, endowed with rich soils and favourable climate, imported many of its foodstuffs because of an over-concentration on sugar production.[19]

In the years after Fulgencio Batista returned to power in 1952 by *coup d'état*, the island was politically stable but resting on a cauldron of discontent that was about to overflow. Batista was solidly pro-American – at times embarrassingly so – and even the widespread political opposition to Batista seemed to be man-ageable as long as Batista controlled the highly personalist armed forces. Militaristic, repressive, and corrupt as the regime was, Batista was confident of the security of his government by the mid-1950s, overly confident as history was to prove. When, on 26 July 1953, the youthful Fidel Castro led his motley band of revolutionaries against the Moncada barracks in Santiago de Cuba, Castro not only lived to tell the tale but also was ultimately allowed to go into exile to plot a return to the country and the launching of another revolutionary initiative – this one the most successful in the history of the western hemisphere and dramatic in its impact on international relations.

As Castro suggested in his "History Will Absolve Me" speech at his trial following the Moncada barracks attack, his revolution had little clear direction in 1953, a sense of social justice and opposition to Batista, militarism, and the strength of the foreign – largely American – presence in Cuba. Such nationalism was deeply rooted in Cuban culture, and given the strength of the U.S. presence it was inevitable that American interests would be the main target of that nation-alism. As historian Franklin Knight observes, although the main owners of sugar production were Cuban (60 percent), foreign interests controlled 75 percent of all arable land, most of which was planted in sugar, and 90 percent of essential services.[20] Beyond a strong sense of Cuban nationalism, which was by far the most important signal of what was to come after 1959, there was no programme and certainly nothing that hinted at a later socialism let alone orientation toward the communist bloc. None of the Castro compatriots who followed him into the Moncada barracks débâcle was a member of the Cuban Communist Party or of the communist youth movement in Cuba. Besides, at that stage in the 1950s Castro was only a minor element in the political opposition to Batista, opposition that was manifest in frequent demonstrations by labour, students, intellectuals who were drawn to the Cuban Communist Party, and the more feeble protests of the largely politically bankrupt traditional political parties.

Less than two years after his sentencing to the Cuban prison colony on the Isle of Pines, Castro and his surviving compatriots went into exile in Mexico, just a year after the overthrow of Arbenz in Guatemala. It was a further reflection of the looseness of the inter-American security system in the 1950s that Castro, without intervention by either Mexican or U.S. authorities, trained his next invasion force on Mexican soil, from which he launched the yacht *Granma* in late 1956 for eastern Cuba; there the rugged terrain of the Sierra Maestra mountains provided sanctuary for the evolving revolutionary movement against Batista's slowing crumbling credibility and military potence.

Unlike the situation that prevailed in Guatemala, U.S. authorities were unable to control the political or military dynamic of the Cuban situation. Neither the CIA nor the Military Defence Assistance Program, of which Cuba was a beneficiary in the 1950s, proved adequate instruments for the occasion, in part because the Military Assistance Program was designed to deal with a foreign threat to hemispheric security rather than with a political culture in radical transition. Ironically, the U.S. clearly hastened Batista's collapse in 1958; as Castro's revolution spread from the Sierra Maestra into every province in the country, the U.S. government denied Batista the use of U.S. military materiel, including bombers, and personnel trained under the Military Assistance Program, because their use was to be restricted to hemispheric defence. The United States followed those restrictions with a full arms embargo and then recall of U.S. Ambassador Arthur Gardner.[21] Unlike 1933, when the U.S. was able to capture the revolutionary movement and turn it to its own advantage, in 1958 a combination of Batista's refusal to resign and the momentum of the revolution made it impossible for U.S. authorities to shape the course of events. The end for Batista and, as it turned out, the old order came in the context of a massive general strike on 1 January 1959. Ironically, it was not the Cuban revolution itself that ultimately made the external threat a reality after 1960 but rather the U.S. failure to understand the nature of and to cope with the strength of Cuban nationalism and the weakness of the traditional political, social and military institutions on the island.

Dominican Republic

When Cuba "fell" to Castro's forces in early 1959 security in the Caribbean assumed a greater urgency for the United States and other major western powers. Unlike the precarious control which Batista exercised in the 1950s in Cuba, in the Dominican Republic Rafael Trujillo maintained a firm grip on the helm of power, partly because of consistent support from the Truman and Eisenhower administrations. There was some moral support for Dominican dissidents from anti-Trujillo governments in Costa Rica, Cuba, Guatemala, Haiti – under President Estimé, who had succeeded Lescot – and Venezuela, but such moral support proved of little consequence. Trujillo's tough stance on Communists conformed with both U.S. and Vatican preferences.

In 1952 Trujillo's younger brother Hector became nominal President in 1952, leaving Rafael free to pursue his ambitions on a larger stage. He made several visits to the United States, meeting with Presidents Truman and Eisenhower and their senior officials, as well as congressional leaders. In 1955, Vice-President Nixon paid a courtesy visit to the Dominican Republic, and although the 1956 kidnapping in New York and subsequent murder in the Dominican Republic of Trujillo critic Jesús de Galinda concerned President Eisenhower, it did not seriously affect relations between their two countries. Trujillo visited Generalissimo Franco in Spain and Pope Pius XII at the Vatican, who reportedly gave him a friendly reception, and he shortly concluded a concordat with the Vatican.[22]

The concordat served the purposes of both parties. Trujillo obtained an annulment for his first marriage; the Church achieved what it wanted as well – a commitment that under Dominican law, parties who married in a Roman Catholic Church would not be eligible for divorce.[23]

By early 1960, however, relations deteriorated. The concordat of 1954 divided the Archdiocese of Ciudad Trujillo into five dioceses. It had been one matter for Trujillo to control or intimidate the lone Archbishop of Santo Domingo; it proved impossible to dominate five bishops. Then late in October, little more than a year after John XXIII had replaced Pius XII on the papal throne, Archbishop Lino Zanini arrived in the Dominican Republic as papal nuncio. On Sunday morning 31 January 1960, most priests read from the pulpit a letter from Zanini that condemned the Trujillo government. The impact on public opinion was formidable.[24]

Archbishop Zanini had cut his diplomatic teeth under Pius XII, who sent him to Argentina. Not long after Zanini's arrival, the Church quarrelled with Argentine dictator Juan Perón. Ironically, when Perón fell from power he took refuge in the Dominican Republic only to find that Zanini had subsequently been appointed there as well. Perón decided that it was time to move again, this time to Franco's Spain. Perón told Trujillo:

> It was that man who caused my downfall. Wherever that man puts his foot, he causes disturbances. Watch yourself carefully.[25]

One missionary priest from the United States, Father James Alan Clark, noted that 188 of the 266 Roman Catholic clergy in the Dominican Republic were foreigners, principally Spanish, Canadian, American, Dutch, or Cuban. The fact that their families lived in other countries, wrote Clark, reduced the threat of reprisals to their next of kin.[26] However, the Galinda assassination had demonstrated that Trujillo agents operated well beyond the shores of the Dominican Republic. The clergy and Archbishop Zanini deserve credit for their courageous act of defiance.

By 1958, relations between the Eisenhower administration and Trujillo also began to cool. As the year began, U.S. interests in the Dominican Republic included that country's proximity to the Panama Canal, a guided missile tracking station in the north, and Dominican support for U.S. policies at the United Nations and elsewhere.[27] However, in December 1958, Lear B. Reed, CIA Chief of Station in Ciudad Trujillo, offered assistance to Dominicans who had tried to kill Trujillo. When Fidel Castro gained power in Cuba and the United States sought Latin American support against his dictatorship, it appeared incongruous that successive U.S. governments could maintain their support for a repressive right-wing dictatorship in the Dominican Republic.[28]

In March 1960, the Eisenhower administration sent retired U.S. Army General Edwin S. Clark to Ciudad Trujillo in a fruitless attempt to persuade Trujillo to resign voluntarily. U.S. intelligence sources indicated that opposition to Trujillo was substantial, and, as in the case of Batista, the Eisenhower administration preferred that he leave power at a time that the transfer of power might be controlled and U.S. security interests protected. If he had not already done so, Washington feared, he might crush any reasonable opponent friendly to the United States and leave only communists to succeed him. When Trujillo clung to office, Eisenhower, Secretary of State Christian Herter, and Clark discussed "a plan for removing Trujillo from control of the country, and to establish in his position a controlling junta which would immediately call for free elections and make an attempt to get the country on a truly democratic basis."[29]

That same year, the Organization of American States imposed sanctions upon the Dominican Republic after Trujillo organized a plot (which failed) to assassinate Romulo Betancourt, President of Venezuela.[30] The Eisenhower administration felt very strongly that the Dominican Republic should not be allowed to increase its sugar exports to the United States as U.S. purchases of Cuban sugar terminated. Additional purchases from the Dominican Republic, thought Eisenhower, would "seriously embarrass . . . the United States in the conduct of our foreign relations throughout the hemisphere."[31] Thus, an increasing number of the Dominican elite had reasons to favour Trujillo's elimination, for either moral or financial reasons.

While relations with the United States were strained, there were others to whom Trujillo could turn. On 3 March 1959, D. H. T. Hildyard, Head of the American Department at the Foreign Office in London, told a Canadian official "that Trujillo had always been very friendly to the United Kingdom and that, while not necessarily approving of his government, the U.K. could still do business with him."[32] At the same time, the British government favoured an arms embargo in the Caribbean, and the Canadian government refused to deliver twelve aged Vampire jets.[33] W. W. McVittie, British Ambassador in Ciudad Trujillo, attributed the "very friendly" relations between the United Kingdom and the Dominican Republic to sugar purchases by Tate and Lyle Limited. McVittie also commented on Trujillo's relations with other European countries:

> Relations were excellent with Franco's Spain, who, copying the Vatican, penetrate this country by propaganda (Hispanidad) and by infiltration of priests. France maintains a large Embassy and is making efforts in the cultural field. Japan is in favour, being a large sugar buyer, and is expanding her trade. The interests of Canada, West Germany and Italy are also mainly commercial.[34]

In 1958 and 1959, McVittie noted, the Bank of Nova Scotia made loans worth tens of millions of dollars to the Trujillo regime.[35] Nevertheless, leaders of European and North American countries would not visit Ciudad Trujillo, and the Dominican dictator strengthened his ties with lesser countries. Late in 1958, the Liberian Foreign Minister paid a state visit, following which the Dominican Republic and Liberia agreed to establish embassies in each other's capitals.[36] Always anxious to promote his legitimacy, Chiang Kai Shek from the Republic of China (Taiwan) sent his son Chiang Wego to the Dominican Republic in 1959. Chiang Jr. visited Trujillo and his brother, the nominal President, but he met people from the Chinese community of the Dominican Republic, reportedly very supportive of the government in Taipei.[37]

Hence, Trujillo, unlike Batista, weathered the opposition of the 1950s, but more difficult times lay ahead. The international experience with Trujillo's regime underlined the uneasy alliance that existed in the Cold War years between the democratic major powers and the often corrupt, authoritarian regimes they supported – or at least felt they had to tolerate – in the Caribbean basin. The main goals of major power diplomacy in the region remained political stability and free market economies, which they believed were the essential bulwarks against communism.

Haiti

Several major forces determined Haiti's international situation in the Cold War years: proximity to and dependence on the United States with its own Cold War preoccupations; even closer proximity to and constant concern with the security threat posed by a hostile Dominican government on its borders; the continuing influence of French culture and radical political ideology on Haitian politics and in its labour movement; and the nation's endemic economic problems.[38] Preoccupation with the threat of the Dominican Republic made

Haitian leaders extremely sensitive to balance of power considerations in the Caribbean basin, seeking assurances of support from the United States, but also attempting to buttress that U.S. support with the allegiance of anti-Trujillo governments in the region as well as from anti-Trujillo Dominican exile groups. Hence, various pre-Duvalier governments in Haiti sought close relations with such countries as Cuba and Venezuela. From the perspective of U.S. officials, stability in Haiti was the primary if elusive goal throughout the post-Cold War years as they sought to remove the preconditions that they believed would foster communist support.

In August 1946, the Haitian Congress chose Dumarsais Estimé as president. Estimé, although black, was acceptable to mulattos, and this was a strong point in his favour, but his reliance on support from nationalists and the poor made it difficult for him to balance the demands of the foreign sector in Haiti with domestic pressures. On balance he moved away from strongly nationalistic policies that would have threatened foreign capital in agriculture, landholding, and foreign involvement in such areas as domestic retail. One moderate black faction, the *authentiques*, wanted to collaborate with mulattos; others, the *irredentistes*, sought to replace them. Estimé managed to improve educational and health facilities, and his Minister of Labour, a medical doctor named François Duvalier, sought *irredentiste* support.

Estimé survived as President until 1950 but he did so with mounting domestic and international pressures. Domestically the country suffered from declining world coffee and sugar prices, which in turn reduced domestic income, increased unemployment and along with it labour unrest in a sector that was already radicalized with the formation of Mouvement Ouvrier Paysan (MOP). Haiti's delicate situation relative to the Dominican Republic was complicated further by a shift to more conservative regimes in the Caribbean basin.[39] Romulo Betancourt was out of power in Venezuela; Colombia was embroiled in a civil war with the Conservatives in power; in Nicaragua, Anastasio Somoza was seen as supportive of Trujillo and in his own right engineered an abortive coup in neighbouring Costa Rica, with its longstanding liberal traditions, leaving only Cuba as a possible counterweight against Trujillo. Yet, Estimé's main opposition was from the privileged classes that felt threatened by the support he received from radical labour and political groups. In 1950 the Haitian army removed Estimé and Congress selected as President Colonel Paul Magloire, a black officer with strong political connections and with cabinet experience in Estimé's government. Duvalier became leader of the *irredentistes*.

Magloire's end was rather ignominious. Controversy developed in 1956 over the date when his mandate was to end, and when the army abandoned him, he went into exile. Ten months of chaos followed, and when it ended in September 1957, François Duvalier won election as President of Haiti. The presidential election was Haiti's first which involved a popular electorate (rather than Congress or the army) directly. The army assisted his rise to power through electoral fraud because it thought he would be the easiest of the candidates to manipulate, and following the election two of the defeated candidates received death sentences.[40] Duvalier then reorganized the army so that from his point of view it would be more trustworthy, and he also organized his own personalist security and terrorist force, the notorious Tonton-Macoutes.

During his fourteen years in power before passing the torch to his son, Duvalier's base of support rested with the black community. Black intellectuals and landowners saw in him something to admire. He himself claimed to represent the black middle class, not the impoverished masses. Duvalier distrusted the mulattos, who in turn distrusted him. As President, Duvalier encouraged such African traditions as voodoo, which became respectable. (Mulattos ridiculed it and promoted European values.) He redesigned the flag, replacing the blue with black. He opened embassies in Africa, where he sent supporters of dubious loyalty. Although he personally spoke French, Duvalier encouraged the use of Creole dialects as a manifestation of Haitian national pride.

On matters of substance, Duvalier was more traditional. Many Haitians continued to depend upon foreign churches for hospital care and schooling. One of Duvalier's ideas for earning income for the impoverished masses was the establishment of a United States naval base which might replace the one at Guantánamo Bay in Castro's Cuba. However, the Americans decided to keep the Cuban base and did not accept his invitation. Duvalier granted concessions to American oil prospectors, allowed Mafioso a casino, let the Reynolds Mining Company (with bauxite interests) and SEDREN, which mined copper, to retain segregated housing and to pay Haitian workers less than expatriates for similar work. Only when the government of President John F. Kennedy appeared sympathetic to a 1963 attempt by Juan Bosch, President of the Dominican Republic, to depose Duvalier did Duvalier show sober second thoughts about the American connection. By contrast, one of François Duvalier's few meaningful economic reforms was land redistribution to peasants on L'Ile de la Gonave.

Novelist Graham Greene, an authority on Duvalier's Haiti, suggests that Duvalier resorted to tyranny and terror in response to threats against his life. For instance, in 1958 eight men from Florida – only three of them Haitians – came close to ousting him; all eight died in the attempt. In 1963, there was a threat against the Duvalier children.[41] Whether as a response to such threats or as simply a means to enforce his control, by 1964 Duvalier's agents were killing more than 300 people each month.[42]

By the end of the 1950s Haitian politics conformed to that of the region, with the most obvious exceptions being Costa Rica and Cuba after early 1959: authoritarian; frequently violent in the treatment of political dissent; nationalistic and yet open to foreign influence and power; impoverished; and highly unstable politically. Of all the countries of the region Haiti had each of those characteristics in the extreme, but the magnitude of crisis that would necessitate foreign intervention in Haiti was still two decades away.

Panama

Because of the canal, Panama occupied one of the two most important strategic locations in the Caribbean. The other was Guantánamo in Cuba. In addition, the United States had constructed several air bases in Panama during World War II, largely to defend the canal. In the bilateral post-war relationship between the two countries, the canal and the American bases were the main bargaining chips in Panama's quest for a greater degree of autonomy in its own affairs as well as enhanced benefits from canal operations. There were a number of important contextual issues that also drove the relationship, including communist activity in the country in the late 1940s and 1950s, periodic economic recession, the almost constant manoeuvring for political power within the country, and pervasive Panamanian nationalism, normally focused on canal-related matters.

From 1949 until his resignation in 1951 Arnulfo Arias held the presidency, and, in spite of his previously anti-American attitudes and association with the Patriotic Front Party (PFP), which he founded in 1944, supported U.S. Cold War policies in the region, including at least rhetorical support for the U.S. presence in Korea. The PFP was instrumental in Panamanian rejection of the Defence Sites Agreement in 1947 but by 1952 had shifted its support away from Arias.[43]

Arias's short-lived government did little to address the ongoing sources of social and economic problems in Panama or Panamanian–U.S. tensions relating to the status of the canal and U.S. bases, with the result that when Arias' chief of police (the only military force in the country), José Antonio Remón, gained an electoral victory in 1952, American officials anticipated some challenges to the U.S. presence. The election period was also marred by intensified communist activity in the country, activity that was exacerbated by severe economic recession. The U.S. Ambassador was sufficiently concerned that he recommended immediate economic assistance to the country to reduce unemployment. The Department of State had already launched an anti-communist campaign that Acheson described as of "significant proportions."[44]

The Communist Party in Panama was in reality extremely weak. The U.S. State Department believed that the movement had "at least indirect communication with Moscow" through the Czech legation at Caracas and the Panamanian Federation of Workers was affiliated with the major communist labour federations, the Latin American Confederation of Labour (CTAL) and the global World Federation of Trade Unions (WFTU). Yet the Communist Party itself had only an estimated 500 members of whom no more than 50 were considered "hard core." Still, American officials feared that the Party could exercise considerable influence beyond its numbers because of the more general intellectual acceptance of Marxist ideology among Panamanian nationalist intellectuals. The main concern was that by working through students and teachers, communists would gain control of the Patriotic Front.[45]

As President after 1952, Remón undertook a number of reforms, including a restructuring of his country's economy and a reorganization of the police force.

Remón warned Eisenhower that the relationship between Panama and the United States required major changes, and to avoid violence, Eisenhower agreed to talks to resolve issues outstanding since the 1930s.

The 1936 treaty had failed to resolve other contentious issues, some of them controversial since 1903. As far as the Remón government was concerned, U.S. citizens held too many Canal Zone jobs for which Panamanians were qualified. There were two rates of pay in the Canal Zone – a lower one for Panamanians and a higher one for Americans. Compounding these problems were others of recent origin. The Panama Canal Company stopped providing housing for employees who were not U.S. citizens, and as these people sought new accommodation in Panama City and Colón, they faced and inadvertently helped to create a housing shortage. These same employees lost many of their perks, including free tuition for their children, and the less disposable income they had, the worse the impact on Panama's economy was bound to be. Remón wanted the Canal Zone to contribute significantly to Panama's economy, and he knew how to exert pressure. As negotiators were about to depart for Washington late in the summer of 1953, Remón encouraged 100,000 demonstrators to bid them a fond farewell. In October of that same year, Remón met in Washington with Eisenhower and John Foster Dulles.

The Eisenhower and Remón administrations concluded another treaty which modified, but did not abrogate, the Hay-Bunau-Varilla Treaty of 1903. The 1955 treaty, duly approved by appropriate authorities in Panama and the U.S. Senate, despite the assassination of President Remón, allowed the Panamanian government to tax Panamanian employees of the Panama Canal Company. It provided for an increase in the rent which the United States paid for the Canal Zone from $430,000 (a result of the 1936 treaty) to $1.93 million. It also promised a bridge over the Panama Canal (opened in 1962), and equal pay for equal work regardless of nationality.[46]

The Eisenhower-Remón Treaty proved only a temporary measure. It allowed the United States to maintain the military base outside the Canal Zone at Rio Hato, acquired during World War II and more important than ever for the defence of the canal once the Soviet Union acquired long-range aircraft and nuclear weapons. More provocatively, it maintained the Canal Zone under U.S. control. U.S. citizens would continue to live in prosperous American-style suburbs within easy walking distance of the slums of Panama City and Colón. U.S. legislation to provide equal pay for equal work passed Congress in 1958, but it allowed U.S. employees expensive fringe benefits to which their Panamanian employees were not entitled. Many Panamanians resented the continuing presence of Americans in well-paid jobs, while they languished at the bottom of the pyramid.

Events in Egypt, where a nationalistic government seized the Suez Canal 26 July 1956 and then, with the help of the United Nations, successfully resisted an Anglo-French attempt to reoccupy the Suez Canal Zone, also impressed Panamanians. Eisenhower and Dulles were furious that Panamanian and

Egyptian officials should be talking to each other, and despite the large number of ocean-going vessels still registered in Panama, Dulles managed to exclude Panama from the Suez Canal Users' Association which met in London 7 August 1956, less than three months before the Anglo-French invasion. Eisenhower and Dulles thought that talks with the Nicaraguan government on a possible new canal might warn the Panamanians not to overplay their hand.

On 2 May 1958, Panamanian students attempted to raise their flag at fifty different points in the Canal Zone. That same year, President Eisenhower's brother Milton visited Panama. When he returned to the United States, he warned of further trouble. President Eisenhower accepted his recommendations – more economic benefits for Panama and Panamanians and the flying of Panama's flag at designated locations inside the Canal Zone – but Congress did not. Riots ensued the following year on Panama's independence day, 3 November.

Eisenhower knew that further concessions were necessary. After all, Fidel Castro had come to power in Cuba ten months earlier, and the United States government would not want Panamanian anti-Americanism to produce a Cuba-like environment on the isthmus. Eisenhower promised higher wages for Panamanian workers in the Canal Zone, offered money for employees' homes, and allowed the Panamanian flag to fly inside the Canal Zone, at a place near Panama City called Shaler's Triangle. Dulles' successor as Secretary of State, Christian Herter, expressed interest in a sea-level canal.[47]

A secret report of the National Security Council dated 29 December 1960, less than one month before Eisenhower vacated office, noted that for reasons both military and commercial, a canal in Panama was a necessity. The Canal Zone, the report continued, offered a convenient site for the training of soldiers from Latin American countries, and it allowed a U.S. military presence in Latin America.

Unfortunately, the report continued, there were serious problems. Panama's economy was overly dependent upon jobs in the Canal Zone, upon Americans and Panamanians with jobs in the Canal Zone, and upon tourists and sailors whose ships were passing through the Canal Zone. Panama's oligarchy, about twenty extended families of Spanish descent, deflected hostility from the black and mestizo majority by blaming the United States for Panama's problems. Because of the oligarchy, anti-U.S. sentiment was increasing, as was the influence of Colonel Nasser's United Arab Republic and Fidel Castro's Cuba. The existing canal was unable to cope with the volume of traffic and the large aircraft carriers and oil tankers then in service. It was also vulnerable to sabotage or worse by the Soviet Union or its friends.

The report made several recommendations. Its most important was construction of a new sea-level canal, to be dug with nuclear explosives before 1980. Such a canal, the report continued, would have to be in Panama, probably well east of the current one. Larger countries such as Mexico or Colombia, across whose territory it was physically possible to construct an inter-oceanic canal, would demand a greater degree of influence over its operations than U.S. interests would allow. The "Nicaragua" route would require co-operation from too many countries. While it was unlikely that the Panamanian government would grant the degree of control which the United States currently enjoyed over the Canal Zone, the United States probably would not need such control. A sea-level canal would lack the intricate technology of the existing canal and would be less vulnerable to neglect or sabotage. Perhaps Panama might permit limited U.S. control of the sea-level canal in exchange for U.S. withdrawal from the existing Canal Zone (apart from the military bases there). Planning for such a canal must begin at once. The U.S. government should encourage more enlightened policies on the part of the Panamanian oligarchy, for a greater degree of social justice was a prerequisite to stability. Finally, tactful behaviour on the part of the Zonians – the Americans who lived in the Canal Zone – would help to defuse tensions.[48] This report provided the basis of the Kennedy administration's thinking on Panama.

Puerto Rico

Throughout Puerto Rico's twentieth-century history, the "status question" has been an ongoing issue, and there have been three principal political factions. On one side there have been those who favoured independence. To *independentistas*, Puerto Ricans have an honourable heritage of their own which can best be preserved through independence; the U.S. military draft to which Puerto Ricans have been liable was obnoxious; arguably Puerto Rico might prosper more than it has if a Puerto Rican government were free to impose or withhold its own tariffs. *Independentistas* have included Eugenio Maria de Hostos, an intellectual of the last Spanish and first American days, whose prestige remains high; the controversial Pedro Albizu Campos, a nationalist of the 1920s and 1930s; Ruben Berrios of the modern Puerto Rican Independence Party; and Juan Mari Bras, of the pro-Cuban Puerto Rican Socialist Party. They have also included violent enthusiasts who carried the struggle to Washington, DC. There they attempted to assassinate President Harry Truman in 1950 and to shoot members of the House of Representatives in 1954. On the other side have been those who favoured statehood for Puerto Rico; these included José Celso Barbosa (a black man) when the Foraker Act became law, as well as members of the New Progressive Party, which has won four of Puerto Rico's eleven gubernatorial elections since 1952. They argue that statehood would send a message of stability to potential investors and give Puerto Rico greater influence in Washington, where so many important decisions affecting Puerto Rican life and welfare are made.

In the middle stand the Popular Democrats, founded by Luís Muñoz Marin, son of Luís Muñoz Rivera, who had promoted increased autonomy for Puerto Rico during the final years of Spanish rule. The second Muñoz decided that desirable as independence might be on emotional grounds, the fight against poverty had to be Puerto Rico's highest priority. Independence could wait. Meanwhile, Puerto Ricans could enjoy guaranteed access to the mainland for their surplus population and for products produced on the island. They could benefit from federal relief and public works programmes, while, at the same time, avoiding federal taxes. By tradition, Americans could not suffer taxation without representation, and as long as Puerto Ricans lacked voting representation in Washington, Muñoz favoured what he called "Commonwealth status" for his homeland. This meant that Puerto Ricans would elect their governor on the day that Americans elect their president, and the insular government would have the same authority in Puerto Rico that a state government would have on the mainland, even if Puerto Rican influence in Washington was minimal.

Commonwealth status took effect in 1952. The following year, the General Assembly of the United Nations agreed that Puerto Ricans had "effectively exercised their right of self-determination" and that that part of the United Nations charter which dealt with non-self-governing territories did not apply to Puerto Rico.[49] Muñoz himself won Puerto Rico's first four gubernatorial elections (1948, 1952, 1956, 1960), and successors within the party won four of the remaining seven (1964, 1972, 1984, 1988). The party also won 1967 and 1993 plebiscites in which voters were asked to choose among Commonwealth status, statehood, and independence.[50]

Yet hardly surprisingly, when Puerto Ricans have gone to the polls, there has usually been more at stake than the status question – a euphemism for the island's relationship with the United States. The Popular Democrats won the 1967 plebiscite which dealt solely and clearly with the status question, then lost the 1968 gubernatorial election to a candidate who favoured statehood.

As governor, Muñoz Marin favoured an economic policy known as "Operation Bootstrap." Large corporations would receive tax incentives to open factories in Puerto Rico, where wages were generally lower than in the United States. From Puerto Rico they could ship goods to the United States market without any tariff barrier. In the short run, Puerto Rico boomed. The Cuban revolution of 1959 also proved beneficial to Puerto Rico as American tourists eager for a Spanish style – but safe – tropical vacation considered Puerto Rico a happy alternative to the politically inaccessible Cuba. Muñoz won four elections, then handed authority to a duly elected successor from his own party, Roberto Sanchez. However, after twenty years in La Forteleza (the governor's palace), during which Muñoz and Sanchez were bound to make some controversial decisions which would antagonize an increasing number of people, the Popular Democrats understand-ably lost support. At the same time, Puerto Ricans compared their standard of living to that of other United States citizens, not to that of residents of other Caribbean islands, and they registered dissatisfaction that their per capita income was consistently lower than that of the poorest state. Finally, Governor Sanchez's divorce became such a public issue that he broke with his party and ran against it as a candidate for the newly created People's Party. Both the Popular Democrats and Sanchez went down to defeat, and the New Progressive Party, led by a distinguished pianist, Luis Ferre, triumphed.

British Guiana

The Cold War preoccupations that characterized the "American" Caribbean were equally germane in the British sphere of influence. In the case of British Guiana, Cold War issues were exacerbated by traditional ethnic tensions between the East Indian and "Afro-Saxon" communities. The colony held economic and strategic importance for both Great Britain and the United States. Following the war the United States retained leased-base areas, including an important air base. Like its neighbour Surinam, British Guiana was also an important source of bauxite, gold and diamonds. Hence both American and British authorities reacted with some alarm when the country appeared in 1953 to be moving toward a communist-leaning government, and although the British were the main actors in the events that ensued, the United States expanded its technical assistance programme to the colony to complement British efforts to undercut the economic conditions that were believed to feed communism. Britain took the situation there sufficiently seriously that its 1954 White Paper noted, in connection with British Guiana and Kenya, the continuing need to devote a substantial portion of its engineering production to defence.[51]

In 1953, British Guiana's dominant political party was the People's Progressive Party, still led by Jagan. Jagan's and the party's power rested in part on the support of the Guiana Industrial Workers' Union (GIWU) and the rival Man Power Citizen's Association (MOCA), representing the colony's sugar field workers. Organized labour also divided along Cold War lines. The British Guiana Trade Union Council (GBTUC), formed in 1940, at the urging of the British TUC, joined the World Federation of Trade Unions in 1948. However, when the British body quit the WFTU two years later in response to its pro-communist leanings, the BGTUC refused to follow suit. Indeed, leaders of several unions that actually comprised the BGTUC – including Jagan himself – served as observers within the European Federation of Trade Unions (EFTU) between 1951 and 1953. This served to widen the rift between Jagan's GIWU and the MOCA, which had recently affiliated with the International Confederation of Free Trade Unions. It also prompted a split within the BGTUC itself, between the supporters of Jagan and the People's Progressive Party (PPP) on the one hand and the anti-communists on the other. In 1953, anti-communist elements acted to dissolve the GBTUC rather than let it remain under Jagan's control.

It was against this backdrop of political and labour tension that British Guiana held its first elections under universal suffrage in the spring of 1953. Led by Jagan, the PPP won eighteen out of twenty-four seats in the legislative assembly, although its percentage of the popular vote was only 51 percent. What precipitated crisis for Jagan's government was his party's determination to force through the assembly legislation compelling employers to concede recognition of the GIWU. The powers of the legislative assembly were limited, for while it could pass legislation, the legislation did not become law until and unless it won approval from the legislative council, consisting of people appointed by the governor, and by the governor himself, appointed by the British government. The governor in 1953 was Sir Alfred Savage, initially appointed by Britain's post-war Labour government and retained by the Conservatives when they took office in 1951.

Nevertheless, the British government of Sir Winston Churchill was not inclined to gamble. Stalin died in 1953; it was also the year the Korean War ended, a time of continuing tension between the Soviet Union and western countries. Apart from his unwillingness to preside over the dissolution of the British Empire, indeed apart from the extensive British investments in British Guiana, Churchill believed there was adequate reason for concern over Jagan's communist leanings. A Colonial Office document summarized the British government perspective on Jagan and the PPP. Even before the People's Progressive Party's victory at the polls, the document noted, Churchill's cabinet had been aware of ties between PPP officials and Moscow. Nevertheless, the British government had allowed the PPP to assume office, and Governor Savage had done his best to work with Jagan and his associates. Unfortunately, from Savage's perspective, PPP officials then intensified their linkages with the Soviet bloc. Savage enumerated for the Colonial Office the litany of evidence of Jagan's Soviet bloc leanings:

> Mrs. Jagan, who is secretary of the party and was a member of the Young Communist League when in America, attended the third world congress of the Women's International Democratic Federation (Communist) in Copenhagen in June and later visited Rumania. Mr. Rory Westmaas is vice-president of the P.P.P. and organizer of the local "peace committee" and the Pioneer Youth League. He has recently been to a Communist-organized international youth conference in Bucharest. Dr. Jagan visited East Berlin to attend an international youth conference held under Communist auspices in 1951. . . . In the last May Day procession, members of the party carried portraits of Stalin, Mao Tse-tung, and M. Malenkov [Georgi Malenkov, Stalin's immediate successor]. In an official Ministerial broadcast Dr. Jagan said that he was . . . "a great admirer of the Soviet Union, people's China, and the people's democracies . . . "
>
> At the same time, under Mrs. Jagan's leadership, the Communists in the P.P.P. have organized it into small cells for recruitment, indoctrination, political agitation, and the maintenance of discipline on Communist lines. A Pioneer Youth League, affiliated to the World Federation of Democratic Youth (Communist), has been set up for the political training of the young.[52]

The statement noted that PPP ministers encouraged strikers in the sugar industry, and that the economy of British Guiana had become chaotic.

On 6 October 1953, the Colonial Office issued a statement that because of communists in high places, even in Jagan's cabinet, British Guiana faced the possibility of bloodshed. To prevent such an eventuality, the British government was sending soldiers and sailors to Georgetown.

On 8 October, about 600 Royal Welsh Fusiliers along with British Marines arrived in Georgetown and assumed positions around such strategic buildings as Government House and the radio station. The next day, the Colonial Office announced that it had suspended British Guiana's constitution and dismissed the PPP ministers. Governor Savage would assume "emergency powers." Four days later, police raided the homes of some forty PPP leaders as well as party headquarters and party offices in other parts of the colony.[53]

U.S. interest in British Guiana's 1953 crisis was limited. As British Guiana was only a colony at the time, the highest post which the United States government could have had there at the time would have been a consulate-general. There was no U.S. consulate-general, nor even a consulate. Vice-Consul Kenedon Steins had to file his reports from Georgetown through the U.S. consulate-general in Port of Spain, Trinidad. Archival evidence indicates that Steins had to rely on newspapers and published reports for most of his information. In 1953, the colony's trade with the United States was but a fraction of British Guiana's trade with Canada, by far the most important trading partner (Table 2).

Canadians who had major investments in British Guiana shared the British concern about the PPP's electoral triumph in British Guiana. The Aluminum Company of Canada owned the Demerara Bauxite Company (Demba) at Mackenzie in British Guiana and thought that because of its contribution to the colonial economy, one of its officials ought to have a seat on the legislative council. Alcan repeatedly informed Governor Savage of its disappointment that he was not appointing any of *its* people, and Alcan officers thought that Governor Savage himself was far too leftist, far too sympathetic to unions and socialists, to be kept in his job by a Conservative government. It was shocking that Governor Savage would say "that Socialism is here to stay and that all of us might as well accept that fact." Nor did Canadian business people like the PPP charge that "Only two real Negroes, and not a single Indian, are employed in the Royal Bank

Table 2 Value of British Guiana's exports, 1953 (in $BWI)[54]

To	First half of 1953	Third quarter of 1953
United Kingdom	52,415	92,902
Canada	8,788,183	5,133,361
Netherlands	189,525	
Norway	7,210	
France	64,262	
United States	1,891,749	1,321,884
Total	10,929,082	6,612,409

of Canada, and Barclay's bank, in any clerical position." Said one Alcan official, British Guiana should realize that "other countries, after experiments with Government ownership and controls, now seem to be eager . . . to leave the job to private enterprise. . . . If private enterprise is to have a chance to do its stuff, it shouldn't be unduly hampered by Governmental controls."[55]

By the time the British restored constitutional government in 1957, the PPP had split. Jagan retained the loyalty of most East Indians, but Forbes Burnham led the people of African descent into a new party, the People's National Congress (PNC). The rest of the population was splintered among people of Amerindian, Chinese, and European descent. Because most people in British Guiana voted along racial lines, and because more than half the people were of East Indian descent, the PPP won a majority of the seats in the elections of 1957 and 1961. The transition to independence was well advanced in other parts of the Commonwealth Caribbean, but Conservative governments in the United Kingdom (led in turn by Sir Winston Churchill, Anthony Eden, and Harold Macmillan) were reluctant to see British Guiana achieve independence under Cheddi Jagan.[56]

Post-war developments in British Guiana underlined the extent to which broader international considerations and conflicts could influence events. The Jagan situation was also ironic since his attachment to Marxism was a product of his education in the United States and not a response solely to indigenous circumstances in the Caribbean. In fact, Jagan had little support in other Caribbean colonies and countries and was even barred from Trinidad. His experience did mirror, however, labour developments throughout the Caribbean basin in the Cold War years in the tension that emerged between pro-and anti-communist factions as well as in the international response to that rivalry.

Jamaica

Beneath an appearance of political stability, strong undercurrents of dissent and factionalism kept the Jamaican political scene and labour movement in a state of flux in the post-war era. As in the case of British Guiana, these destabilizing forces often reflected the larger ideological tensions of the Cold War.

Since adoption of the 1944 constitution, Jamaica has had two principal political parties – the left-of-centre People's National Party (PNP) and the more conservative Jamaican Labour Party (JLP). Jamaica also dominated trade union development within the British Caribbean. Membership of the BITU, the region's largest union, was more than 50,000, or 80 percent of the island's trade unionists, and it grew another 60 percent between 1944 and 1949. By 1956, Jamaica accounted for over half of all trade unionists in the British Caribbean. The post-war era witnessed a continuation and intensification of the split within the Jamaican labour movement between the BITU-JLP under Alexander Bustamente and the JTUC-PNP under Norman Manley. The elections of 1949 marked the solidification of the split within Jamaican labour.

In 1952 the JTUC expelled leading executive members Ken Hill, Frank Hill, Richard Hart and Arthur Henry for their pro-communist leanings and for opposing a move to affiliate with the ICFTU. Together they comprised an influential power bloc within the labour movement. Their opposition to joining the ICFTU precipitated the formation of the breakaway National Labour Congress and, in 1955, the National Workers' Union (NWU). Freed of the taint of communism that the Hills, Hart and Henry had cast on the JTUC, the new organization proved to be immensely successful. The new organization appealed particularly to skilled workers who identified themselves with the middle class ideals of the PNP. It also benefited from financial help provided by the United Steel Workers of America, which was keen to organize local bauxite workers, and from the Cuban Sugar Workers Union, which helped to arrange an organizing drive of Jamaica's sugar estates in 1955. This strong international support enabled the NWU to challenge the BITU in its traditional stronghold. By 1955 membership in the NWU was over 24,000, and that increase enhanced electoral support for the PNP, which, led by Norman Manley, defeated the JLP for the first time in that year's elections.[57]

Although the PNP was nominally socialist, at no point did its struggle with the JLP threaten to convert Jamaica into a socialist state. As Michael Kaufman notes: "from the start the socialism of the PNP was bound by an allegiance to the British empire, to traditions of Westminster government, and to many of the existing economic relations of Jamaica." The purge from the JTUC of its Communist leaders in 1942 revealed that the PNP–NWU alliance might fight for social democracy but not social revolution. Jamaica's place within the international arena restricted the scope of struggle for its labour movement in the years after World War II.[58]

Trinidad and Tobago

Of considerably less significance to the Cold War context in which the process of self-government and decolonization evolved, Trinidad and Tobago none-theless evinced many of the same characteristics of the more important countries in the region. A series of constitutional reforms followed the war, all of which widened the franchise and transferred power to Trinidad's electorate. By this time, the Labour government of Clement Attlee was bowing to pressure to terminate British rule on the Indian subcontinent and in the Middle East, and Attlee decided that the British people lacked both the strength and the will to maintain their empire as it had been. While Trinidad did not gain independence as quickly as India, Pakistan, or Israel, its people did make political gains. In the elections of 1946, all adults (defined as people of at least 21 years of age) were eligible to vote. By 1950, elected members constituted a majority of both the Legislative and Executive Councils, although with the assistance of the non-elected members, the governor need not accept the advice of the elected majority.

Responsible government arrived in 1956 under Dr. Eric Williams, a Marxist former history professor from Howard University in Washington, DC. His largely black People's National Movement won thirteen of the twenty-four seats in the legislature, defeating the largely Hindu People's Democratic Party led by Bhadase Maraj, and a number of smaller groups. As Chief Minister, Dr. Williams maintained the confidence of the business community through his conservative policies and the appointment of white business people to positions in government.[59]

As in other countries and colonies in the region, in Trinidad there were Cold War conflicts relating to trade union affiliations with international organizations. Unlike Jamaica, Trinidad experienced a plurality of trade unions rather than a bifurcated system, and there was less connection on the island between politics and trade unionism. There was, nonetheless, conflict over the labour movement's international affiliations. In 1946, the Trinidad and Tobago Trades Union Council (TTTUC) complied with the suggestion of its British counterpart and affiliated with the World Federation of Labour. When the British TUC subsequently left the pro-communist organization, the TTTUC, led by Russian sympathizers John Rojas (President of the Oilfield Workers' Union) and Quinton O'Conner (President of the Federated Workers' Union), refused to follow its lead. However, six small Trinidad unions did transfer their support to the anti-communist ICFTU in 1951, affiliating with it as the Trinidad and Tobago Federation of Trade Unions. Led by waterfront workers, this body had some 13,000 members. Their leadership already threatened by this defection, Rojas and O'Conner later yielded to pressure from employers, the government and their own members and withdrew from the WFTU. The decision helped stem the trend toward factionalism, and in 1957 the rival groups rejoined to form the Trinidad and Tobago Trade Union Congress under the presidency of Rojas.

West Indian Federation

In 1957, acting on a decade-old initiative by the British Colonial Office, Jamaica, Barbados, Trinidad, the Windward and Leeward Islands entered into a federal union, the West Indies Federation (WIF). British Honduras and Guiana both sent observers to the 1956 conference but did not join the federation. Jamaica, remote from most of the other partners, had more than half the population and more than half the surface area. Only the tiny Turks and Caicos Islands and the tinier Cayman Islands shared locations in the western Caribbean with Jamaica, and the Turks and Caicos were on the far side of Cuba. Until World War II, Jamaica's links with the eastern Caribbean had been so minimal that mail had to travel via England, New York, or Halifax. The WIF was primarily a British idea, driven in large part by a desire to facilitate self-government and economic independence for unprofitable colonies with a minimum of hardship to those small islands which would not be viable on their own.[60]

Jamaicans precipitated its disintegration within four years, deciding by referendum on the fate of the short-lived federation. Their dissatisfaction is understandable. Residents of the major British West Indian island felt isolated from the distant federal capital, Port of Spain, Trinidad. They were also under-represented in the federation's House of Representatives. Although Jamaica had 52 percent of the population, it initially had only 38 percent of the seats, 48 percent following reapportionment in 1960. Like each of the other islands (except Montserrat), Jamaica had only two seats in the Senate. Jamaicans held only two of the eleven federal cabinet posts, one of them a Minister without Portfolio. Moreover, Sir Alexander Bustamante, who served as leader of both Jamaica's Labour Party and the Federal Labour Party, developed a personal antipathy to a fellow Labourite, Albert Gomes of Trinidad. Bustamante declared, "I would sooner associate with scorpions than stay leader of a party which includes Gomes. Jamaica is my first love, not the federation."[61] To maintain his base of support in Jamaica, Bustamante's rival there, Prime Minister Norman Manley, had to soften his longstanding support for federation and speak more forcefully on behalf of Jamaican interests. Both Bustamante and Manley held seats in the Jamaican, rather than the federal, House of Representatives.

Pressures within Jamaica reached the point where Manley felt obliged to call a referendum on that island's possible secession from the federation. Bustamante campaigned enthusiastically in favour of separation, Manley less wholeheartedly in favour of federation. Manley indicated that whatever the result, he would not regard it as a vote of confidence but would remain in office. Bustamante warned that the federation meant the domination of Jamaica by smaller islands, which would siphon Jamaica's relative wealth – earned largely through the mining of bauxite, tourism, and agricultural exports – to their impoverished people. Jamaicans could not keep what they had within the federation, said Bustamante. Manley argued that independence would be more costly to Jamaica than federation, because other islands were helping to share necessary government expenses. Manley also noted that self-interest obliged Jamaica to pay its share of the newly established inter-island University of the West Indies and the federal ships which linked the various islands whether Jamaica was part of the federation or not. Those arguments failed to persuade Jamaicans, only 60.8 percent of whom bothered to cast their ballots. Of those who did, 54.1 percent voted for secession and 45.9 percent for federation. By contrast, 73 percent participated in Jamaica's general election of 1961, in which Bustamante's JLP defeated Manley's PNP.

Trinidad followed Jamaica out of the West Indies Federation, and on 2 February 1962, British Colonial Secretary Reginald Maudling told the House of Commons that the federation would be dissolved. Legislation to that effect passed the House of Commons in March and April, with the dissolution effective 31 May 1962. Jamaica gained full independence later that same year. Along with Guyana and Belize, the former members of the federation later entered a common market – the Caribbean Free Trade Area (CARIFTA), now the Caribbean Community and Common Market (CARICOM) – in 1968, but politically they remain separate.

Emigration and migration

One of the major themes of the post-war years was the large-scale movement of peoples within the region as well as out-migration. This was one of the areas of post-1945 Caribbean history that was totally unrelated to the politics of the Cold War, although in retrospect this migration may prove to have been far more historically significant in cultural, economic and political terms than the half-century preoccupation with the demons of communism. In the decades following World War II migration within the Caribbean and emigration to Europe and North America intensified. Historically, migrations in the Caribbean basin involved both movement within and departures from the region. In the nineteenth and twentieth centuries, such specific economic developments as the growth of banana plantations in Central America, the massive labour needs of Panama Canal construction early in the century, or the substantial longer-term labour requirements of sugar cultivation and production, all stimulated intra-regional movements of peoples. Indeed, prior to the end of the nineteenth century, significant labour migrations tended to be entirely within the region,[62] but decolonization, economic depression, employment opportunities elsewhere, combined with frequent civil unrest to stimulate an outward movement of peoples, frequently but not always the most skilled, educated and mobile segments of the population. Industrialization and economic development initiatives, such as Operation Bootstrap in Puerto Rico, encouraged an already existing trend toward urbanization and out-migration and further impoverishment of the rural populations. Yet, largely because of the tightening of North American immigration policies, it was not been primarily the rural and urban poor that emigrated outside the region in the post-war era; rather, the middle classes of the region have been more strategically situated to meet immigration requirements in the United States and Canada. During periods of crisis, however, as for instance the Central American wars in the 1980s, the Haitian coup and civil war in the same decade or Castro's occasional "liberation" of the inmates of Cuban prisons, it has been the poor and disadvantaged that have found their way to North American shores. In the case of emigration to Canada, such movements have been facilitated by the high priority placed in Canadian immigration policy on family unification as well as some specialized programmes to attract seasonal farm and domestic workers, although policies have generally favoured the skilled and professional migrant from the West Indies.[63]

In the British West Indies, a series of Development Plans since 1946 had an impact on out-migration similar to that of Operation Bootstrap in Puerto Rico. For British territories, the plight of would-be emigrants to the United Kingdom was, however, severely curtailed in 1962 when Britain adopted legislation – the Commonwealth Immigrants Act – effectively closing the door on immigrants from the region. Fortunately for prospective emigrants, at the same time that Britain was curtailing immigration in the 1960s the United States and Canada were liberalizing their policies. Further, as negative as the impact of immigration restriction may have been on local peoples seeking to enhance their economic conditions, those who did manage to emigrate permanently or as transient labour appear to have had a positive impact on their home economies through wage remittances to families, enhanced education and training for those who returned, and simply the reduced pressure on employment their departures provided. Moreover, the British West Indies countries have maintained an interest in the well-being of their nationals who have emigrated, as Diane Marshall has noted for the experience of those peoples from St. Kitts and Antigua which U.S. officials sought to expel from the U.S. Virgin Islands in the 1970s.[64]

For the United States Puerto Rico occupied a unique situation. Residents of the American island were most profoundly affected by the post-war developmentalism that characterized the area, but since they were also American citizens migration to the United States did not prove the obstacle that it may have been for residents of the other Caribbean colonies and nations, although migrants from the French colonies enjoyed the same citizenship status. The combination of Operation Bootstrap with the decline of the sugar industry that had occurred in the 1930s provided both longer-term and immediate cause for the migration. The migrants were also heavily rural in background. In the half-century prior to 1946 only slightly more than 100,000 Puerto Ricans had made the move; yet in the years from 1946 to 1972 the migrants numbered over 1 million, representing one-third of the island's population. Approximately 70 percent of the migrants went to New York City, to areas where Puerto Rican migrants had already established themselves.[65]

Since Operation Bootstrap was a model for development in the region by the 1960s it was not surprising that the other islands would experience similar out-migration. Between 1950 and 1972 approximately 3 million people left their island homes, 2.3 million of them destined for the United States, followed by the United Kingdom, which absorbed more than 300,000, France with 200,000, and Canada, which became home to some 120,000 islanders. The majority of the migrants to the United States in those years were Puerto Ricans (860,000), followed by Cubans (620,000), although most of the latter emigrated in the aftermath of the Cuban revolution. In the same period more than 250,000 people moved to the United States from the Dominican Republic, 200,000 from each of Haiti and Jamaica, and 65,000 from Trinidad and Tobago.[66]

The British, French, and Dutch experiences differed primarily because of the distinct colonial ties and resulting citizenship in the case of the French and Dutch colonies. As well, Caribbean migration to Europe has been less significant numerically than migration to North America.[67] The primary origins of Caribbean migrants to the United Kingdom between 1950 and 1972 was Jamaica (168,600) followed by Barbados (28,400), Guyana (28,100), and Trinidad and Tobago (23,800). The Caribbean migration to Canada prior to 1972 was similar to the migration to the United Kingdom although on a much smaller scale, with the majority of migrants coming from Trinidad and Tobago (40,000) followed closely by Jamaica (35,000), Guyana (18,000), and Haiti (15,000). The migration to France from these countries was negligible, with only 5,000 from French Guiana and another 4,000 from Haiti. Conversely, the migration from Martinique and Guadeloupe after 1946, predominantly Afro-Caribbean, was more substantial, with the majority arriving after official French policy encouraged the movement in 1963. By the mid-1980s, in fact, there were as many French West Indians in metropolitan France as in the islands. Many of these migrants occupied lower level public service positions in France, thus filling a socio-economic place above the North African migrants. Such migrants not only answered a labour need in France but also relieved some of the social and economic pressures created by overpopulation and unemployment in the islands.[68]

V. S. Naipaul in *The Middle Passage* captured accurately another distinction among the colonial and migration experiences of the Caribbean societies, also hinting at the racial tensions associated in the European countries in the 1960s and 1970s, when he suggested that "In the French territories he aimed at Frenchness; in the Dutch territories at Dutchness; in the English territories he aimed at simple whiteness and modernity, Englishness being impossible."[69]

High levels of out-migration combined with migration within the region as well as rural to urban movement in each society to make a profound social, economic and political impact on the recipient as well as sending societies. For the migrants themselves, in the short term the out-migration often created groups of marginalized and alienated people, caught between an old, familiar culture and a new, more hostile one. Of course, patterns of chain migration and ethnic clustering in the receiving societies tended to mitigate somewhat the shock of migration, yet all too frequently such ethnic clustering was the result not of cultural preference but of economic deprivation and racial discrimination. For some groups such as the Puerto Ricans and Cubans, there were already well-established Puerto Rican and Cuban communities in the United States, as was the case with the British West Indians who emigrated to the United Kingdom or post-World War II Jamaican emigrants to the United States, who moved into an environment that had already been influenced by Marcus Garvey's generation. Jamaican migration to the UK in the early and mid-1950s was predominantly male, with comparatively few children. In 1958–9 the male–female migration reached a closer equilibrium, with one child for every four female migrants, suggesting a higher incidence of married couple migration in those years before falling back after 1960 to the earlier pattern. Significantly, as with many earlier international population movements, there was also a high rate of return migration. In the case of Jamaicans, for instance, in 1959 the return migration to Jamaica from the UK was one-sixth of those emigrating, although the level declined sharply in the early 1960s.[70]

Conclusion

It was the Cuban revolution which most dramatically altered the international and domestic history of the Caribbean basin after 1959. Between 1945 and Fidel Castro coming to power in Cuba, the main international concern in the region was the threat rather than the reality of communism. The Cold War thus provided the main context within which international relations and domestic politics evolved, but the Cold War was for residents of the Caribbean a vague notion that had only limited application to the realities of their daily existence. Even for the main power brokers in Caribbean domestic politics, and in spite of the amount of attention occasioned by the Guatemalan situation in 1954, Cold War issues were tangential. More immediate issues involved economic development, the role of foreign capital, the continuation of colonialism, the distribution of wealth and political influence. Not ironically those broader concerns fused with Cold War preoccupations in the aftermath of the Cuban revolution and mobilized the United States to a far more active role in the region than it had followed since the interventionist years prior to World War II.

1 Early foreign petroleum development in Colombia: ESSO (Tropical oil, a standard oil of New Jersey subsidiary) servicing Colombian agriculture, Cundinamarca (1935) (courtesy of ESSO Inter-America, Coral Gables, Florida)

2 San Felipe – 16th century fortress guards Cartagena

3 German Junker hydroplane on the Magdalena River, SCADTA Airlines (1925),
courtesy of the U.S. National Archives and Records Service, Record Group 165,
Records of the War Department, General and Special Staffs

4 Bridge of the Americas

5 Panama Canal from railroad

6 Former homes of indentured labourers near Ecclesville (1976) – now destroyed

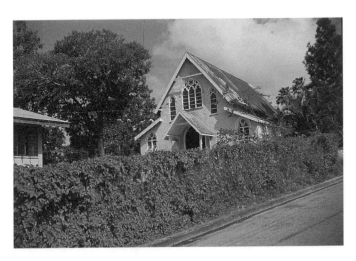

7 Aramalya Presbyterian church – reflects Nova Scotia and East Indian influence

8 Port of Spain carnival – showing celebrants carrying flags with swastikas (1996)

9 British army base, Punta Gorda, on the Belize–Guatemala border (1978)

10 "Without internationalism there would have been no Cuban revolution and without internationalism the proletariat would not have been revolutionaries"

11 Linden – bauxite production (1974)

12 Sandinista election banner for incumbent president Daniel Ortega:
caption reads "Everything will be better: Daniel President"

13 Sandinista campaign rally in rural Nicaragua near the town of Esteli

14 Bonao school built by Falconbridge Dominicana (1971)

15 Canadian Destroyers in San Juan harbor (1972)

5

THE CUBAN REVOLUTION AND CARIBBEAN BASIN RELATIONS, 1960–79

The Cuban revolution was the single most important development in inter-American relations in the twentieth century. Not only did the "success" of the revolution against U.S. pressures provide inspiration for other insurgent movements in the Americas but the orientation of Cuban foreign policy made it possible for the Soviet Union for the first time to establish a definite strategic presence in the area. In the process the Cold War preoccupations in Latin America that had previously seemed only marginally threatening, in spite of John Foster Dulles's blustering over Guatemala in the 1950s, now assumed major proportions. Clearly the most dramatic and real threat of conflict occurred with the Cuban Missile Crisis in October 1962, but even in the decades following that major crisis, Cuban–Soviet engagement in the Caribbean region remained a major preoccupation of the United States.

Some authors have identified the Soviet Union as a major player in the region since the early 1960s. Timothy Ashby, for instance, writing in 1987 in the midst of the Central American crisis, contended that "since 1960 the Soviet Union has established a degree of influence approaching hegemony over several heretofore independent nations in the Western Hemisphere."[1] His specific list included Cuba, Grenada, and Nicaragua, of which only Cuba was relevant to the pre-1979 years. The Cuban–Soviet–U.S. interplay was the main theme in the international history of the region through the 1980s, although this chapter closes with the overthrow of Nicaraguan dictator Anastasio Somoza by the Sandinista National Liberation Front (FSLN) forces in 1979.

The Cuban revolution was the most critical issue of the post-1959 years, and many other bilateral and multilateral issues cannot be entirely separated from the impact of the revolution on the region. The continuing fear of nationalism, in particular of the nationalization of foreign investment in the region, continued throughout this period. The rise of the Organization of Petroleum Exporting Countries (OPEC) in the 1960s, the major oil shortage that followed the 1973 Yom Kippur Arab–Israeli War in the Middle East, the Venezuelan shift toward a far more nationalistic position toward oil investments than it had pursued before the 1960s, and the nationalization of Guyanese bauxite, among other developments, all suggested that foreign interests in the region were more vulnerable than at any previous time.

The Cuban revolution also exacerbated older issues of political and economic instability. In Colombia, for instance, as it gradually emerged at the end of the 1950s from almost two decades of civil war between Liberals and Conservatives, the Cuban revolution injected a new element of concern over subversion into an already volatile domestic situation. In 1958, Liberals and Conservatives reached an uneasy accord establishing a National Front government, under which the two parties would alternate in office and exclude other parties from the electoral process. As the country struggled to regain political stability and to address a wide range of economic development, agricultural and fiscal reforms, and questions of social dislocation, the advent of new Cuban and Maoist-inspired guerrilla movements added a crucial new variable in the political dynamic.

New issues also came to the forefront gradually in the post-1960 years. One was the impact of illegal narcotics trafficking on the economics, politics, and foreign policies of the region. Colombia became the main processor and distributor of cocaine in these years, although the main foreign policy impact came in the 1980s, with the result that the Colombian situation is discussed in a subsequent chapter.

Longstanding problems also remained, including the persistent issue of out-migration of people from the region, primarily to the United States. Until British governments introduced restrictive legislation in the 1960s, residents of the British West Indies (now the Commonwealth Caribbean) could move freely to the United Kingdom. News that a colony was to receive independence usually sparked an exodus of people prior to the due date. Cubans, most of them middle class, disgruntled with the Castro regime flooded into Miami, Puerto Rico, New Jersey, Texas, and elsewhere in the United States in the course of the 1960s, first admitted by the Eisenhower administration as political refugees. Guyanese seeking better economic opportunities than were available under Forbes Burnham moved to the United States and Canada. East Indian Trinidadians had ties with Canada through the Canadian Presbyterian Mission and took advantage of that connection to move to Canada. More than a decade later there had been so many "tourists" from relatively prosperous and democratic Trinidad and Tobago that the Canadian government required visitors to obtain visas.

In the 1970s, economic difficulties in Jamaica prompted thousands of migrants to move to Canada and the United States. In 1977, as the bauxite industry collapsed and crime discouraged tourism, the *Miami Herald* estimated that between twenty-five and thirty Jamaican families were moving to the United States through Miami every week, the majority Jamaican ethnics: people of Chinese, Lebanese, Syrian, East Indian, or European descent. Official figures indicated that there were 8,000 Jamaican adults who had become legal residents of Florida, but the media claimed that the number of illegal residents more than doubled that figure. Apart from Mexico, Jamaica sent more illegal immigrants to the United States than any other country.[2] Of course, for the Jamaicans, the pattern of seasonal migration had already been well established before the end of World War II. Between 1943 and the late 1970s, some 500,000 Jamaicans picked fruit in the northeastern states and cut sugar cane in the South. During Manley's first government (1972–80), they came at the rate of 12,000–13,000 each year, and many also went to the Niagara fruit belt in Canada, some remaining illegally.[3]

The United States responded in a variety of ways to this transformation in the region. One was to strengthen police forces to cope with rising crime rates, including the international traffic in narcotics. There was also increasing political demand for tightened immigration policies, at least increased control over illegal migrants. More specific to foreign policy, American officials also intensified their commitment to counter-insurgency training for local military and police forces. Another was the broader application of the Alliance for Progress, with the stated objectives of alleviating those economic and social conditions which marginalized a significant segment of the region's peoples from the mainstream of the political economy and created the preconditions for the infusion of Cuban and Soviet-led communism into the area.

One novel dimension of the Alliance was the establishment of the Peace Corps during the Kennedy administration. Young volunteers went to Latin American countries to work in rural and urban development projects and train local peoples in a variety of fields. Working at the grassroots and in the local languages, Peace Corps workers were in many instances able to establish close personal bonds with the local population on a level that was impossible for senior American officials or the private corporations; such bonds produced both short-and longer-term benefits. Colombia in the 1960s came to be known as a "showcase" for the Alliance for Progress, but all countries of the region felt the impact of the programme. For many the Alliance proved disappointing and a failure; certainly it waned during the Johnson administration with the escalation of the Vietnam conflict, and the Nixon administration effectively killed the Alliance.[4]

Beyond the formal political and institutional presence of the United States in the Caribbean basin, North American and European popular culture continued to interact with more traditional Afro-and Indo-Caribbean cultures. The impact of U.S. popular culture in the post-1960s through radio, television, film, magazines, and sport is impossible to measure empirically, but there is little doubt that it has had a massive impact in the region. Radio has tended to be more indigenous and, at least in poorer, more remote areas, more accessible to the masses, but the advent of widely available North American television programming and the VCR (video cassette recorder) has a revolutionary effect. Yet, the impact outside the region of Bob Marley and reggae music has been equally profound. The North American cultural presence of course predated the advent of television. One thinks of the old man's preoccupation with the New York Yankees in Hemingway's *The Old Man and the Sea*. But that was only an early example of the impact of professional and amateur baseball in the region. It is no coincidence that professional teams of the United States and Canada are heavily staffed by

Cubans, Puerto Ricans, Dominicans, and Venezuelans among others, but not by players from the British or French Caribbean, suggesting that language was not the only cultural filter.

Rex Nettleford, writing in *Caribbean Review*, indicated that "some predict a progressive Americanization of the region in things of the most fundamental importance to the life and being of its inhabitants." He observed that the Jamaican Prime Minister in 1983 was reported as welcoming the significant amount of American television programming on the Jamaican Broadcasting Corporation as helping "to keep his nation stable." The advent of the ubiquitous satellite dish has further enhanced the impact of American television and through it American lifestyles and values – at least the lifestyles and values which television programming project. In the British Caribbean, as Nettleford notes, pre-World War II American influence had to compete with a more vigorous British presence in everything from sport – where cricket and soccer dominated the local scene – to religion, a pattern that was strongly reinforced among the region's middle and upper classes by their choice of English and Scottish universities and grammar schools. If American television is considered a threat in the stronger cultures of the region, such as Jamaica, which does have a channel devoted to Jamaican culture, other countries are even more vulnerable. In Grand Bahama, for instance, there was no local television programming in the late 1980s. In the same period in Antigua/Barbuda, 60 percent of programming was American; the privately owned cable channel showed only U.S. programmes. In Trinidad 80 percent of television in the late 1980s was foreign content, and in Dominica that rose to 100 percent.[5] Larger, wealthier, and more self-confident countries such as Mexico and Colombia have not experienced this level of infiltration; indeed, Mexico is a significant exporter of culture not only in the Caribbean basin but also to the United States.

Profound as the impact of "foreign" culture may have been in the Caribbean region, one must not neglect the persistence of indigenous cultures nor the efforts that have been made to preserve and strengthen those cultures. The establishment of the multicountry University of the West Indies is one notable example of the effort to understand and disseminate West Indian cultures and history, including the delivery of programmes to those countries without formal campuses.[6] Nor is the flow of culture entirely unidirectional, as the appeal in North America and Europe of such leading authors as V. S. Naipaul and Gabriel García Márquez indicates. Indeed the well-known influence of William Faulkner on García Márquez also underlines the complex nature of culture flows.

Important as this broader cultural context has been for the peoples of the region, the main issue of the post-1960s years remained the spill-over effects of the Cuban revolution. Indeed, on one level it could be argued that the intensification of American cultural influences in the Caribbean basin were a product of the Cold War in general and the Cuban revolution in particular. The United States greeted the Cuban situation with escalating animosity in the late Eisenhower and Kennedy presidencies. President Eisenhower refused to meet with the only recently victorious Castro in April 1959 when the latter visited Washington, although Vice-President Nixon hosted the Cuban leader. The following year the President authorized the CIA to engage in planning an invasion of Cuba by Guatemalan-based, anti-Castro Cuban nationals, thus setting in motion an operation that Kennedy inherited when he took office in 1961. By that time, the Eisenhower and Castro administrations were engaged in economic warfare, with the United States cutting the Cuban sugar quota in 1960 and Cuba retaliating by nationalizing sugar mills and turning to the Soviet Union for economic assistance.

In 1959–60, Cuban ties with the Soviet Union and also, to the consternation of Moscow, with the People's Republic of China (PRC), grew closer. By 1961, Castro was clearly moving by necessity into the Soviet economic and strategic orbit. The shift was not a sudden one but rather a development that grew out of mutual needs. As early as 1959, during an exhibition of Soviet science in Mexico City, Soviet officials met with Cuban representatives and later moved the exhibition on to Havana. The Soviet Union then sent technicians to Cuba, carefully selecting Spanish-speaking descendants of Spanish Civil War Republican exiles to the USSR. In May 1960, the Soviet Union recognized the Castro government; significantly, the first Soviet Ambassador to Havana had previously been expelled from Canada for espionage. In July that year, Khrushchev stated that the Soviet Union "would do everything to support Cuba in her struggle. . . . Now the United States is not so unreachable as she once was." In the same month, Castro made public his plans to carry the revolution into other countries in Latin America. As early as November 1960 CIA director Allen Dulles reported to the National Security Council (NSC), following insurgent activities in Guatemala against the repressive and incompetent government of Ydigoras Fuentes and in Nicaragua against President Luis Somoza (son of Anastasio Somoza, killed in 1956, and brother of Anastasio Somoza who ruled Nicaragua from 1963 to 1979), that "Castro-itis" was affecting Central America and parts of South America, although even the NSC discounted Cuban involvement in the Guatemalan incident.[7]

Whether Castro was pushed into the Soviet camp by hostile U.S. actions in 1960–1 or whether his vigorous anti-American nationalism would have led him there inexorably will likely never be satisfactorily answered. Certainly there are those, such as U.S. Ambassador to Cuba Philip Bonsal, who adhere to the idea that it was U.S. policy that "lost" Cuba to the Soviets. At the time of the Bay of Pigs planning in the Kennedy administration, some leading American statesmen such as Senate Foreign Relations Committee chairman J. William Fulbright did not believe that Castro constituted a strategic threat to the United States at that juncture. Such views were not only in a minority among U.S. leaders, but, as Arthur Schlesinger, Jr., described Fulbright's position, were considered "old-fashioned" among the action intellectuals that dominated the Kennedy administration. Schlesinger himself, as a Kennedy adviser, opposed the surrogate invasion not on principle but because he did not anticipate success.[8]

Voices of dissent or not, the critical fact is that both Presidents Eisenhower and

Kennedy were personally opposed to Castro and the Cuban revolution as were their key advisers and policy makers, with the result that the two sides quickly moved toward confrontation. With endorsement from the Kennedy administration, more than 1,400 CIA-trained Cuban nationals in April 1961 launched a disastrous invasion of Cuba. Within two days the fiasco was over. Without U.S. air cover, Castro's air force decimated the landing and supply vessels, and the few insurgents who managed to move beyond the beaches at the Bay of Pigs were quickly captured. It was an international public relations nightmare for an embarrassed but no less emboldened Kennedy administration. Most significantly, the attack and the lack of contrition on the part of the U.S. government increased the likelihood that Castro would seek any means to deter another invasion.

Less than a year and a half after the Bay of Pigs invasion the world watched and waited in stunned anxiety while the two superpowers confronted one another over the placement of Soviet offensive nuclear missiles at Cuban sites. Castro's commitment to Marxism-Leninism may have been tactical and pragmatic not ideological, but there is little doubt of his long-time commitment to anti-imperialism and anti-Americanism, and he would have sought to export revolution with or without the assistance of the Soviet Union.

Nikita Khrushchev provides a clear account of Soviet thinking at the time of the decision to place offensive weapons in Cuba. "I was haunted," he recalled in his memoirs, "by the knowledge that the Americans could not stomach having Castro's Cuba right next to them. They would do something. They had the strength and they had the means." As he suggested in his memoir of the subsequent missile crisis, "Cuba was threatened by the saber-rattling militarists of the Pentagon." Khrushchev assigned Defence Minister General Rodion Y. Malinovsky to head a small planning team to implement the placement of forty-two missiles, each with a one-megaton warhead. As Kennedy informed an alarmed nation, the medium-range ballistic missiles could reach Washington, DC, and the Panama Canal; the intermediate-range missiles could reach from Hudson's Bay in the north to Lima, Peru, in the south. As the Soviet leader recalled, they looked at a map and selected the launch sites and then identified the targets that would inflict the "maximum damage" and "inspire terror." At the same time, they installed in Cuba the latest anti-aircraft weapons, coastal defence missiles and tank units to resist any invasion. To all of this, in Khrushchev's view, "Castro gave his approval."[9] There is no hint in Khrushchev's memoirs that this was a Cuban initiative or decision. But where the Soviets miscalculated was in the success of U.S. intelligence to detect the deployment before the missile installations were complete, thus seriously weakening the Soviet bargaining position when the U.S. confronted the Soviet leaders and demanded the withdrawal of the missiles. At the time of the U.S. detection, the nuclear warheads had not reached Cuba, but the Soviet Union pressed on with the shipment and the forty-two missiles were installed.[10]

In addition to the critical issue of possible thermonuclear war, the crisis revealed the cracks in the Soviet–Castro relationship. Nikita Khrushchev observed in his memoirs that in the midst of the missile crisis Castro wanted the Soviets to engage in a pre-emptive strike against the United States to prevent an invasion of or attack on the missile sites in Cuba. As the Soviet Premier commented, Castro's insistence revealed that he failed to understand Soviet strategic objectives, which were to deter an attack on Cuba, not to provoke a nuclear war between the superpowers. "All we wanted," he claimed, "was to give the new progressive system created in Cuba by Fidel Castro a chance to work." But when he learned that Castro was actually prepared to wage nuclear war in defence of the system, "Only then did I realize," Khrushchev wrote, "that our friend Castro, whom I respect for his honesty and directness, had failed to understand us correctly."[11] He might have added that the Soviets had also failed to understand Castro, and in fairness to Castro, Khrushchev's memoirs indicate that Castro had been initially opposed to the Soviet proposal to place nuclear weapons on Cuban soil.[12]

The powers pulled back from the brink in October 1962, but the Cuban Missile Crisis itself, not solely the U.S. success in having Soviet nuclear weapons withdrawn from Cuban soil, altered the strategic relationship in the Caribbean basin. The informal understanding between Kennedy and Khrushchev that the United States would not invade Cuba in return for the removal of the missiles, provided both Cuba and the Soviet Union with reasonable security and a tactical base from which to sponsor insurgent operations throughout the region, although Cuba tended to be the militant force. As one author suggests, Cuba became an "unsinkable aircraft carrier," a "weapons depot and conduit" for the projection of Soviet power in the western hemisphere.[13]

Factors other than the informal understanding between the USSR and the United States in the resolution of the missile crisis contributed to Castro's security. In 1964–5, the Johnson administration, according to *New York Times* columnist Tad Szulc, was planning a second invasion of Cuba using U.S.-trained and equipped Cuban exile forces based in Guatemala and Nicaragua. The invasion was to be co-ordinated with the assassination of Castro. Szulc claimed that the invasion was cancelled when a rebellion occurred in the Dominican Republic, which in turn occasioned U.S. intervention; thereafter, Vietnam absorbed U.S. attention.[14]

After 1960, the Soviet Union took a more aggressive and active approach to Latin America as a whole. In 1961, the Russians established a Latin American Institute in Moscow, which over the next two decades developed one of the world's largest research programmes on Latin America and also, in co-operation with other government agencies, offered such programmes as training for Latin American students and scholars. The Soviet Union also moved beyond a new scholarly interest in the Caribbean and Latin America. In 1964, the Russians and Cubans held a conference in Havana that was attended by representatives of all Latin American communist parties except for Maoist factions.[15]

The Cuban–Soviet relationship was not without turbulence, however, especially as Castro became increasingly irritated in the course of the 1960s by the persistent view in the Third World – especially strongly articulated by the PRC – that the Cuban regime was no more than a puppet of Moscow. Divergence between the two was over more than perception, however. The Soviet Union was prepared to support revolutionary activity against repressive regimes in Latin America but not against liberal, reformist governments, although it had a rather broad definition of what constituted a repressive regime. Hence, in the course of the 1960s Moscow endorsed Cuban-supported activities in Venezuela, Colombia, Guatemala, Honduras, and Haiti, but Castro wanted both more autonomy as well as a wider field of operations. Soviet Premier Alexei Kosygin, concerned with Castro's stance, sought to mend differences during a visit to Havana in 1967. There was even speculation that Argentine-born Ernesto "Che" Guevara (one of the main Castro revolutionary leaders in the late 1950s and a prominent cabinet member in the Castro governments of the early 1960s) was, during his insurgent operations in Bolivia, betrayed to Bolivian authorities in late 1967 by a Soviet agent as a caution to Castro not to deviate too far from the Soviet line.

By 1968, Castro seemed once more back in the Soviet fold and supported the Soviet crushing of Czech resistance that year following the Prague Spring. Four years later, Cuba was admitted to the Soviet Council for Mutual Economic Assistance, the only member outside the main Soviet bloc in Eurasia. By 1975, Soviets and eastern Europeans had largely assumed control of the management of the Cuban economy, and Soviet foreign aid continued to flow in massive volume. By the end of the decade it is estimated that one-half of all Soviet foreign assistance was directed to Cuba. As well, Cuba continued to be an important forward base for Soviet military vessels. By the mid-1970s, the harbour at Cienfuegos had been sufficiently developed to provide a regular base for Soviet surface vessels and submarines.[16]

In the course of the 1960s and 1970s, the United States and its allies isolated Cuba from normal relations in the western hemisphere. The OAS expelled Cuba in 1962 and imposed an economic blockade. It was not only the authoritarian regimes in the Americas that supported this approach. Liberal and reformist governments such as those of Romulo Betancourt in Venezuela and Alberto Lleras Camargo in Colombia strongly condemned Castro and his effort to foment rebellion in the Americas – including in their countries – and supported the expulsion of Cuba from the OAS. But the ostracism was not universal. Canada continued diplomatic relations with Cuba throughout the crisis, although the more important reality was that Canada's continued presence in Havana provided an important source of information for the United States on Cuban affairs.[17]

Dominican Republic

The Castro revolution in Cuba as well as the changing dynamic in east–west relations generally, including the Vietnam War, provided the critical context for U.S. relations with the Dominican Republic.[18] One month after the failed Bay of

Pigs invasion, Dominican army officers shot and killed long-time Dominican dictator Rafael Trujillo. Arthur Schlesinger, Jr., reported that the "assassination took Washington by surprise," but others have their doubts on that score.[19]

With Cuban problems dominating U.S. security concerns in the Caribbean, officials viewed with alarm any additional volatile situation in the region. Members of the Trujillo family jockeyed for position until November 1961 when President Kennedy sent naval vessels within sight of Santo Domingo (as Ciudad Trujillo had been renamed). The Trujillos took the hint and went into exile. In May 1962, President Kennedy approved a plan for presidential elections later in the year and the inauguration of a new Dominican President in February 1963. Both President Kennedy and Ambassador John Bartlow Martin were desperately anxious to exclude from power both the "Castro/Communists" on the left and Trujillistas on the right.[20] In the ensuing elections, Juan Bosch, a liberal reformer who had spent many of the Trujillo years in exile, won the presidency. He held it for only a few months of 1963 before conspirators ousted him. In protest, the Kennedy administration recalled its ambassador. Weeks later, Lyndon B. Johnson succeeded the assassinated John F. Kennedy, and his administration restored full diplomatic relations with the junta which had ousted Bosch. Both Secretary of State Dean Rusk and historian Piero Gleijeses agree that President Kennedy would have done likewise, that there was more continuity than disparity between the Kennedy and Johnson policies toward the Dominican Republic.[21]

In April 1965, Bosch's supporters attempted a counter-coup to enable the elected president to complete his term, but President Johnson sent the Marines back into the Dominican Republic and blocked such a development. In his memoirs, Johnson argued that the month before his death, President Kennedy had foreseen the possible "need" for such interventions in a number of small Caribbean and Central American countries and ordered the Defense Department to make contingency plans. The availability of such plans facilitated the occupation of the Dominican Republic. Johnson's initial concern when the Dominican factions began to shoot at each other was the safety of resident Americans, but the larger concern was that the Dominican Republic might follow Cuba into the Soviet bloc. There were "at least 1,500" dedicated communists involved in the fighting, wrote Johnson, and a determined well-organized minority might overpower a much larger number of less competent or less committed people. Communists, U.S. officials feared, would use Bosch to gain power.[22]

President Johnson's intervention remains highly controversial. Personally, he considered the military action a great success. The Dominican Republic did not go the way of Cuba, and the Marines withdrew the following year.[23] Military historian Lawrence A. Yates says that, despite subsequent problems (which were many), President Johnson avoided the two extremes: a second Cuba or a second Hungary (imposition of an unpopular government upon an unwilling people through long-term military occupation).[24]

Others disagree. Criticized at the time as an over-reaction by *New York Times* reporter Tad Szulc,[25] Johnson faces charges of exaggeration from his own

Secretary of State, Dean Rusk,[26] and from Rusk's biographer.[27] Seven years later, Abraham F. Lowenthal began a book on the 1965 intervention with the words, "I regard the U.S. military intervention in the Dominican Republic as a tragic event, costly to the Dominican Republic, to the United States, and to inter-American relations."[28]

Historian Piero Gleijeses is scathing in his criticism. Johnson's Ambassador in Santo Domingo, Tapley Bennett, "seemed to know no one . . . to the left of the Rotary Club." Very friendly to President Donald Reid Cabral, a businessman who headed the junta, Bennett had never met Bosch yet "felt a violent hostility" against him.[29] Of former Ambassador Martin, Gleijeses says: "In a few hours, Martin 'understood' everything."[30] Gleijeses sees two principal reasons for the intervention. If the Johnson administration was engaging (as it was in 1965) in a massive build-up in Vietnam, half a world away, it could not risk a second Cuba in its backyard and retain any credibility. At the same time, President Johnson "had no reason to distrust the reports of his embassy."[31]

The aftermath of the intervention produced a degree of political stability more satisfactory to American officials. U.S.-sponsored presidential elections in 1966 brought to power Joaquín Balaguer – Trujillo's last puppet President – over Bosch.

An associate of Trujillo's since 1937, Balaguer and his goon squad, *La Banda*, terrorized individuals and groups in ways that the police could not. Despite a constitutional provision that the incumbent President could not run for re-election, Balaguer did so in 1970, 1974, and 1978, on each occasion amidst claims of electoral corruption, although this did not seem to bother the government of President Richard Nixon, who provided aid to Balaguer's police.

The Balaguer presidency did stimulate a significant infusion of foreign investment, not all of it from the United States.[32] The largest single investor was a mining corporation registered in Canada, Falconbridge – backed by capital from the United States and the World Bank, as well as Canada. On one occasion before Falconbridge Dominicana began production of ferronickel late in 1971, the Balaguer government sent soldiers to break a strike so that the company could salvage its $195 million investment. "Excellent co-operation has been received from all officials of the Dominican Republic," said the 1970 Annual Report of Falconbridge Nickel Mines Limited.

Falconbridge Dominicana created hundreds of jobs at Bonao and contributed to the modernization of the community. It also diversified the Dominican economy, making it less dependent upon sugar and tobacco.[33] Nor was it alone. The Royal Bank of Canada had entered the Dominican Republic in 1912, the Bank of Nova Scotia during the U.S. occupation of 1916–24. Chase Manhattan and First National City Bank followed from New York in 1962, one year after Trujillo's assassination. The Bank of America arrived from California in 1968, when Balaguer was president.[34] Dominican historian Frank Moya Pons, writing in 1986, marvelled at the economic growth under Balaguer after 1965.[35]

The first major official of the Nixon administration to visit the Dominican Republic was Nelson A. Rockefeller, Governor of New York and a rival of Nixon for the Republican Party's presidential nomination. Nixon asked Rockefeller, who had decades in Latin American experience both in governmental service and in connection with his family's business interests, to report on the issues confronting the region.

Under extremely tight security, Rockefeller met President Balaguer in July 1969; the latter warned of political instability and Cuban penetration of his country. Balaguer informed Rockefeller that communism was a "serious danger," that Cuba was "training young people," who went to Cuba via Mexico, in all phases of communist activity, including sabotage and guerrilla warfare. Significantly, Balaguer urged the Nixon administration to take a more decisive stand against Cuba, since the communists were using Cuba as "a base in the center of the Americas." In Balaguer's view, the United States should either reach an agreement with Cuba on expropriated property and recognize Castro's government, or lead an effective co-ordinated inter-American action to stop Cuban subversion in the region. Rockefeller advised President Nixon, following a meeting with Balaguer's cabinet, that agricultural reform in the country was essential to alter the over-concentration in sugar production and to provide the majority of landless workers access to their own lands.[36]

The Nixon administration certainly accepted Balaguer's argument that dissent in the Dominican Republic was Cuban-inspired and continued to support his repressive regime. Nixon's National Security Adviser and long-time adviser to Rockefeller, Henry Kissinger, wrote in 1971 – at a time that *La Banda* was at the peak of its powers: "Our relationship with the Dominican Republic has been a very satisfactory one on both sides in recent years, and we are doing everything possible to continue that relationship at its present level."[37]

Disgusted with Nixon's support for anti-communist dictators, President Jimmy Carter (1977–81) promoted a policy of concern for human rights. When Dominicans had their regular quadrennial presidential election in 1978, early returns gave the lead to opposition candidate Antonio Guzmán. Suddenly television coverage ceased, and when it returned, Balaguer was ahead. Suspecting the worst, President Carter threatened an end to aid unless the counting was credible. Balaguer and his supporters then permitted Guzmán to win and assume office. A high-profile U.S. delegation attended Guzmán's inauguration as a warning to the Dominican military not to stage a coup.[38]

Panama

The Department of State's national intelligence estimate in 1959 predicted that the United States would "almost certainly be confronted with pressures for revision of arrangements on the Canal Zone and with resistance to any extension of U.S. facilities."[39] Rising Panamanian nationalism, focused on the status of the canal and Canal Zone, provided the main area of dispute between the United

States and Panama after 1960. Although little of the tension pertained specifically to Cold War issues, the Cold War did provide the critical context within
which discussions took place; yet, ironically, by the 1960s the canal was losing
its critical strategic importance to the United States. Historian John Major, one
of the leading academic authorities on the Panama Canal, contended that by 1964
the Panama Canal was no longer militarily vital to the United States because
of a two-ocean navy and the incapacity of the locks to accommodate the new
generation of large vessels.[40]

Although the canal may have become technically obsolete, its strategic
importance to the region remained along with its symbolic value in the Americas.
In addition to the canal itself and the associated defence installations, the United
States, under the 1903 treaty, maintained an air navigation and communications
site on Taboga Island off the Pacific entrance to the canal. Under a separate 1955
treaty, the United States acquired for its exclusive use over a renewable fifteen-
year period Rio Hato, a training area of approximately thirty square miles on the
coast south of Panama City. Panama was the centre for the U.S. Caribbean
Command (Army, Navy, and Air) at Quarry Heights and Fort Amador.[41]
President Kennedy rejected formal bilateral negotiations of new canal treaties
with the Panamanian government of President Roberto F. Chiari (1960–4),
although informal discussions continued for several years.

Quite apart from construction of a sea-level canal by means of nuclear
explosives, there were several contentious issues. Chiari wanted the Panamanian
flag to fly wherever the U.S. flag flew in all parts of the Canal Zone except
military bases. As an indication of Panamanian sovereignty, he even wanted it to
fly outside military bases and on the bow of ships in transit through the canal.
Chiari wanted Zonians to buy their stamps through the Panamanian post office.
He sought more jobs and higher wages for Panamanian workers inside the Zone,
limits on commercial activity by Americans in the Zone, and the return to
Panama of Canal Zone lands not essential to the canal's defence and viability.
Chiari also sought one or two corridors through the Canal Zone, which bisected
his country, and the withholding of income tax payments from Panamanians with
jobs in the Canal Zone. The Panama Canal Company would then pay the money
directly to the government of Panama. The Panamanian government also sought
an increase in the annual payment for the Canal Zone.

There was little progress on these issues during the Kennedy era. Kennedy
rejected the display of Panamanian flags outside military bases or on ships in
transit. Kennedy raised the minimum wage in the Canal Zone, from 61 cents an
hour in 1962 to 70 cents in 1963 and 80 cents in 1964, but he refused to accept
Chiari's proposals of affirmative action for Panamanians and the gradual attrition
of workers from the United States. He agreed to rename the newly constructed
Thatcher Ferry Bridge across the Pacific end of the Panama Canal "the Bridge
of the Americas," and he thought that U.S. authorities should interpret existing
treaties in a liberal manner. He also supported increased financial assistance for
Panama under the Alliance for Progress.[42] There was some support at the time

for a revised treaty from among the directors of the Panama Canal Company, one of whom indicated to Secretary of State Dean Rusk and Under-Secretary of State George Ball, "It is . . . not too soon to give thought to what kind of a new treaty we want, or could negotiate."[43]

Even following widespread rioting in Panama in January 1964 over the flag question and a temporary break in diplomatic relations with the Chiari government, the U.S. government considered negotiation of a Panama Canal Treaty "premature."[44] Even before the students raised the flag, the CIA had been advising President Johnson to expect trouble in Panama late in 1963 or early in 1964, at least in part because of assistance provided to Panamanian communists by Fidel Castro. Moreover, President Johnson had serious doubts about the good faith of the Chiari government. Although the President thought changes on the isthmus were desirable, he did not want to bow to violence.[45]

There was also another factor which no U.S. President seeking re-election could ignore. Despite warnings from Secretary of State Dean Rusk that the status quo in Panama was inflammatory, President Johnson's Republican opponent in 1964 was Arizona Senator Barry Goldwater. Although Goldwater's position softened with time, in 1964 he condemned the Democrats for failing to protect U.S. interests from foreign enemies.[46]

President Johnson handily defeated Senator Goldwater in the November 1964 presidential election, and bilateral U.S.–Panamanian negotiations began early in 1965. At the time, the assumption was that a sea-level canal would replace the existing locks canal. National Security Action Memorandum (NSAM) of 8 January 1965 instructed the Secretary of State to negotiate terms for a sea-level canal not only with the government of Panama, but also with the governments of Colombia, Nicaragua, and Costa Rica. Although the United States would assume responsibility for construction and financing of the sea-level canal, "sovereignty over the canal area would remain in the country or countries through which the canal would pass."[47] At the same time, the United States would be willing to negotiate an end to the 1903 treaty with Panama, but it must remain in effect until the opening of the sea-level canal. Even with the opening of the sea-level canal, the United States would require military bases in Panama. These requirements proved too much for the new Panamanian government of President Marco Robles, elected for a four-year term in 1964. The Johnson and Robles administrations actually initialled draft treaties in 1967, but the draft treaties were stillborn. For reasons only partially related to the canal treaties, the Panamanian Congress impeached President Robles in 1967, and after his impeachment there was no possibility that the Panamanian Congress would ratify the treaties.

When negotiations resumed, there were new players on both sides. It was with the government of Omar Torrijos that Richard Nixon's administration (1969–74) dealt. Ironically, Nelson Rockefeller in his report to Nixon on Panama spoke in highly positive terms about Torrijos, whom Rockefeller found sincerely dedicated to the alleviation of poverty, economic development, and social action.[48] Rockefeller certainly misjudged Torrijos' determination to remain head of the National Guard and outside politics. Once in power, Torrijos absolutely refused to renew the lease on the Rio Hato military base, and Nixon authorized purely exploratory negotiations in 1970 only because the State Department warned that without discussions there might be violence.[49]

There were definite limits on what the Nixon administration would concede in such talks. It wanted the *right*, but without any *obligation*, to construct a sea-level canal across Panama. "Effective U.S. control of canal operations [and] canal defense . . . [were] non-negotiable."[50] While it might (and in fact did) later modify the point, the Nixon administration's starting position would be that any new canal treaty would last indefinitely, without any expiry date. That such negotiations failed is hardly surprising.[51]

On 7 February 1974, Secretary of State Henry Kissinger and Panamanian Foreign Minister Juan Antonio Tack agreed upon a statement of principles. The new treaty would completely replace that of 1903; it would have a time limit; the treaty would eliminate the U.S.-controlled Canal Zone; the United States would acquire for the life of the treaty whatever lands, water, and air space it needed "for the operation, maintenance, protection and defense of the canal and the transit of ships;" Panamanian control of the canal should increase; and the Republic of Panama should receive greater revenues from the canal.[52]

President Gerald Ford (1974–7) made an additional concession which paved the way for a settlement between his successor, Jimmy Carter, and Omar Torrijos. President Nixon had authorized Ambassador Anderson to concede a termination date for any treaty he might negotiate, but he insisted that the life of any new treaty must be "at least fifty years, with provision for an additional 30–50 years if Canal capacity is expanded."[53] President Ford accepted 31 December 1999 as the termination date for U.S. operation (as distinct from defence) of the existing canal, although he insisted that the United States should continue to defend the canal for at least forty. Like his predecessor, Ford considered a sea-level canal as an option rather than a commitment,[54] and by 1975, that option looked increasingly improbable. The Ford administration concluded a series of draft agreements with the Panamanian government, but the talks faltered over Panamanian demands on defence and ended entirely in February 1976 as the U.S. presidential campaign got under way,[55] in large measure because Ford's chief Republican opponent was California Governor Ronald Reagan, an outspoken critic of the proposed new Panama Canal treaties. Ford and his advisers feared that concessions to Panama might deliver the Republican nomination to Ronald Reagan, although in the end it mattered little since Democratic candidate Jimmy Carter defeated Ford in the presidential elections.

On the first full day of the Carter presidency, National Security Adviser Zbigniew Brzezinski began to address the Panama Canal issues.[56] According to Robert Pastor, a member of the National Security Council, "Jimmy Carter spent more time on the Panama Canal Treaties than on any other issue in his first two years in office."[57] Carter believed that the Panama Canal treaties were a matter of urgency and determined to act quickly and decisively.

A Policy Review Memorandum drafted by the National Security Council only five days later observed that the "basic national security interest [of the United States] in Panama is that the Canal remain efficient, secure, neutral, and continuously open to all world shipping at reasonable tolls." In this sense little had changed in the previous century. The report noted that although the canal was an aging facility of declining commercial value, approximately 44 percent of the total tonnage that passed through the Canal originated in and 22 percent was destined for U.S. ports.[58]

The governments signed two Carter–Torrijos treaties in September 1977, one to transfer the Canal to Panamanian control by the end of the century and integrate the Canal Zone into the Republic of Panama, the other to deal with the Canal's defence. Both Carter and Torrijos had to sell the treaties to their respective constituencies, and neither would find the task a simple one. A range of factors contributed to the success of the treaties: the preliminary work of two Republican presidents and Henry Kissinger; support for the treaties by such famous spokesmen of the American right as columnist William F. Buckley and actor John Wayne; warnings that both the canal itself and U.S. commercial investments in Panama would be safer if the treaties were approved. Even with such support and preparation, the U.S. Senate gave the necessary two-thirds vote of approval to the first treaty by the narrow margins of sixty-eight to thirty-two, and on 18 April 1978, the second treaty also cleared the Senate by an identical margin. Through a referendum of 23 October 1977, Panamanian voters, most of whom would have preferred immediate control of the Canal, had already provided the necessary two-thirds vote of approval by a narrow margin.[59] On 1 October 1979, most of the Canal Zone became part of the Republic of Panama, and in April 1982, Panama assumed responsibility for police and judicial activity in the Canal Area (what was left of the Canal Zone).

Haiti

Haiti's importance in the Caribbean in the middle years of the Cold War was substantially increased as a result of the Cuban revolution. Its strategic location combined with political instability and massive poverty to make it appear highly vulnerable to Cuban influence after Castro came to power in early 1959. Although François Duvalier was popularly elected in 1957, marking a departure in the usual cycle of military coups, he rapidly moved toward rule by repression, using the National Police, Presidential Guard, and the secret police as his instruments of governance, counterbalancing the power of the armed forces. When he came to power, Haiti's economy was virtually bankrupt and the situation was made even more severe by the uncertainty of coffee prices, on which the economy depended.

Following a short severing of diplomatic relations in late 1957 as a result of the death of a U.S. citizen at the hands of Duvalier's police, from 1958 on the United States sought to bolster both bilateral relations and the state of the Haitian economy through loans, grants, and military assistance. With the failure of the coffee crop and a drop in international prices in 1959 the situation became acute. With unsettled conditions in the neighbouring Dominican Republic and a small-scale Cuban invasion of Haiti in late summer 1959, U.S. officials had to balance their reservations about shoring up the corrupt and repressive Duvalier regime against their fears of the alternatives to Duvalier. The International Cooperation Agency opposed financial assistance to Duvalier on the grounds the government was not taking a constructive approach to development, but more senior U.S. officials put a higher premium on the threat of Castroism; hence, they opted for Duvalier against the unknown. In 1960, the new U.S. ambassador arrived with pledges of aid money, $5 million for budget support and $4.5 million for additional development projects.[60]

In spite of the Kennedy administration's vigorous commitment to anti-Castro policies in the Caribbean, the Haitian–U.S. relationship deteriorated early in the administration. In 1962, the Kennedy administration all but eliminated U.S. aid to Haiti.[61] Following anti-Duvalier riots in the spring of 1963 and at a time when the newly elected Bosch government in the Dominican Republic was poised to send troops into Haiti, the U.S. government recalled its Ambassador from Port-au-Prince "for consultation," placed warships off the island of Gonaive, and "increased patrol of the Windward Passage to insure against illicit traffic between Cuba and Haiti."[62] Journalist Elizabeth Abbott says that Duvalier celebrated Kennedy's assassination.[63]

Shortly after his inauguration, President Richard M. Nixon sent a former rival, New York Governor Nelson Rockefeller, on a good-will and fact-finding mission throughout Latin America. Hostility, demonstrations, even violence dogged Rockefeller in almost every country. One of the happy exceptions was Haiti. As some 30,000 seemingly friendly Haitians gathered outside the presidential palace in Port-au-Prince, Rockefeller held Duvalier with one hand. Nixon's new Ambassador to Haiti, Dr. Clinton E. Knox, admired Duvalier,[64] and that autumn, National Security Adviser Henry Kissinger summarized President Nixon's position on aid to Haiti. The preference was to increase multilateral aid assistance for economic development and to provide humanitarian assistance through multilateral and private channels, with only minor assistance from USAID through the Embassy.[65]

François Duvalier died in 1971, and his 19-year-old son Jean-Claude Duvalier named himself president-for-life. At first the terror dissipated. The Tonton-Macoutes became less active, and political exiles were able to return to Haiti and live in peace. Although an irresponsible playboy who took little interest in the daily running of government, Jean-Claude Duvalier did maintain a firm degree of control over the local media. Perhaps the most serious charges against him revolved around his own extravagant lifestyle and that of his family, while most Haitians continued to suffer from grinding poverty. His compatriots suffered stunted growth from malnutrition, high levels of infant mortality and disease, while a small elite lived in luxury. While some terror continued and refugees from both poverty and political repression fled the country, a prominent electric sign displayed the message across Port-au-Prince, "Long live Jean-Claude Duvalier, president-for-life."[66]

The Nixon administration found Jean-Claude more than tolerable,[67] and it was not until Jimmy Carter came to office that tensions increased. With Carter's concern for human rights, Carter did not share Nixon's appreciation for Jean-Claude Duvalier's government and he pressed Duvalier to implement some modest reforms. Press controls were slightly relaxed and a number of political prisoners were released from Haitian prisons during the Carter presidency. The changes tended to be cosmetic, however, and in any event the Reagan administration relaxed all pressures on Duvalier during its first term in office.[68]

Behind the political scenes, the social and economic situation in the country continued to deteriorate. Haitians fled the poverty and oppression of their homeland, legally as immigrants and illegally as boat-people. The United States, Canada, and France offered opportunity, the Bahamas and the Dominican Republic miserable conditions but better than what Haitians faced at home. By the end of the 1970s, an estimated 1.5 million Haitians lived in other countries, and many of the 6 million remaining in Haiti sought to join them.[69] Tourism, which had attracted revenue to Haiti during the 1970s, plummeted in the 1980s as foreigners associated Haitians with AIDS.[70] The International Monetary Fund (IMF), the World Bank, and the Canadian government lost patience with the Duvalier government and refused to fund new projects.[71]

More responsible than President Carter for the 1986 collapse of the Duvalier administration was Pope John Paul II, whose papacy began in 1978. The Duvaliers had long sought to "Haitianize" the Roman Catholic clergy in the country, partly because of the long historical identification of the Church with France and imperialism, but the approach returned to haunt them. John Paul's emphasis on human rights, social progress, and the commitment of the Church to those ideals was taken seriously by the Haitian clergy, which gradually became radicalized and an important source of opposition to the Duvalier regime. By the mid-1980s, that opposition had produced the charismatic figure, Jean-Bertrand Aristide, the parish priest of St. Jean Bosco.

Opposition from a radical clergy was only one source of opposition to the Duvalier government by the mid-1980s, however. Agitation for change ranged from the slums of Port-au-Prince to the historic seat of the Haitian revolution in Gonaive and a Reagan administration that was increasingly uncomfortable with the regime. The withdrawal of military support was the final blow to Baby Doc, and he went into exile in early 1986, leaving the country in the poverty and chaos in which his family had found it four decades earlier.[72]

Puerto Rico

As a quasi-colony of the United States, Puerto Rico occupied a minor role in U.S. Cold War policies and in international relations in the Caribbean region. It was nonetheless a strategic holding, and the continuing increase of nationalistic activity on the island was a frequent source of tensions with Washington. Those tensions became particularly acute after the Cuban revolution and when Richard Nixon was in office in the closing but highly volatile years of the Vietnam War. Governor Ferre had problems other than constitutional ones during his four-year term (1969–72). Because the New Progressive Party's mainland partner was the Republican Party, Ferre became an ally of President Nixon's. This had its advantages and disadvantages.

On the one hand, Ferre could persuade the Nixon administration to stop the U.S. Navy and other friendly navies from testing live ammunition on the Puerto Rican island of Culebra, located between the Puerto Rican mainland and the U.S. Virgin Islands. The Culebra tests – which had been taking place since 1936 – were no longer controversial in Puerto Rico; *independentistas*, supporters of statehood, and people in the middle agreed that they were unnecessary and undesirable. On 26 March 1970, Culebra Mayor Ramón Feliciano had written President Nixon to ask that the tests be ended, and Hugh W. Sloan, Jr. of the White House Staff rejected his concerns most emphatically on grounds that "the island is an integral part of the Atlantic Fleet Weapons Range Complex," and an "essential target area."[73]

As preparations for more tests proceeded in late 1970 and early 1971, demonstrators organized. On 28 October 1970, clergy from several denominations picked the Capitolio, seat of the Puerto Rican Congress. Activists arranged events for the very Culebran beaches where the shells would be falling. This time it was the governor, not the mayor, who wrote to President Nixon. Ferre charged that the Defense Department had "not taken into account the environmental or foreign policy ramifications" of the tests, and suggested that the tests were hurting the U.S. image elsewhere in Latin America.

Nixon sent a sympathetic reply and shortly thereafter hosted Governor Ferre at the White House.[74] In January 1971, the Navy and the Puerto Rican government signed an agreement which limited the geographical area for testing live ammunition at Culebra. Nevertheless, the protests on the unaffected beaches of Culebra continued.

Meanwhile, other Republicans became involved, the most notable being Massachusetts Senator Edward W. Brooke. Brooke noted that the Navy itself thought that the 11 January agreement had reduced the effectiveness of the tests by 70 percent and urged Nixon to "terminate this program," cautioning that "Culebra has become a rallying point for a multitude of nationalistic political parties whose goal is to lessen if not eliminate . . . the exploiting influences of the United States in the Caribbean/Latin American area."[75] In April 1971, in response to such pressures, Defense Secretary Melvin Laird ordered an end to "explosive bombardment" of Culebra by 1 January 1972 and an end to tests of any nature by June 1975.[76] The U.S. Navy would, however, continue to test live ammunition on Culebra's sister island, Vieques. The Navy would also maintain the San Juan and Roosevelt Roads Naval Bases on the Puerto Rican mainland.

Governor Ferre had managed to defuse one problem; unfortunately, there were others. Although Puerto Ricans could not vote in U.S. elections, they were subject to the draft, and the Vietnam War became as controversial there as it was on the mainland. When President Nixon ordered the U.S. army into Cambodia in 1970 and trigger-happy soldiers killed students at Kent State University in Ohio, authorities found it prudent that Puerto Rico's National Guard should be placed on a state of alert. In 1972, one student dissident accused of murdering a policeman, Humberto Pagan, jumped bail and fled to Canada. His friends threatened to kidnap the Canadian consul, Glen Shortliffe, and his wife if Pagan were extradited. It was not an auspicious time to favour a closer relationship with the United States. During the 1972 presidential election campaign, Ferre supported President Nixon.[77] Given Commonwealth status, Puerto Ricans could not vote for Nixon or any other presidential candidate, but they could – and did – defeat his supporter, Governor Ferre.

The winner of the 1972 gubernatorial race was another Popular Democrat, Rafael Hernandez Colón. He reopened the constitutional issue, seeking more autonomy for Puerto Rico and fewer responsibilities. On 27 September 1973, by which time U.S. combat forces had withdrawn from Vietnam, but the Watergate scandal was taking its toll on the Nixon administration, President Nixon announced an Ad Hoc Advisory Group on the Status of Puerto Rico. It was not in his interest to have yet another controversy at that time. The U.S. and Puerto Rican governments each appointed seven members, but while the U.S. delegation was bipartisan (three Democrats, three Republicans, and a businessman), all the Puerto Ricans were Popular Democrats. As far as Puerto Ricans were concerned, the Ad Hoc Advisory Group did not represent all shades of public opinion, and it lacked credibility. The Ad Hoc Advisory Group's final report of 14 June 1975, which would have allowed Puerto Rico greater authority to develop its own foreign policy and a larger share of tax revenue, plus exemption from laws subsequently enacted by U.S. authorities, met a cool reception in Washington. Congress was less than sympathetic when Ferre sought exemption from U.S. minimum wage and environmental laws so that low-cost, polluting Puerto Rican factories could produce inexpensive goods for sale in the United States. Many Puerto Ricans also disagreed with the recommendations.

Economic problems and constitutional controversies combined to defeat Hernandez in November 1976, when he sought a second term. Muñoz had launched what he called Operation Bootstrap, whereby Puerto Ricans were to pull themselves out of poverty by their own bootstraps, figuratively speaking. Operation Bootstrap petered out in the 1970s. Puerto Ricans had become members of labour unions affiliated with the American Federation of Labour-Congress of Industrial Organizations, and in so doing, they forced up the price of labour. This factor, along with the high cost of energy after Venezuela – Puerto Rico's principal source of energy – helped establish the Organization of Petroleum Exporting Countries and raise the rates of oil – rendered Puerto Rico less competitive in the United States market.[78]

This time the winner was Carlos Romero Barcelo, Mayor of San Juan and an avowed supporter of statehood. Romero's victory coincided with the defeat of President Gerald Ford, who nevertheless was frustrated with the stalemate on the Puerto Rican status issue and before leaving office declared support for Puerto Rican statehood and submitted a statehood bill to Congress. Puerto Rico was becoming an international embarrassment. The balance of power in the United Nations General Assembly had changed since 1953, especially as dozens of former African colonies became members. Encouraged by Fidel Castro's Cuba, which raised the issue at every opportunity, there was a strong possibility that supporters of Puerto Rican independence might soon persuade the General Assembly to pass a resolution unacceptable to Washington, still reeling from the Vietnam and Watergate débâcles. While the United States could have defied the General Assembly, it was preferable to try to prevent passage of such a resolution, with the result that the Puerto Rican status question remained a live issue for yet another generation.[79]

Challenges in the British Caribbean

Throughout the British Caribbean, but especially in British Guiana (Guyana following independence) and Jamaica, Cold War issues, spiced with strong nationalistic developments throughout the region, dominated the international agenda in the 1960s and 1970s; given U.S. hegemony in the area, such questions were of equal concern to U.S. as to British officials.

In the case of the United States, the Kennedy and Johnson administrations, although preoccupied with the Cuban revolution, shared the hostility of various British Conservative governments under Sir Winston Churchill, Anthony Eden, and Harold Macmillan (as noted in Chapter 4).[80] U.S. officials in the post-Cuban revolutionary years were especially concerned with containing Cuban influence in the region and to deter Caribbean neighbours from emulating Castro's example. Cheddi Jagan's activities in British Guiana, for some foreign observers and policy makers, appeared overly inclined toward the Cuban model. Some U.S. officials believed that there was a democratic solution to the apparently continuing dominance of British Guiana's politics by Cheddi Jagan and the People's Progressive Party (PPP), with which Jagan had won the most recent election in 1961. Kennedy's chief historian and adviser, Arthur Schlesinger, Jr., noted that Jagan had managed to win 57 percent of the seats on the basis of 42.7 percent of the popular vote. As long as his party had one vote more than either of its opponents (there was another party, the United Force, to the right of the PNC), the PPP would win the seat. However, if British Guiana, alone of British possessions, abandoned the British system of parliamentary government and adopted proportional representation based on the entire country, Jagan could be stopped. U.S. officials hoped that the combined strength of the non-East Indian populace plus the extra push which would come from right-wing East Indians would stop Jagan.[81]

The Johnson administration continued the Kennedy policies toward British Guiana. Because Canadians held considerable investments in bauxite, banking, and life insurance in British Guiana, President Johnson wanted – and thought he could have – Canadian co-operation against Jagan. Jamaica and Trinidad had achieved independence in 1962, and pressure to end colonial status in British Guiana was bound to intensify. Less than two weeks into the Johnson presidency, on 4 December 1963, Secretary of State Dean Rusk and Canada's External Affairs Minister Paul Martin discussed British Guiana, and Martin told Rusk that the Canadian government was contemplating the sending of an envoy who would assess the situation. Then Canada might open a mission in Georgetown, and Paul Martin himself might visit, although U.S. officials also feared that an official visit might enhance Jagan's prestige.

The issue seemed sufficiently critical that despite the Christmas season, the State Department summoned officials of the Canadian Embassy in Washington for talks, and U.S. Embassy officials in Ottawa discussed British Guiana with the Department of External Affairs. These talks had advanced to the point that when Prime Minister Lester B. Pearson visited President Johnson at the White House in January 1964, the Johnson White House was fairly confident that neither Martin nor "any other high-ranking Canadian" would visit British Guiana. Despite the fact that White House officials regarded Martin as hopelessly naive about Jagan, on 15 December 1963, Martin told U.S. Embassy officials in Ottawa that he did not want "a second Castro in the region."[82]

The Johnson–Pearson summit resolved any differences over British Guiana quickly, quietly, and amicably. Canada would send its own "commissioner" to British Guiana, Milton Gregg, a former Minister of Labour. (Because Canada and British Guiana were both parts of the Commonwealth, they could not exchange ambassadors, and because British Guiana was still a colony, Gregg would not be a High Commissioner like Canada's Heads of Mission in London, Canberra, and Wellington.) According to the Memorandum of Conversation, Under-Secretary of State George Ball indicated that "the United States thought it was a good idea for Canada to be represented there."[83]

The British government accepted White House concerns and imposed a proportional representation arrangement upon British Guiana. In 1964, the PPP led by Jagan won twenty-four seats; the PNC under Forbes Burnham won twenty-two seats, and the United Force won the remaining seven. Burnham became Prime Minister, and in 1966 the Labour government of Harold Wilson granted British Guiana its independence (thereafter referred to as Guyana).

Jagan remained an unrepentant Soviet-oriented Communist. In 1974, when one of the present authors (Mount) interviewed him at Freedom House, headquarters of the PPP, a banner proclaimed, "Forward with Leninism for a Socialist Guyana!" A table in the waiting room had nothing but communist literature – the *Pyonyang Times* and other North Korean pamphlets and magazines, translations from the Soviet press, North Vietnamese material, and the *Canadian Tribune*. A picture of Lenin hung above Jagan's head as he spoke. In opposition, Jagan did form a working relationship with the Soviet Union, and the U.S.SR recognized the party as communist. But Burnham also moved toward Marxism in the 1960s and 1970s, calling for the establishment of a co-operative socialist republic.

Still, there were a range of domestic tensions in Guyana, distinct from Cold War concerns, that drove the Guyanese political agenda. Honestly or otherwise, Burnham "won" all Guyanese elections until his death in 1985. Regarding the disputed election of 1973, Guyana's High Commissioner to Canada, Dr. Robert Moore (a history professor), explained:

> Of course we [the PNC] cheated. That was the only way we could win. And we had to win. The Great Power in this part of the world [the United States] would not have tolerated a PPP government. The Guyana Defense Force [Guyana's almost totally black army] would not have tolerated Indian government. The people of Georgetown [Guyana's largely black capital city] would not have accepted government by anybody else. We were the only alternative to chaos.[84]

There is a strong case to be made that Burnham began as a moderate but moved steadily to the left during his twenty-one years of authority. At first he promoted Caribbean unity. In 1971, for example, he wrote a Declaration of Grenada, which envisioned closer political links between Guyana and the small Anglophone islands of the eastern Caribbean. He promoted the Caribbean Free Trade Area (CARIFTA) in 1967, which in turn because CARICOM in 1970. CARICOM located its headquarters in Georgetown. Constructive diplomacy of this nature proved short-lived.

Five years after independence, Burnham's government nationalized Demba and Reynolds, the aluminum giants in Guyana. Later he nationalized the British corporation, Booker's, which operated a chain of retail stores and manufactured sugar-related products for export. North American- and European-owned banks and pharmaceutical factories also became property of the government. Burnham granted landing rights to Cuban aircraft carrying combat troops to Angola, and he visited North Korea. He fostered links with Colonel Qaddafi's Libya and opposed the 1983 U.S. military action in Grenada.[85] Burnham liked visitors to call him "Comrade" rather than "Sir."[86] Cuba, North Korea, and East Germany replaced the United States and the United Kingdom as Guyana's principal suppliers of armaments and military training. By the end of the 1970s, Guyana had diplomatic relations with the PRC, Cuba and the U.S.S.R, with several hundred Cuban technicians providing assistance in Guyana.[87]

In the process, Burnham antagonized almost everyone. Successive U.S. governments obstructed Guyanese attempts to borrow from the World Bank and persuaded the International Monetary Fund to impose rigid conditions for any loans. Washington also organized boycotts of Guyanese bauxite and, despite Guyanese objections, sold F-16 fighter aircraft to Venezuela. Other members of CARICOM, who had backed Guyana's territorial claims against Venezuela, were so angry at Burnham's opposition to the 1983 U.S. military intervention in Grenada that they threatened to relocate CARICOM's headquarters. The United States government actually ordered aerial surveillance of Guyana after the Brazilian government charged that there were many Cuban soldiers in Guyana. Nor did Burnham's foreign policy provide substantial benefits to the Guyanese people. World Bank figures from 1988 indicate that between 1980 and 1987, Guyana's gross national product (GNP) had shrunk by 6 percent – worse than the GNPs of all other countries in the world apart from Libya, Mozambique, and Qatar. Trinidad and Tobago, which had supplied Guyana with petroleum products at less than the world price, suspended this arrangement when Guyana could not afford even the reduced price. Rice production fell from 256,000 tons in 1980 to 236,000 tons in 1985. Sugar production fell from 3,831,000 to 3,270,000 tons during the same period.[88] There was little improvement prior to Burnham's death in 1985.

Jamaica

The Cold War affected Jamaica's relations with the United States between 1972 and 1980, when Michael Manley (son of Norman) served as Jamaican Prime Minister. Prime Minister Shearer's JLP government, defeated by Manley's People's National Party (PNP) in the general election of 1972, had been friendly to the Nixon administration in Washington. One source described Shearer as "exceptionally pleased" about a meeting with President Nixon on 11 August 1970, when the two men discussed U.S. Caribbean policy. "I got the impression that he feels he may have been present at a small historical watershed," said Frank Shakespeare of the United States Information Agency."[89] In October that same year, Shearer attended a White House dinner for a number of prominent world leaders, including British Prime Minister Edward Heath, and President Nixon considered a visit to Jamaica early in January 1971.[90]

Given the strategic importance of Jamaican bauxite, especially after Forbes Burnham nationalized Alcan's subsidiary in Guyana, Demerara Bauxite (Demba) in 1971, the Nixon administration reacted strongly to the 1972 electoral victory of the PNP. Would Manley's government nationalize foreign bauxite interests?[91] Although Australia, Guinea, and Brazil were also major producers of bauxite, they were more distant from the United States and strategically more vulnerable suppliers. By 1958, Jamaica held an estimated 17 percent of the world's known bauxite reserves (over 56 percent of the western hemisphere's reserves)[92] By 1966, Jamaica was producing 26 percent of the west's bauxite requirements, half of the output of the Caribbean basin, 36 percent of Alcan's supply. By 1971, Jamaica had become more important to Alcan than Guyana, not only because it produced more bauxite but also because it was closer to the North American mainland, and Alcan had rail connections between its mining operations and plant in the interior to the deep-water port at Esquivel. By 1974, estimates placed the total value of the aluminum company's facilities at more than U.S. $800 million.[93] The Nixon administration also feared "price gouging." The State Department advised Reynolds Aluminum in June 1974 that if bauxite companies could persuade Congress to legislate release of a bauxite stockpile in order to off-set Jamaican price hikes, "they would have administration support." Already the U.S. government was spending $700,000 to find alternate sources of supply, and the administration wanted U.S. aluminum producers to "contribute 50,000 each per year for three years in order to accelerate this research." The administration found support from the aluminum companies quite positive.[94]

The Nixon administration had reason to fear Guyanese influence in Jamaica. An economics professor at the University of the West Indies in Mona, Jamaica, Norman Girvan, had advised Burnham and was an adviser to Manley. Another of Manley's advisers, Patrick Rousseau, also closely monitored events in Guyana. Moreover, in 1970, inspired by OPEC, Burnham had proposed creation of an International Bauxite Association (IBA).[95] Guinea, Surinam, Jamaica, Sierra Leone, and Yugoslavia joined in March 1974, Ghana, Haiti, Indonesia, and Australia later; Brazil declined. In the aftermath of the Yom Kippur Arab–Israeli War in the autumn of 1973, OPEC countries had raised the price of crude oil, and Burnham advocated raising the price of bauxite as a way to offset the cost of oil in the bauxite-producing countries. In 1971, Reynolds had escaped nationalization in Guyana, but there was no guarantee that the axe would not fall either there or in Jamaica, although Manley personally assured Canadian Prime Minister Pierre Trudeau and Secretary of State Henry Kissinger that his government's motives were purely economic and that all multinationals would receive equal treatment.

Early in 1975, by which time Gerald Ford was President, the Jamaican government dropped the other shoe. First, it purchased 51 percent of the Jamaican holdings of the U.S. and Canadian multinationals which had controlled Jamaica's bauxite industry. Then it raised taxes on the bauxite companies, and it sought to purchase some 200,000 acres of their property.[96]

Jamaica was more vulnerable to international pressure, however. Bauxite and alumina constituted 64 percent of Jamaican exports, 13 percent of the gross domestic product (GDP). Australia and Brazil remained outside IBA, and the companies estimated that world reserves were greater than anticipated demand for another century. Hence, when Manley insisted that the companies' tax payments be tripled, he effectively priced Jamaican bauxite out of the market, and over the next decade (1974–84), the Jamaican share of the west's alumina production fell from 11.7 percent to 6 percent.

Fortunately for Jamaica, U.S. dependence upon Jamaica as a source of supply for bauxite created an atmosphere for negotiations rather than reprisals. National Security Adviser Brent Scowcroft favoured a meeting between Vice-President Nelson Rockefeller and Prime Minister Manley, who would be visiting Washington when President Ford was in China. The National Security Council, wrote Scowcroft, was concerned about Manley's friendship with Fidel Castro and Jamaica's support for a United Nations resolution that Zionism was racist.

Nevertheless, politics should not interfere with U.S. needs for bauxite, and half the U.S. aluminum industry's supply of bauxite came from Jamaica. As Scowcroft's indicated, ALCOA, Anaconda, Kaiser, Revere, and Reynolds had a total investment of $660 million in the Jamaican bauxite industry.[97]

Much to the delight of Fidel Castro, Manley's PNP won a second term of office in the Jamaican election of 1976.[98] In January 1977, Jamaica established diplomatic relations with the Soviet Union;[99] in October of that year, Fidel Castro visited Jamaica and Prime Minister Manley bestowed upon him the Order of Jamaica, the highest award his country could bestow upon a foreigner. Fortunately for Manley, Jimmy Carter, a Democrat, occupied the White House by this time, and the Democrats controlled Congress. In June of that year, the U.S. Senate rejected by a margin of fifty-eight to thirty-four a motion sponsored by Utah Republican Orrin Hatch to withhold $10 million in aid because of Manley's friendly relations with Castro.[100] Rosalynn Carter, the President's wife, went to Jamaica and visited Manley in May,[101] and in November the Agency for International Development extended $63.3 million to the Jamaican government for developmental assistance.[102] The following month, Manley returned to Washington and met President Carter and Secretary of State Cyrus Vance.[103]

The main U.S. objectives from the meeting were several: to encourage a co-operative attitude on Jamaica's part in its role as leader of the G-77 (the non-aligned nations); to reinforce Manley's recent tendency to take a more pragmatic line in foreign policy; and to encourage him to take the necessary economic measures, no matter how difficult they may be, to put Jamaica on the road to economic recovery. At the same time, U.S. officials believed strongly that Manley had to be made to understand that "unbridled and injudicious rhetoric" on his part could set off political reactions in the United States that would be impossible to control.[104]

In February 1978, Manley referred to Jamaica as a "friend" of the United States but warned that Jamaica must be free to pursue the "socialist path" which it had chosen.[105] Unfortunately for Jamaicans in general and the Manley government in particular, by 1980 that "socialist path" had led to economic chaos and social instability. Jamaicans migrated in droves; Kingston became more violent than usual; the bankrupt government turned to the Inter-American Development Bank for a loan which enabled it to avoid immediate default on its debt of one hundred and $10 million but discussion with the IMF failed. Confronted with these economic realities, the Manley government agreed to reduce its tax demands on Reynolds, Alcan, Kaiser, Alpart, and Anaconda.[106]

Even had the Carter administration been more willing to help Manley's Jamaica, there was a limit to what it could do without provoking problems at home. In November 1978, financial adviser Stu Eizenstat received a letter about tariffs on rum. Al Stern of the White House staff had heard about a tentative agreement between Jamaica and the United States to lower the tariff by some

30 percent. If this were to happen, feared Stern, Jamaican rum might flood the United States while rum from Puerto Rico and the U.S. Virgin Islands sat on the shelves unsold.[107]

Throughout 1980, polls had indicated that the Jamaican Labour Party (JLP) led by Edward Seaga would win Jamaica's parliamentary elections,[108] and when the elections took place 30 October 1980, the margin of victory exceeded even the JLP's highest expectations. With 53 percent of the popular vote, the JLP won fifty-one of sixty seats.[109]

Manley won personal re-election and survived as Leader of the Opposition, with consequences for a later date, but few in Washington regretted the JLP victory. The Carter administration and, more importantly, advisers to Ronald Reagan saw the election as a defeat for "revolutionary socialism."[110] The Seaga government invited the IMF to send envoys to Jamaica to discuss reconstruction and promised support to the private sector. In mid-April 1981, the International Monetary Fund approved a $640 million loan in support of the JLP government's economic policies.[111]

In the last days of the Carter administration, as the President's attention focused exclusively on attempts to negotiate the release of American diplomats held hostage in Iran, the U.S. extended a $40 million loan to assist Jamaica's economic recovery.[112] On President Reagan's first full day of office, the White House announced a visit by Prime Minister Seaga the following week.[113] The meeting ended with two agreements to help the Jamaican economy.[114] Eight large international banks, the largest of which was Citibank from New York, extended $70 million in credit to Jamaica and refinanced an additional $103 million in Jamaican loans.[115] The World Bank offered $37 million.[116]

Trinidad and Tobago

Until 1990, Trinidad's foreign relations were dull in comparison with those of many less fortunate societies. Dr. Eric Williams, Prime Minister of Trinidad and Tobago from 1956 until his death in 1981, believed in the West Indian Federation. However, Jamaica's withdrawal from the federation led to Trinidad's, and after the break-up, Trinidadian authorities felt little responsibility toward their impoverished neighbours. Dr. Williams and his colleagues in the People's National Movement (PNM) government were cautious, non-provocative, and constructive in their dealings with other countries, although in 1972, Trinidad and Tobago joined Jamaica, Guyana, and Barbados in establishing diplomatic relations with Castro's Cuba.[117]

As well, efforts to achieve co-operation among the countries of the West Indies survived the collapse of the formal federation. In 1968, for instance, the ten nations that had participated in the federation formed the Caribbean Free Trade Area, and Belize joined three years later. The association actually went well beyond – at least in principle – trade relations, incorporating commitments to achieve co-operation among the participants in production, in establishing common services in such areas as sea and air transport, health, culture and communications, labour relations, and foreign policy.[118]

There were constructive achievements in the Williams era. The government persuaded the U.S. Navy to leave the base at Chaguaramas, despite the ninety-nine-year lease which the British had granted. In 1967, Trinidad and Tobago became the first Anglophone country after the United States itself to join the Organization of American States. The others followed, and Trinidad and Tobago lobbied successfully for the admission of Guyana and Belize, despite the territorial disputes with Venezuela and Guatemala. In 1970, Dr. Williams invited Venezuelan and Guyanese officials to meet in Port of Spain to discuss that contentious issue. Neither Dr. Williams himself nor any member of his cabinet tried to serve as an intermediary, but they did give the Venezuelan and Guyanese delegations a place where they could talk to each other, and where they did manage to hammer out a *modus vivendi*. The United Nations Economic Commission for Latin America met in Trinidad and Tobago in 1975. At that, its first meeting in the Anglophone Caribbean, Trinidad and Cuba led a successful effort to create a Caribbean Development and Cooperation Committee, including most of the independent island countries. However, Williams was suspicious of Venezuelan imperialism as well as of socialism in Guyana, Bishop's government in Grenada, and Michael Manley's Jamaica (1972–80). So intense, however, was the perception of isolation on the part of Williams and his PNM successor, George Chambers, from Grenadian matters that when the crisis came in 1983, the neighbouring islands wrote Trinidad and Tobago out of the script. They dealt directly with the Reagan administration in Washington rather than with their erstwhile leader in Port of Spain.

Conclusions

Cold War issues dominated the international history of the Caribbean basin in the 1960s and 1970s, particularly following the Cuban revolution. The Cold War and the response to Fidelismo, however, were only the major issues in these years, and a variety of other questions and developments characterized the political, strategic, economic, and cultural dynamic of the region. Prominent among those other issues were the constant tensions associated with nationalism and decolonization. Much of the insular and the remnants of continental empires – at least the formal vestiges of empire – were transformed in the course of the 1950–80 period, leaving most nations independent but still the product of their formal imperial connections. Where former British, French, and Dutch empires had once ruled, and in some instances continued to do so, the United States had established informal empire, characterized not by imperial administration, except in Puerto Rico and the Virgin Islands, but rather by the dominance of its strategic, economic, and increasingly by its cultural presence in the region. Other issues were closely connected to the other major forces shaping the history of the area: migration, race relations, economic development, poverty alleviation, illegal international narcotics trafficking. Such issues acquired increasingly strategic importance quite independent of the impact of the Cuban revolution, and this became especially striking in the context of the Central American crisis in the 1980s.

6

FROM REVOLUTION TO THE
END OF THE COLD WAR

On 19 July 1979, the Sandinista army marched in triumph into Managua, having finally routed the forces of Anastasio Somoza. Other than Castro's revolution and defeat of Batista in 1959, there was no more significant event in the post-World War II international history of the region. Nicaragua, under a Sandinista government from 1979 through the February 1990 elections, became the fulcrum in east–west relations. Initially, it was a test of the superpowers' ability to shape the politics of the Third World; finally, it became one of the major symbols for superpower collaboration in bringing an end to a half-century of Cold War as the Soviet Union under Mikhail Gorbachev moved away from the domestic and foreign policies of the Brezhnev era. For almost a decade, the Nicaraguan revolution and the determined U.S. effort to contain Sandinista and Castro-ist export of insurgency in the area was rarely out of the headlines. Such importance was intensified by the concurrent and related major insurgencies in El Salvador and Guatemala. The conflict drew into the maelstrom of debate and negotiation not only the United States, the Soviet Union, and Cuba – the main players in the drama as it unfolded – but all of the Central American countries, the Caribbean rim nations, including Mexico, Canada, a number of European nations, the members of the Organization of American States and the UN.[1]

Dominant as the Nicaraguan crisis became in the Caribbean basin in the 1980s, it was neither the only significant development nor the only nation which was transformed in the course of these years. In the United States, the election of Ronald Reagan in 1980s began a decade of Republican control of the White House and a return in foreign policy to the rhetoric of the Cold War, increased military spending, and a hard-line against the Soviet Union and its surrogates in the western hemisphere and elsewhere. The U.S.–Organization of Eastern Caribbean States invasion of Grenada in 1985 and the Bush administration's invasion of Manuel Noriega's Panama in December 1989 symbolized the willingness of the Republican administrations of the decade to use military force to gain what they believed had been lost by diplomacy and politics.

Economically, the 1980s were years of crisis for much of Latin America – the "lost decade" – occasioned in large part by over-borrowing in previous decades in anticipation of future growth and, in a number of instances, brought on by the collapse of prices for major export commodities such as oil after 1984. Mexico was especially hurt by the economic downturn of the decade and set the pace for the hemisphere in moving under presidents Miguel de la Madrid and Carlos Salinas de Gortari from its state-dominated but mixed economy to a more open, market-driven economic structure, in the process shedding many of its several thousand state enterprises. Other countries in the region followed the Mexican model, with the major exceptions of Cuba and Nicaragua, both of which adhered to statism and command economies for reasons of ideology and national security. Colombia, already with a well-developed and diversified economy, including the economic impact of illegal narcotics trafficking, managed to escape the major debt crisis of the 1980s.

International efforts to control narcotics smuggling and distribution provided another major theme of the decade. Narcotics acquired its prominence in large part because of the significant impact the wealth and power generated by the cocaine traffic had on the political and strategic dynamic of the region. Narcotics could assist in fuelling insurgencies otherwise hard-pressed to pay for badly needed weapons, and the narcotics traffickers themselves were a major disruptive source of military power. The issue simply impacted on so many countries in the region. With sources of supply in Peru, Bolivia, and Ecuador, and with Colombia the major processing area for cocaine, narcotics trafficking reached into every country of the Caribbean and Central America, impacting on their economies, politics, police and military, and culture. In Colombia, the major narcotics cartels were quickly linked with the guerrilla insurgencies that had been part of the Colombian political scene for several decades. In Mexico–U.S. relations, cross-border narcotics smuggling rivalled illegal migration in the bilateral relationship. The harder line taken by the United States in the Reagan-Bush years in their approach to international narcotics as a national security issue moved the issue closer to the top of the political agenda, with the result that narcotics trafficking played a part in much of the inter-American dynamic in the course of the decade.

The Central American crisis

The fallout from the Sandinista overthrow of the Somoza regime touched every country in the region in the course of the decade, with the major impact being in neighbouring countries in Central America. The Sandinista National Liberation Front (FSLN) government in Nicaragua, along with Cuba, lent substantial assistance to insurgent forces in El Salvador, where the United States continued to provide extensive military support to a series of corrupt, repressive, or ineffectual governments. Honduras became the main staging ground for anti-Sandinista forces (the Contras) supported by the United States; Costa Rica also found itself used as a cross-border base for Contra operations at various stages as it had been for the FSLN during its years of operations against Somoza. The United States further bolstered an already bloated Guatemalan military in the course of the decade in order to contain its own insurgent forces. The strengthening of the

Guatemalan military, combined with the general crisis in the region, also served to enhance Anglo-American cooperation in the Reagan-Thatcher years. Newly independent Belize, for instance (1981), with only 160,000 inhabitants adjacent to a country with 40,000 soldiers, seemed even more vulnerable with the military build-up on its borders even though Guatemala had no international support for its claims to Belize other than that offered by Israel. Nonetheless, Britain and Guatemala broke diplomatic relations prior to Belize's independence and did not resume relations until 1986. Confronted with challenges in El Salvador and Nicaragua, the Reagan administration was also anxious to have a British military presence in Belize. Prime Minister Thatcher thus retained a substantial force in Belize through the decade. By 1987, there were almost 2,000 troop, Harrier jets, Puma and Gazelle helicopters, tanks and armoured personnel carriers, an air defence system utilizing Rapier missiles and a Royal Navy frigate that regularly patrolled the country's coast. Britain also provided Belize with a substantial loan to enable the expansion of the airport to permit large British jets to land additional forces in the event of an emergency. At the same time, the U.S. presence also increased. Between independence and the end of the decade, U.S. diplomatic personnel in Belize increased from seven to fifty. The Peace Corps presence was one of the highest per capita of any commitment in the hemisphere. The United States established a Voice of America radio relay station at Punta Gorda in 1985 to aim anti-Sandinista propaganda at Nicaragua and co-operated with U.S. Drug Enforcement Agency officials in eradicating marijuana crops. U.S. aid and invest-ment increased in the same period, and the United States became Belize's largest trading partner, accounting for half its imports and exports, with the Caribbean Basin Initiative encouraging the sale of Belize manufactured products to the United States.[2]

The regional powers also assumed an important mediating role in these years in an effort to bring peace, stability, and some prosperity to the region. Especially important in this regard were Costa Rica – notably under President Oscar Arias – Colombia, Venezuela, and Panama. In early 1983, the foreign ministers of these countries formed what came to be known as the Contadora Group.[3] It sought mediation and diplomacy over armed conflict, placed pressure on the governments of the region to negotiate with opposition groups and to pursue electoral solutions to confrontations, and provided a vehicle for other nations, including Canada, to advance the cause of peace.

The evolution of U.S. policy

As Robert A. Pastor, former National Security Adviser for Latin America in the Carter administration, observed, anticipating that the demise of Somoza in Nicaragua would precipitate a crisis, between September 1978 and July 1979 the National Security Council held twenty-five sessions to address the issues and the policy options. Pastor contends that the Carter administration was under no illusions about the Sandinista National Liberation Front. The administration viewed the FSLN leadership as tied to a Marxist-Leninist view of the world and linked to Cuban and Brezhnev era Soviet foreign policies, even though the FSLN had sought to broaden its political base of support in the year before the overthrow of Somoza. The alternative to an FSLN victory in the short term, however, was even less attractive. If Somoza were propped up further, U.S. officials believed, his government would engage in vicious repression of opposition and make inevitable further crisis and an FSLN victory in the longer term in any event.[4]

Given this dilemma, the Carter administration sought to achieve a peaceful transfer of power through the mediation of the OAS and its regional members. Given Somoza's refusal to co-operate, the administration escalated its pressure on Somoza, cutting off aid and ending military support, at precisely the time that, largely unknown to U.S. officials, the FSLN was receiving substantial military supplies from Cuba through Panama and Costa Rica. With the FSLN factions united under Cuban pressure, and with the fresh supply of arms, in June 1979 the Sandinistas engaged in a major and ultimately successful offensive against Somoza's National Guard. In this late stage of the military conflict, the Carter administration continued to press for a negotiated settlement and a coalition government, unacceptable to Somoza, the FSLN or to Panama, Costa Rica, Venezuela and Mexico. By mid-July Somoza fled to Miami; the FSLN assumed power, and the real crisis of the next decade began as the U.S. sought to come to terms with the Nicaraguan situation as well as its impact on regional and east–west relations.

The contrast between the approach of the Carter administration and its Republican successor under Ronald Reagan was marked. Here the lessons of Cuba hung heavily in their historical memories; but they drew different conclusions, with the Carter administration attempting to understand and contend with the internal forces of change within each country and the regional implications of the Nicaraguan revolution. The Carter administration emphasized diplomacy and negotiation over military solutions. The Reagan and Bush administrations, conversely, viewed the Central American situation exclusively as part of the east–west, U.S.–Soviet/Cuban conflict and opted for largely military solutions to the conflict. Determined to avoid the mistakes of the 1960s toward Cuba and to keep Nicaragua out of the Cuban–Soviet camp, Carter continued to work for negotiations, to encourage the FSLN to broaden further its political base and not to lend support to insurgencies elsewhere in Central America, especially El Salvador and Guatemala. The small aid package that Congress finally approved for Nicaragua was conditional on the administration monitoring Nicaraguan behaviour toward its neighbours.[5]

The pressures on Carter to move to a more aggressive stance were substantial in 1979–80. The Sandinista victory in Nicaragua was followed that year by the victory of the New Jewel Movement of Maurice Bishop in Grenada and its immediate overtures to Castro. At the same time the CIA discovered a Soviet brigade in Cuba, raising the east–west stakes at an awkward time, when the Salt

II Arms Limitation agreement concluded by Carter and Brezhnev was making its way through the U.S. Senate. When the non-aligned nations met in September 1979 Bishop, Castro and Daniel Ortega sought, unsuccessfully as it turned out, to shift the focus of the movement toward a harder anti-American, pro-Soviet line. Here the Carter administration listened more carefully than would the Reagan administration to the advice it received from other countries in the region, with the suggestion that the FSLN government in Nicaragua be accommodated but that Bishop's New Jewel Movement government be isolated by providing assistance to other countries in the area.[6]

The Carter administration had no real opportunity to test the longer-term viability of its policies in the Caribbean basin with the electoral loss to Ronald Reagan and the Republicans in 1980. Moreover, following the Soviet invasion of Afghanistan in late 1979 and the Iranian hostage-taking crisis, the administration seemed semi-paralyzed until its demise. The Reagan administration came to office committed in the electoral campaign to a new, more aggressive approach designed to restore American prestige, reverse a perceived decline in U.S. strength, and assert American power in the world. Those rather vague notions of a revived Wilsonian moralism and rekindled Cold War rhetoric came to be embodied in the Reagan Doctrine. In its simplest terms, the Reagan Doctrine involved a shift from détente to an offensive against Soviet-bloc interests, especially in the Third World. The administration pledged to stand by its "democratic" allies and to resist Soviet-inspired aggression against those democratic forces from, as Reagan indicated in 1985, Afghanistan to Nicaragua.[7]

The implications were clear: there would be no tolerance for what was portrayed as Soviet–Cuban insurgencies and revolutions in the Caribbean region. The administration moved quickly in 1981 to bolster anti-Sandinista elements in Nicaragua or in bases in neighbouring countries. Funded entirely by the U.S. government, Contra leaders were trained in Florida and in major U.S. bases constructed in Honduras to provide strategic proximity to Nicaraguan borders. Over the next decade, the U.S. poured hundreds of millions of dollars into support for the Contra "freedom fighters" against Nicaragua. The results were negligible. The Contra war cost thousands of lives, many of which were innocent civilians caught between contending forces in the northern towns and villages of Nicaragua, and contributed to the further impoverishment of the Nicaraguan people; but it failed to produce a military victory or to destabilize the Sandinista government in Managua. The war, including the scandal surrounding the illegal diversion of funds to the Contras from weapons sales to Iran under the direction of Oliver North, served little value except to discredit the United States in the eyes of the international community and to undermine rather than enhance U.S. prestige in the world.

At the same time that the Reagan administration fought its surrogate war against the Sandinista government of Nicaragua, it bolstered the governments of El Salvador and Guatemala in their efforts to contain their own insurgent forces. Reagan inherited from the Carter administration in El Salvador a situation that had continued to deteriorate and in which the post-1979 involvement of Nicaraguan weapons seriously undermined the Carter preference for negotiation. Distracted as he was in the last year of his presidency by Afghanistan and the American hostages in Teheran, Carter sought in El Salvador to restrain the military, bolster civilian forces under Christian Democrat José Napoleon Duarte, the leader of the ruling junta, and to encourage meaningful agrarian and other reforms to undercut the appeal of the FMLN and the Revolutionary Democratic Front (FDR). But the absence of a vital political centre in El Salvador, with the flight, fear or death of many of those who might have led the centre, made it difficult to avoid continued military conflict and political polarization. Under the circumstances, the Salvadoran military and right-wing death squads held the balance of power and used it to engage in massive repression of the civilian population. Carter was further undermined by the support that the Salvadoran guerrillas received from Nicaragua for their unsuccessful January 1981 offensive. That Nicaraguan link to the FMLN-FDR provided the Reagan administration with the wedge it needed to take a harder military line in the region.

From 1981 on, the Reagan administration reinforced the Salvadoran military, failing to understand that the critical issue in El Salvador at that stage was not the defeat of the insurgents, who had been defeated in their January offensive, but rather the need to strengthen Duarte and the civilian political sector against the Salvadoran military and the extreme right led by Roberto D'Aubuisson. In his early 1984 Report of the National Bipartisan Commission on Central America, former Secretary of State Henry Kissinger recommended reinforcing the Contras, on grounds that the Soviet Union and Cuba were using Nicaragua as a base for penetration of the region, with El Salvador the "target of first opportunity."[8] That conclusion overwhelmed the other recommendations that the U.S. address the pressing human and economic needs of the region as well as the need to encourage political reforms. By insisting on the primacy of supporting the military, Reagan and Secretary of State Alexander Haig further undermined the capacity of the Salvadoran civilian moderates to hold the extremists in check.[9]

There was virtually no shift in policy toward El Salvador throughout the Reagan administration, although the administration, and to some extent the Salvadoran military, found itself constrained occasionally by congressional insistence that aid be limited to humanitarian support and tied to concrete evidence of improvements in the Salvadoran human rights performance. U.S. policy was an abysmal failure in El Salvador in terms of its stated objectives. The FMLN-FDR were never subdued though the focus remained on a military solution; rather, even at the time of the 1991 congressional elections, the insurgents held large segments of the country and carried out daring raids against U.S. as well as Salvadoran forces. At the same time the activities of the right-wing death squads intensified and the political centre fragmented. Duarte returned to a feeble presidency following disputed elections in 1984 and barely hung on to power through his term in 1989. Human rights were not protected;

agrarian reform was not implemented in any meaningful manner, and those who sought such reforms within the country risked their lives in doing so.

Equally serious was the lack of encouragement U.S. officials provided for the international community in its efforts to find peaceful, negotiated solutions to the crises. Those initiatives derived from several quarters. As noted earlier, Colombian, Mexico, Venezuela and Panamanian leaders established the Contadora Group in 1983 and achieved considerable success over the next two years in gaining the support of the Central American countries to a negotiated settlement based on a withdrawal of all foreign support for the conflicts, end the shipment of arms to the combatants, and work toward the reduction of militarism in the region. Their fear was that U.S. policy had produced precisely the opposite of its stated objectives: a reduction of east–west tensions; an end to the militarization of the area; and the defeat of the insurgent groups. Instead, the armies of Nicaragua and El Salvador had greatly increased in size and influence and the armed insurgencies had also made substantial inroads. The closest neighbours of Nicaragua and El Salvador had a good deal to fear from the direction in which U.S. policy seemed to be leading the area: militarism, massive instability, refugees, increased poverty and disease, and ruined economies with the U.S.-imposed economic blockade of Nicaragua. The U.S. greeted such initiatives with polite scepticism, as naive if well-intentioned overtures.

Several factors gradually pressed the contending parties toward at least an uneasy truce and ultimate peace. One major factor was the demise of the Reagan administration at the end of 1988 and a shift to George Bush. A second was the dramatic shift in Soviet policies under Mikhail Gorbachev in the course of the decade, the increasing acceptance in U.S. official circles of the sincerity and seriousness of the Gorbachev commitment, and a degree of great power collaboration in the quest for peace. A third was the persistent efforts on the part of the regional countries and the international community to bring sanity, balance and a negotiated rather than military solution to problems that had only been worsened by a decade of hard-line approaches.

In February 1986, the original members of the Contadora countries, frustrated at the lack of interest in their efforts from the United States, found support among the representatives of four non-regional powers – Brazil, Peru, Uruguay, and Argentina. Although they met with Secretary of State Shultz and urged the United States to move toward a negotiated settlement, Reagan declined to respond to the initiative. Instead, a few months later Congress as well seemed to move to a more militant stance, approving $100 million in aid to the Contras, most of it for military assistance.

Discouraged but undaunted, the regional countries pressed ahead with their initiatives. The newly elected President of Guatemala, Vinicio Cerezo, brought his fellow presidents to Esquipulas in May of that year in an effort to explore common interests, including the idea of a Central American parliament as well as the means of promoting peace in the region. In August 1987, the five Central

American countries, led primarily by President Oscar Arias of Costa Rica, signed the Esquipulas II accord, in which they agreed that there should be negotiations leading to a cease-fire, the disbanding of irregular military forces, and the establishment of both national reconciliation commissions and an international commission for verification follow-up. The Reagan administration continued to oppose this approach, arguing that only military pressure on the Sandinistas would bring a settlement to the area.[10] The international community was, by this juncture, beginning to have a more substantial impact on the regional dynamic, leading ultimately to a series of cease-fires in Nicaragua and the February 1990 elections that were officially supervised by the UN, the OAS, and a small but influential Carter group.

In other contexts the international community voiced its displeasure with the manner in which the United States was conducting its Central American operations. In a thinly veiled critique of European reservations about U.S. actions in Central America, the Kissinger Commission report observed that although European nations had historic interests in the area, and Britain retained a military presence, none of them had a real security concern with developments in Central America. Kissinger's admonitions did not silence that international voice, however muted it may have been. In June 1986, the World Court found that the United States had violated international law, intervening in the internal affairs of a sovereign nation, by training, financing and arming the Contras. A UN resolution calling on the United States to heed the ruling of the court was tabled when it became evident the United States would not honour the decision, but such close neighbours and allies as Canada voted in favour of the resolution. Other allies, including Britain, France, and West Germany, abstained from the vote; only Israel and El Salvador cast ballots on the U.S. side.[11]

The evolution of Soviet policy

The major transition that occurred in Soviet foreign and domestic policies during the Gorbachev years was critical to a resolution of the Central American crisis, although American policy makers in the Reagan-Bush administrations remained skeptical of Soviet objectives.[12] Part of the problem in deciphering Soviet intentions in the region, as elsewhere, was the dual track on which Soviet involvement occurred, with the International Department of the Central Committee of the Communist Party of the Soviet Union (CPSU) working closely with local communist parties, and the Soviet Foreign Ministry pursuing its separate and occasionally divergent policies toward an area. Only in Cuba and Nicaragua was there a unified policy because of the close bilateral relationships (Map 4). The other complication for the Soviet Union in Central America was the fact that in the 1980s it had formal diplomatic relations with only Costa Rica and Nicaragua. Regardless of such distinctions of policy orientation and application within the Soviet system, certainly Gorbachev's global policies were a marked shift from those of Leonid Brezhnev, which had been expansionist and militaristic. The

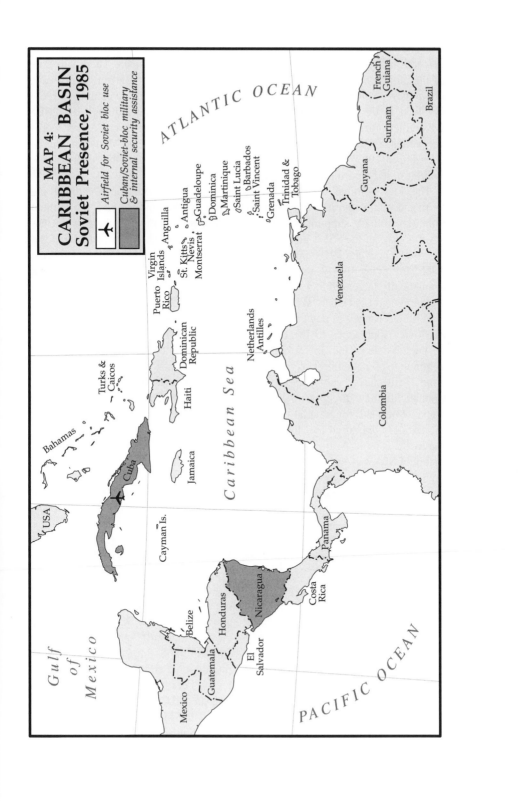

MAP 4:
CARIBBEAN BASIN
Soviet Presence, 1985

✈ Airfield for Soviet bloc use

Cuban/Soviet-bloc military
& internal security assistance

Brezhnev regime celebrated the Sandinista victory over Somoza because of its perception that the FSLN had firm roots in Marxism-Leninism. There was none of the initial ambiguity that had greeted Castro's defeat of Batista twenty years previously. Yet the Soviet Union was also cautious in becoming directly involved in the Nicaraguan situation, with the result that although the FSLN government received official recognition only one day after it came to power, it was almost a decade before any ranking Soviet officials visited Managua. On that occasion in 1987, Boris Yeltsin, then simply a candidate member of the Soviet Politburo, led a parliamentary delegation to Managua.[13]

The low political and diplomatic profile which both the Brezhnev and Gorbachev administrations maintained in Managua did not preclude commitment, although military support even through Cuba was relatively minor in the first several years of the FSLN government. Soviet weapons shipments which reached Nicaragua between 1979 and 1982 totalled less than $8 million, although by June 1985, following two years of CIA-funded Contra operations, that value had dramatically increased to $600 million, including shipments from East Germany, Bulgaria, and Czechoslovakia.[14]

With Gorbachev in power after 1985 there was a marked shift in the direction of Soviet approaches to the region. In part the shift was occasioned by the desperate state of the Soviet economy and its inability or refusal to attempt to continue to escalate the arms race with the United States. In part, the shift derived from Gorbachev's very personal view that the Soviet Union had to move in dramatically new directions. Although weapons shipments to Nicaragua through Cuba continued for several years, both the Cubans and Nicaraguans were increasingly pressured by Moscow to open their economies and to integrate into the world system. At the same time the message from Moscow to Managua was that the FSLN government had to find a political solution to its situation, not rely on military victory. Gorbachev also rejected violence as a means to revolutionary change, including the export of revolution. There were several signals of Soviet intent in the course of 1988–9. The first was a letter from Gorbachev to Costa Rican President Oscar Arias in April 1988 insisting that the Soviet Union was not sending weapons to insurgent forces in Guatemala and El Salvador.[15] A second was the June meeting of the Congress of People's Deputies where it was stressed that the U.S.S.R had to integrate into the world economy and to accept the economic principles associated with such integration. A third came in a personal letter from Gorbachev to Bush in October, in which the Soviet leader stressed that there had been no arms shipments from the U.S.S.R since the year before, although Nicaragua continued to receive foodstuffs and oil products, on which it was dependent. That fact was confirmed by U.S. officials in the fall of 1989 at the time that Nicaragua and the international community were working feverishly to put the machinery in place for the February 1990 elections.[16]

If Soviet intent was clear by 1989, Nicaraguan and Cuban compliance was less certain, either ideologically in the rejection of the idea of "revolution without borders," or in terms of arms shipments to El Salvador, which appear to have continued through 1989. In October of that year, Soviet Foreign Minister Shevardnadze met on several occasions with President Ortega, the Sandinista National Directorate and the diplomatic corps in an effort to press the Soviet perspective. Several developments placed additional strains on the new Soviet–American co-operation. One was the fact that Moscow found it difficult to bring Havana and Nicaragua into line. Nicaragua continued to be a major source of weapons for the FMLN's new offensive in late 1989–90, threatening to cool the Bush–Gorbachev discussions at their Malta summit meeting late in 1989, although Bush appears to have accepted Gorbachev's assurances that Moscow was sincerely trying to prevent such deliveries.[17] A second was the precipitous U.S. invasion of Panama in an effort to overthrow Manuel Noriega in December 1989, an action that gained widespread condemnation in the international community. Adding further tension was the illegal entry by U.S. forces into the Nicaraguan ambassador's residence in Panama during the invasion. Nonetheless, Moscow was committed to winding down the war in Central America and intensified its pressures on Managua by withholding emergency funds and insisting that the FSLN government sign the Central American accord at San Isidro, Costa Rica, in mid-December.[18]

In fairness to Nicaraguan leaders, they had since 1981 made overtures to western European governments for expanded trade and financial assistance, with limited results. Nicaragua also turned to Japan to study the feasibility of an isthmian canal through Nicaragua, a revival of a century-old idea.[19] Between the seizure of power in 1979 and 1986, western European governments provided only $600 million in economic and financial assistance to Nicaragua. This failure of support derived in part from western European disappointment with the increased militarization of the Nicaraguan economy, the country's close ties to Cuba and the more radical leaders in the Third World, and the failure to fall in line with the initiatives of the Contadora group. To what extent Nicaragua's orientation was the result of ideological commitment rather than the necessities of a nation besieged by the surrogate forces of the United States is open to debate.

Although the Bush administration made no commitment to accept the results of the February 1990 elections in Nicaragua, the Gorbachev administration was magnanimous in its approach. The coalition opposition forces, the National Opposition Union (UNO), united behind presidential candidate Violeta de Chamorro, won a narrow and controversial victory in the internationally monitored national election, thus ending a decade of Sandinista governance. Moscow congratulated both winners and losers. Ortega received an expression of appreciation for his devotion to the Nicaraguan people, their well-being and sovereignty, and for his willingness to encourage true political pluralism. Moscow also expressed the hope that under President Chamorro there would be continued positive bilateral relations, a sentiment that Chamorro reciprocated. The next year Moscow made another major overture to Washington, offering to assist in preparing an inventory of pre-1989 Soviet weapons that were still held by the Nicaraguan armed forces.[20]

At the U.S.–Soviet summit in Washington in June 1990, the two nations turned their attention to the El Salvador war. As in Nicaragua both major powers were anxious to realize a political settlement. The Moscow-controlled El Salvador Communist Party was the most moderate force in the insurgent coalition in El Salvador, and as a reflection of the capacity of the U.S.S.R to influence the insurgents, the FMLN also agreed at this stage to return Soviet surface-to-air missiles that had been supplied by Nicaragua. Gorbachev was less successful in pressing for an expanded Soviet role in the negotiations in El Salvador and in obtaining formal diplomatic relations between the two countries, in part because of the opposition of President Cristiani and his right-wing supporters.[21]

Nonetheless, with the Nicaraguan conflict largely resolved by this stage, the way had been paved to resolution of the insurgency in El Salvador, although a major factor in leading to an accord was the awareness on both sides that the conflict was not winnable. With the critical involvement of Mexico and UN officials in the course of 1991, negotiations between the FMLN and the El Salvador government made significant headway. At the end of December 1991, following extensive UN-mediated negotiations and internationally supervised congressional and local elections earlier in the year, the parties signed an agreement in New York to end what had been essentially a twelve-year-old civil war. That war had cost the lives of more than 75,000 Salvadorans and ravaged the countryside and the nation's economic infrastructure. One would be hard pressed to identify the gains made by either side as a result of the war. The agreement also reflected the expanded role that the international community had acquired in the region in the course of the 1980s, with, as in Nicaragua, the UN assuming the responsibility to monitor the disarmament process, facilitate the reintegration of insurgents into the society, and to investigate violations of human rights by the military. Although little came of the latter part of the mandate, the agreement provided for the establishment of a national police force to reduce some of the military's responsibility for areas that were more of a policing nature. The agreement also gave assurances that there would be concrete measures taken to advance the cause of land reform, always at the heart of the civil war.[22]

Grenada

In the same year that the U.S. authorized CIA sponsorship of the Contras in an effort to remove the Sandinistas from power, the Reagan administration demonstrated in Grenada that it was prepared to use military force in the region to achieve its foreign policy objectives and to remove what it saw as a communist threat on its doorstep. Although the events leading to the 1983 U.S. invasion remain controversial, the evidence is now strong that the Bishop government was engaged in activities that threatened the security of the region. Whether means short of invasion would have been equally successful in altering the situation remains open to debate.

Tensions between Grenada and the United States began to develop during the Carter presidency. In March 1979, the New Jewel Movement (NJM) led by Maurice Bishop staged a successful *coup d'état*.[23] Serious problems emerged one month before Bishop's coup. In February 1979, agents of the U.S. Bureau of Alcohol, Tobacco, and Firearms (ATF) in Baltimore arrested and charged two Grenadians whom they suspected of smuggling arms to Grenada. Two ATF officials went to Grenada to help Eric Gairy's police identify and question other members of the NJM. Gairy's goons killed Bishop's father, and fearing further reprisals because of the arms smuggling, the NJM leadership voted to stage the coup right away. According to Pastor, Bishop thought that the attempt would be premature and voted in the negative, but the affirmative majority included Bernard Coard and Hudson Austin. The coup was successful. ATF fell under the jurisdiction of the Treasury Department, and the State Department knew nothing about either the arrests or the NJM.

Within days, leaders of other eastern Caribbean islands suspected a leftist orientation on the part of the NJM leadership and met in Barbados for discussions. Bishop provided assurances to them as well as to the U.S. Ambassador for the eastern Caribbean, Frank Ortiz, who lived in Barbados. Yet Radio Grenada became Radio Free Grenada, and members of the National Security Council in Washington thought that it was broadcasting communist propaganda. When Ortiz went to Grenada and discussed various forms of U.S. aid with Bishop, Bishop refused to promise the elections on which Ortiz insisted. Nevertheless, the State Department accepted Ortiz's advice to be patient for fear of pushing the NJM government into partnership with Fidel Castro.

Two days after the visit of Ortiz, Bishop indicated that he would not respect the constitution. Instead, he introduced "ten fundamental People's Laws" which gave the People's Revolutionary Army arbitrary power to make arrests. He also discontinued the Peace Corps Program and showed no interest in other forms of aid which he and Ortiz had discussed.

The Bishop government then arrested political opponents and began to import Cuban weapons via Guyana. Along with the weapons, Cubans also began to arrive, as early as 4 April 1979. Claiming the need to prevent a counter-revolution led by Gairy, Bishop said that his government would also seek weapons from the United States, the United Kingdom, Canada, and Venezuela, but he announced on 9 April that he had asked Fidel Castro's government to train Grenadian soldiers.

The State Department told Ortiz to warn Bishop that close Grenadian–Cuban relations would create problems with the United States. In an effort to maintain a close bilateral relationship between the two countries, Ortiz again offered the services of the Peace Corps and the Agency for International Development, but Bishop was not interested. Nor was Bishop ready to commit himself on elections, and continued to express concern about the possibility of Gairy attempting a political return, in spite of Ortiz's assurances that the U.S. government would not allow Gairy to leave the United States and attempt a comeback. Bishop nevertheless indicated that Cuban assistance offered the best guarantee that Gairy would never return, and, according to Pastor, Bishop lied when asked whether he had already received Cuban arms. On 13 April, Bishop delivered his first anti-American speech, condemning Ortiz's objections to Cuban assistance. For its part, the Carter administration helped other countries of the eastern Caribbean develop a Coast Guard while British advisers trained police forces on other islands.[24]

Nor was the Carter administration alone in its difficulties with the NJM government. Documents captured after the 1983 invasion indicated that the NJM assigned an official from Grenada's Ministry of the Interior, Michael Roberts, to keep Grenada's churches under surveillance. On 15 March 1983, Roberts concluded that the churches were "the main political source of internal counter revolution." Roberts' superior, Major Keith Roberts, reached a similar conclusion. Keith Roberts noted the enormous popularity of Bishop Sydney Charles, the highest ranking Roman Catholic official, in a country where more than half the population was Roman Catholic. As early as 1980–1, the Roman Catholic Church included prayers for Grenada's political prisoners suffering from arbitrary arrest. Under the NJM government and for the first time in Grenadian history, Anglicans marched with the Roman Catholics in the Corpus Christi parade. The NJM found this ominous.[25]

It is impossible to explain the U.S. military intervention of 1983 in Grenada without some reference to a fairly wide context. Since 1959, successive U.S. presidents had failed to dislodge the pro-Soviet regime of Cuba's Fidel Castro, who had, in the interval, sent troops to assist African revolutionaries. The U.S. effort to prevent a communist victory in South Vietnam had failed. In 1979, the Cuban-backed Sandinistas had won control of Nicaragua, Islamic militants had captured the U.S. Embassy in Teheran along with most of the people who worked there, and Soviet forces had invaded Afghanistan. Events in Teheran and Afghanistan humiliated President Carter in the eyes of the American electorate and guaranteed the electoral victory of Ronald Reagan.

Reagan then launched a $1.5 trillion military build-up and wanted desperately to make his country appear powerful and effective. Within half an hour of his inauguration, the Iranians freed their hostages. However, Marines whom President Reagan dispatched to Lebanon, which was in the midst of a civil war, were less fortunate. A suicide-bomber drove a truck loaded with explosives into the compound where they slept, killing more than 200.[26] Given this context, a military victory somewhere, even in Grenada, was likely to enhance Reagan's chances in the 1984 presidential elections. It may also be relevant that some of the people who later became famous for their illegal and under-handed actions in the Iran-Contra scandal – notably National Security Adviser Bud McFarlane, Admiral John Poindexter and Lieutenant-Colonel Oliver North – advised the President.[27] Another indicted Iran-Contra conspirator, Caspar Weinberger, was Secretary of Defense. CIA Chief William Casey, who was to die while under investigation for complicity in Iran-Contra, was another adviser to the President.

It is by no means certain that the Reagan administration intervened in Grenada for reasons of political expediency. However, that possibility should not be ignored. At the very least, it must have been obvious to U.S. decision-makers that a victory in Grenada would allow the President to claim a success, the first unqualified U.S. military victory since 1945.

On the other hand, it is impossible to dismiss the Reagan administration's concerns out of hand. Grenada was a small Caribbean island, "twice the size of the District of Columbia" in the words of President Reagan, with an estimated population of 110,000.[28] Independent since 1974, it remained a member of the British Commonwealth of Nations. Prime Minister Maurice Bishop had gained power through a *coup d'état*, allowed no elections and admitted to having jailed without charge "up to 40" political opponents.[29] Bishop's government admitted hundreds of Cubans, some of whom were soldiers. It also attracted Soviets, East Germans, North Koreans, and Libyans.[30] Years later, dissident KGB officer Oleg Kalugin reported that East German agents assisted terrorists in a manner unacceptable even to the KGB.[31] North Korea's principal export was weaponry, and its advisers' major areas of expertise were military organization and police surveillance.[32]

More serious conflicts between the Reagan administration and Libya lay in the future, but already there was reason for concern about Libyan agents in the Caribbean. At a later date, leaders of eastern Caribbean allies of the United States informed visiting members of the United States Congress of their concern about possible Cuban-Libyan-North Korean subversion in the region.[33] *Washington Post* reporter Bob Woodward has suggested that the CIA had bribed one of these allies, Dominican Prime Minister Eugenia Charles, with $100,000.[34] Even if this accusation is valid, Charles was not the only leader of the Commonwealth Caribbean to support President Reagan; one of the few exceptions was Guyana's Forbes Burnham. Moreover, there actually were valid grounds for concern about possible Cuban-Libyan-North Korean activity.

Certain other facts are irrefutable. At Point Salines in Grenada, Cubans were constructing an airport which could handle Cuban jetliners with soldiers headed to Africa or Libyan aircraft on their way to Nicaragua.[35] Also in Grenada was St. George's University School of Medicine, most of whose 1,500 students were Americans whose applications to study medicine in the United States had been rejected. The Faculty at St. George's was also American.[36] Yet, before the crisis of October 1983, the Reagan administration did not monitor Grenada very closely. The CIA had few if any observers in Grenada, and the nearest U.S. Embassy was the one in Bridgetown, Barbados. White House and the State Department depended upon British sources for information on Grenada, and the British and U.S. Ambassadors in Bridgetown were hardly on speaking terms.[37] To the dismay of Secretary of State George Shultz, the information provided by British intelligence which seemed so persuasive to American decision-makers seemed less than persuasive to British Prime Minister Margaret Thatcher. Thatcher thought that her friends in Washington were exaggerating the Cuban potential in Grenada and were endangering the lives of British subjects in Grenada. Whatever problems there were in Grenada, Mrs Thatcher indicated, had been there for some years, and it might have been more than coincidental that President Reagan announced military action only two days after the Marines' violent deaths in Beirut.[38] Members of the U.S. Senate Select Committee on Intelligence, Republican and Democrat, agreed with Thatcher that evidence of a planned Cuban takeover of Grenada was lacking. Nor did the Senators find evidence of Cuban plans to export terrorism from Grenada.[39]

As early as July 1981, the Reagan administration ordered Marines to prepare for the invasion of Grenada and the adjacent Grenadine islands with an amphibious attack at the Puerto Rican island of Vieques against an enemy identified as "Amber and the Amberines." There were similar exercises in 1982 and 1983.[40] Whenever the invasion appeared necessary, the Reagan administration would be ready. The following year, President Reagan clearly indicated that Grenada would not be eligible for the benefits of his Caribbean Basin Initiative.[41]

Matters came to a head when a coup of 19 October transferred authority from Prime Minister Bishop to his deputy, Bernard Coard, and the commander of Grenada's tiny army, General Hudson Austin. The mutineers led by Coard and Austin arrested, then murdered, Bishop. Apparently aware that many might see an inconsistency between President Reagan's earlier rhetoric about the Bishop government and his current concern about Bishop's deposition and death, the President explained that Coard and Austin were even worse than Bishop had been, an interpretation with which Secretary of State Shultz concurred.[42] President Reagan then sent 1,900 soldiers and Marines to Grenada, to work with 300 soldiers from friendly nations of the Commonwealth Caribbean.[43] Within days the invasion force consisted of 1,200 Marines and 4,800 soldiers.[44]

Responding to public concerns about the military action, Reagan explained that the airport at Point Salines would, when finished, constitute a menace to the western hemisphere. He also mentioned a "warehouse [which] contained weapons and ammunition stacked almost to the ceiling." Soviets and Cubans had supplied the weaponry, charged the president, who added, "We got there just in time."[45] Furthermore, he did not want the Grenadian government to kidnap the Americans at the medical school and to keep them as hostages.

These points are open to argument. Grenadian officials and a British contractor said that Grenadians wanted a modern airport which could handle long-distance jets for purposes of tourism.[46] In 1983, tourists could easily fly from their homes in Europe or North America to Jamaica, Barbados, Saint Lucia, and a number of other Caribbean islands. Only those with abundant time and money could afford the indefinite layover at a jetport to await the short-haul connecting flight by propeller aircraft to Grenada. Canadian, Mexican, Venezuelan, and even U.S. contractors were involved in construction of the jet-friendly runways, and development of tourism was certainly a plausible motive.[47] Yet, while it was possible to appreciate the need for a new airport, the involvement of Cuban builders while the war in Angola was taking place did offer grounds for suspicion.

As for the Americans at the medical school, early reports in the *New York Times* indicated that many of them, like Margaret Thatcher, thought that a military campaign would be more dangerous than beneficial. Among these was Charles R. Modica, chancellor of St. George's School of Medicine. The intervention, said Dr. Modica, was "very unnecessary" as the Coard-Austin government had assured the safety of the students.[48] Parents of the medical students feared for their sons and daughters should there be an exchanged of gunfire and appealed to President Reagan to act with caution.[49] The first students to "be rescued" indicated that the student body itself was divided on the issue.[50] The White House itself admitted that the Coard-Austin government had offered its co-operation in the evacuation of the medical students, but because it considered that government untrustworthy, the Reagan administration declined the offer.[51] Moreover, if a rescue mission of faculty and students had really been the objective, the Marines might have made an Entebbe-type grab-and-rescue raid. Instead, the army remained in Grenada until June 1985, almost two full years after the initial military action.

The virtual ban on media coverage also raises suspicion. Aware of President Johnson's difficulties from adversarial reporting out of Vietnam and the Dominican Republic, the Reagan administration refused to allow journalists to go to Grenada until days after the worst of the fighting had ended. According to the *New York Times*, the Coard-Austin government had expelled all western reporters, and President Reagan would not let them return until military commanders determined that Grenada would be safe for them. When six enterprising U.S. reporters chartered a boat and landed, U.S. forces sent them away. Radio Havana and ham operators were the principal sources of information, said the *New York Times*, for some time after the invasion.[52]

As far as the Reagan administration was concerned, the benefits outweighed the costs of the operation. Most seriously from its point of view, there were eighteen U.S. military fatalities and one hundred and fifteen injuries. (An estimated twenty-four Cubans also died in combat.)[53] It was hardly good public relations that the forty-five Grenadian casualties included at least twelve patients in a mental hospital, bombed by mistake at the time of the intervention.[54] The United States had to use its veto to defeat a Security Council vote (eleven to one) of disapproval of the invasion,[55] but, in the absence of a veto, it could not prevent the UN General Assembly from passing an identical resolution.[56] The invasion was also highly unpopular at the Organization of American States.[57] As a reprisal, the military government of Communist Poland withdrew permission for nine literary scholars to attend a conference at Illinois University on the nineteenth-century poet Cyprjan Norwid.[58] In the United Kingdom, the Netherlands, and West Germany, opponents of cruise missile deployment capitalized on the Grenada intervention to question the wisdom of U.S. foreign policy in general.[59] Whether the intervention was legal is dubious. For what it was worth, leading Democrats accused the President of non-compliance with the War Powers Act when he ordered the military action in Grenada.[60] The Senate

159

gave after-the-fact approval a few days later.[61] The Reagan administration used Article VIII of the charter of the Organization of Eastern Caribbean States (OECS) to justify its intervention. Section 5 of Article VIII reads:

> The decisions and directives of the Defence and Security Committee shall be *unanimous* and shall be binding on all subordinate institutions of the organization unless otherwise determined by the Authority.[62] (italics added)

Member states of the OECS included Grenada, as well as Antigua, Dominica, Montserrat, St. Kitts/Nevis, Saint Lucia, Saint Vincent and the Grenadines. Unless Governor-General Sir Paul Scoon spoke for Grenada – a most dubious idea given the role of the Queen and her representatives in the late twentieth century – Grenada withheld its assent, and the invitation to the United States lacked "unanimous" support. Nor did St. Kitts/Nevis and Montserrat take part in the vote, and it is indeed questionable whether the OECS lived up to the principle of unanimity. Barbados and Jamaica, whose governments supported the U.S. intervention and sent troops to assist, did not belong to the OECS.

Actually, the OECS charter itself might have been invalid. The Secretariat of the United Nations advises:

> Under Article 102 of the Charter of the United Nations every treaty and every international agreement entered into by any Member of the United Nations . . . shall, as soon as possible, be registered with the Secretariat and published by it. Furthermore, no party to a treaty or international agreement subject to registration which has not been registered may invoke that treaty or agreement before any organ of the United Nations.[63]

As there is every indication that OECS member states had not registered the 1981 treaty with the United Nations, it probably lacked legal validity[64]

Yet, most of these "difficulties" pale into insignificance. President Reagan won a decisive military victory and eliminated an undesirable government, and the anniversary of this success occurred practically on the eve of the 1984 presidential election. President Reagan carried forty-nine states in that election, while his opponent, former Vice-President Walter Mondale – a critic of the invasion[65] – carried only his own state, Minnesota. To the extent that Grenada was an issue, it worked in President Reagan's favour. To some extent, the invasion also had positive repercussions on the South American mainland. Within hours of the Grenada intervention, the leader of Suriname – Lieutenant-Colonel Desi Bouterse – announced suspension of all agreements between his country and Cuba. At the same time, Bouterse declared the Cuban Ambassador in Parimaribo *persona non grata*, ostensibly to prevent the Cubans from doing to him what they had ostensibly arranged for Maurice Bishop[66] The success of a literary conference would not have been a high priority for the Reagan White House, aware as it was that intellectuals tended to favour the Democrats in any event. Of greater consequence, the European allies did agree to accept cruise missiles on their territory.

Whether or not the military action against the Coard government in Grenada was justifiable on strategic, national security grounds, as the Reagan administration contended, will long be the subject of dispute. The action was, nonetheless, entirely consistent with the world view, ideology and foreign policy strategies of the administration, ideas and strategies that were in the process of being applied in Central America and would in 1989 be applied in the Bush administration's military action against Noriega's Panama. By the mid-1980s the United States seemed to have returned to an age of gunboat diplomacy that had not been seen since the blustery era of Theodore Roosevelt.

Panama

As noted in an earlier chapter, Panama by the 1980s had lost much of the major strategic significance it had held prior to the 1950s, but a U.S. military presence in Panama was desirable for reasons not directly related to the Canal. Panama also served as an intelligence base, particularly so that the U.S. could monitor Castro's Cuba.[67] From Panama, the National Security Administration could eavesdrop on most of Latin America.[68] Even if Fidel Castro's government were to disappear, presumably there would be others whom U.S. governments might want to keep under surveillance. The military bases would be very useful for such purposes. The Canal Zone was served as a training facility where Americans instructed Latin American service personnel. However, the U.S. military presence in the twenty-first century would require another round of negotiations, and that round precipitated the fight between President George Bush and General Manuel Noriega, strongman of Panama after Omar Torrijos's death in 1981. Noriega was a most adaptable individual, who served and profited from, at one time or another, the CIA, Israeli interests, Fidel Castro, Colonel Qaddafi, and the Medellín narcotics cartel.[69]

Manuel Noriega was of considerable importance to both the Reagan and Bush administrations. President Reagan wanted to destabilize the Sandinista government in Nicaragua, but Congress would not co-operate. Under the circumstances, the Reagan administration funnelled weapons to Noriega, who forwarded them to the Nicaraguan Contras. Israelis also co-operated in forwarding arms to the Contras, and Noriega worked closely with Michael Harari, an agent of Israel's Mossad, who became an adviser to Noriega and provided security training to those around him.[70] Noriega took advantage of his friendship with the Reagan administration to funnel drugs for Colombian drug lords. At the same time, he sold visas and passports to Cubans and Libyans so that they could go to the United States.[71] The war against drugs was a high Reagan administration priority, and when Congress voted in 1986 to allow aid to the Contras, Noriega's assistance was no longer desirable. Indeed, Noriega became an embarrassment and a liability. Increasing tyranny at home, including the decapitation of critic Hugo Spadafora, further damaged his image.

It was also in the American interest that democracy should return to Panama. A democratically elected government would have a degree of legitimacy which Noriega, as an individual, lacked. On his own he could hardly commit his country to any treaty for a U.S. military presence in the twenty-first century. A return to democracy, however, did not come easily. The Reagan administration imposed sanctions against Panama, which since 1970 had successfully become attractive to international banking operations. Yet, despite the shortage of currency in Panama (the unit of currency remains the U.S. dollar), Noriega remained in power, in part at least because Japan, Libya, and Mexico lent him money. No promise of a well-financed retirement or any other bribe would prompt Noriega to step down and go into exile. The U.S. government reportedly paid $10 million to finance the campaign of Noriega's opponents in the presidential elections of May 1989, but, when his candidate lost, Noriega annulled the elections and continued to govern. The OAS worked unsuccessfully for the next several months in an effort to return Panama to constitutional order, thus making more likely unilateral action by the United States. President Bush failed to act when Noriega survived a coup attempt in October, after which some three dozen conspirators lost their lives. However, on 15 December 1989, Panama's National Assembly, dominated by Noriega, declared that "a state of war" between Panama and the United States already existed, and the next day, the National Guard shot an off-duty U.S. army officer.

The winner of the 1989 presidential election, Guillermo Endara, took the oath of office at a U.S. military base, and less than an hour later, on 20 December, Bush mounted a military invasion of Panama, the goals of which were to arrest Noriega for drug-trafficking and to smash the National Guard. Around 13,000 combat forces arrived on the isthmus and joined an equivalent number who were already there. Preceded by an extensive aerial bombardment of Panama, U.S. ground forces fought and searched until 4 January 1990, when Noriega surrendered and went as a prisoner to Miami to face trial on drug charges. An estimated 500 to 1,000 Panamanian civilians died in the fighting, while 10,000 to 18,000 others lost their homes.[72]

Because of the casualties, the property damage, and the dubious legality of "Operation Just Cause" there was widespread criticism. At the O.A.S., the United States stood alone, while twenty countries voted their disapproval and six abstained. The United Kingdom and France joined the U.S. in thwarting a Sino-Soviet resolution of disapproval at the UN Security Council, but the General Assembly passed a similar resolution by a margin of seventy-five to twenty, with forty abstentions. President Endara requested $1.5 billion to rebuild the damaged areas, especially the Panama City district of El Chorrillo whose wooden houses had burned with considerable loss of life. A CBS poll indicated that 92 percent of Panamanians regarded the military action as a liberation rather than an invasion.[73] Unfortunately for President Endara, however, Operation Just Cause was shortly followed by the collapse of communist governments in eastern Europe and with the end of the Sandinista government in Nicaragua, with the result that U.S. aid was modest and slow coming, leaving the country in serious economic circumstances, with an estimated 150,000 people – 30–40 percent of the population – unemployed, and the Panamanian treasury empty. Equally serious for the future was the fact that despite initial attempts to disband the National Guard and lessen its role as a political arbiter, 80 percent of the Guard became part of the reorganized post-invasion police force.[74] Noriega was gone from power, but the basic realities of Panamanian life and politics had altered little.

Narcotics and national security

The Panamanian situation with Manuel Noriega in the 1980s underlined the close relationship that existed between international narcotics trafficking and U.S. national security. The Reagan and Bush administrations employed primarily military and police operations, concentrating on interdiction of narcotics traffic both in international space as well as at U.S. borders. At the same time, the United States pressured producing nations and those that were the main sources of supply – Colombia, Peru, and Bolivia – to adopt the same military strategy preferred by U.S. officials. This approach was controversial not only abroad, where traditional military forces, priding themselves on their traditional national defence roles, were reticent to become involved in what they considered a police issue, but also domestically in the United States. There the debate centred on the comparative value of a military approach versus increased funding for and attention to drug education and the eradication of the social and economic ills within the country that increased the demand for cocaine, heroin, and marijuana.

The international dimensions of the debate were especially evident in U.S.–Colombian relations in the 1980s. President Carter sent Drug Enforcement Agency officials to Bogotá in 1978 in what administration officials touted as a new initiative on narcotics, and both the U.S. and Colombia during the next several years increased their efforts to control international trafficking. In his inaugural address to Colombians in August 1978, President Gabriel Turbay pledged co-operation with the United States, although he stressed that success depended on U.S. financial support and efforts to control consumption within the United States. Colombia already had a bilateral narcotics control agreement with the United States dating from 1961 and proceeded to conclude similar undertakings with neighbouring Venezuela, Ecuador, and Peru. In 1979 Colombian and American officials began working on a bilateral extradition treaty that would remain controversial in Colombian politics for the remainder of the decade.[75]

U.S. funding for and preoccupation with drug-control activities increased in the course of the 1980s, especially because of ties between the Medellín cartel and the guerrilla movement within Colombia (the Narc–FARC connection identified by U.S. Ambassador Tambs during the Reagan administration), but also because of demonstrated linkages with Nicaragua, Panama, and Cuba. Other than attempting to prevent drug-laundered monies from reaching the hands of guerrilla insurgents in Central America and the Caribbean, U.S. officials concentrated on interdiction, crop eradication, military, police and judicial training programmes, all of which put only a minor dent in the international traffic. In spite of the stepped-up security and other programmes, including the capture and death or incarceration of major drug cartel leaders, the amount of increasingly inexpensive cocaine reaching North American consumers showed no sign of abating.

The Latin American drug producing and exporting countries were slow to accept responsibility for the traffic and even slower to accept that the narcotics were having a devastating impact on their own social and political situations, but this gradually changed in the course of the decade as they committed more energy and resources to narcotics control. In the United States, Congress sought to move slightly away from the purely military approach of the Reagan administration. In 1988, Congress passed an Omnibus Drug Act, which highlighted the internal impact of drug use in the United States by increasing federal funding for education and health programmes.[76] The Bush administration, however, remained largely faithful to the Reagan approach, with its emphasis on interdiction and crop destruction in the Andean region, although the administration also recognized the necessity of providing incentive and support for peasants to develop alternative crops to the highly lucrative coca production.

For Colombia, the narcotics issue reached crisis proportions in mid-1989 during the lead-up to presidential elections, with the assassination of three presidential candidates and uncontrolled intimidation of both candidates and voters. The result was a massive military and police action in an effort to bring the cartels under control. There were widespread arrests, confiscation of property of known traffickers, and efforts to destroy coca processing plants. Although partially successful, the war on the cartels spawned a significant increase in violence, as the cartels, with their substantial wealth and modern weapons, retaliated against government forces. Gradually, in a desperate effort to restore peace, the government and the cartels returned to an uneasy truce.

In February 1990, the Presidents of Colombia, Peru, and Bolivia met with George Bush at the historic walled city of Cartagena on Colombia's coast to discuss the narcotics situation. The conference came close to failing before it began. Alan Garcia of Peru was incensed both because of the U.S. invasion of Panama in December 1989 and the Bush administration's deployment of an aircraft carrier battle group off the Colombian coast to interdict drug shipments. With the battle group withdrawn to Florida, the Cartagena meeting proceeded. There was reason to hail the meeting as a success. In a joint communiqué, the four presidents announced the formation of the "anti-drug cartel," and Bush committed the administration to a five-year, multibillion dollar assistance programme that mixed military support with vital economic assistance. The Latin American presidents successfully pressed their case that military interdiction was only a holding action, that it was essential to strike at the heart of the problem by altering the economic balance in the area through expanded trade opportunities and support for alternative crops. Bush responded well. A few months after the Cartagena accord, the administration unilaterally dropped U.S. import barriers on a lengthy list of commodities identified by his colleagues at Cartagena.[77] Narcotics trafficking was not under control, but the major parties had reached a new level of cooperation and appeared to be moving in a constructive direction.

Dominican Republic

Volatile as Dominican politics remained in the course of the 1980s, it avoided the instability that had contributed to the Johnson administration's military intervention in 1965. The decade began auspiciously, with President Guzmán's announcement in mid-1981 that, unlike his ambitious predecessors, Trujillo and Balaguer, he would be a one-term president and would not seek re-election the following year. Salvador Jorge Blanco became the candidate who supported Guzmán's policies during the 1982 presidential elections and emerged victorious following a brief campaign against Joaquin Balaguer.

Jorge Blanco's term (1982–6) coincided with serious economic problems, as the prices of sugar, nickel, and tobacco – three important export commodities – tumbled on world markets. Large numbers of Dominicans became boat-people who tried to sail to Puerto Rico and, often, make their way from there to the United States. In April 1984, dozens of people died, scores suffered injury, and hundreds faced arrest as a result of riots to protest government orders to triple the price of all imported goods. Police intensified their security precautions, arresting individuals and closing radio and television stations. The Blanco administration found itself caught between the International Monetary Fund, which demanded further austerity measures, and the Dominican population, which threatened further violence. Slowly the government conceded what the IMF wanted; more violence ensued and tension remained high. This situation continued through 1985, when the International League for Human Rights and the Dominican Committee on Human Rights critically reported to the United Nations on the human rights record of Jorge Blanco and his associates. Finally, when the next presidential election took place 16 May 1986, the electorate turned once again to Joaquin Balaguer over Jacobo Majluta of Jorge Blanco's Dominican Revolutionary Party. Juan Bosch, who also attempted a comeback, badly trailed the two leaders.[78] When Balaguer assumed office 16 August 1986, he appointed Donald Reid Cabral – who had replaced the ousted Bosch and served as President from 1963 to 1965 – as his Foreign Minister. Dominicans were reaching into the past to what seemed, with benefit of distance, a happier era.

In order to attract foreign investment and stimulate employment, the Dominican government established export free zones, where investors receive exemption from taxes and certain other Dominican laws. Almost all the goods produced in the zones are exported, and exports to the United States more than tripled during the first three years of Balaguer's restored presidency: from $205 million in 1985 (Jorge's last full year) to $692 million in 1989.[79] Exports included clothing, electrical supplies, leather products, and industry-related commodities. President Reagan's Caribbean Basin Initiative encouraged such commerce. At the same time, tourism soared, from 67,000 tourists in 1970 to more than 1 million in 1989,[80] and the Balaguer government successfully sought investment from and promoted trade with Japan, Germany, Spain, Brazil, and Argentina. As the twentieth century ends, Spain has become the Dominican Republic's second largest trading partner, behind the Netherlands, and the United States, by far the most significant. Puerto Rico, once a sister colony of Spain, is the fourth largest partner.[81] Venezuela and Mexico supply oil. Unemployment, inflation, and debt remain major problems because of the high birthrate.[82]

It would appear that since Balaguer recaptured the presidency in 1986, the cause of Dominican democracy has suffered. Commenting on the election of 1990, the U.S. State Department noted that Balaguer, the purported winner, had "little more than one-third of the vote in what was essentially a four-way race." There were, however, "unproven allegations that fraud had occurred."[83] When Balaguer claimed yet another victory after the election of 1994, President Bill Clinton's State Department was even more critical, expressing disappointment with the process and raising concerns about the evidence of continuing violations of human and civil rights.[84] Two observers of the modern Dominican Republic, Howard J. Wiarda and Michael J. Kryzanek, indicate that Dominican treatment of migrant Haitian sugar workers remains abominable.[85]

Notwithstanding the poor Dominican human rights record, the Reagan administration found President Balaguer a useful ally in its anti-communist crusades. In meetings with Reagan administration officials in Washington, Balaguer reminded his hosts that the Dominican Republic had no diplomatic relations with Castro. President Reagan thanked him for hosting "the first two rounds of peace talks between the government of Nicaragua and the freedom fighters." President Reagan also thanked Balaguer for his "very early opposition" to Panamanian dictator Manuel Noriega.[86] However, the administrations of Presidents Ronald Reagan and George Bush slashed aid to the Dominican Republic, from $104 million in 1987 to $24 million in 1990.[87] Good deeds were not enough in an era when the communist threat was disappearing.

Terrorism in Trinidad and Tobago

Until 1990, Trinidad's foreign relations were dull in comparison with those of many less fortunate societies. Dr. Eric Williams, Prime Minister of Trinidad and Tobago from 1956 until his death in 1981, and his government were cautious, non-provocative, and constructive in their dealings with other countries. If there is any criticism, it is that they and the successor government led from 1981 to 1986 by George Chambers, also of the Peoples's National Movement (PNM), maintained such a low international profile that they were ineffective. In the 1986 elections, the National Alliance for Reconstruction (NAR) led by A. N. R. Robinson defeated the PNM and formed the government. One area of continuity was that of Cuban policy. Williams' successors maintained their relations with Cuba.[88] Sahadeo Basdeo, Minister of External Affairs in the Robinson cabinet from 1988 to 1991, has noted Cuba's economic plight in the post-Cold War environment and urged a normalization of relations between the United States and Cuba in the interest of all parties. In his view, an end to the embargo would increase the probability of a peaceful transition from communist to post-communist rule.[89]

In 1990, however, the overly complacent Robinson government found itself the target of Libyan-backed subversion. For five days and nights, Libyan-assisted terrorists held members of Prime Minister Robinson's cabinet at gunpoint in the Red House, the centre of government activity in Port of Spain.

In 1990, an estimated 6 percent of the people of Trinidad and Tobago were Muslim. Most Muslims were descendants of labourers recruited in India between 1845 and 1917 to work as labourers on the sugar estates. Trinidad's East Indian community (about 40 percent of the total population) was overwhelmingly Hindu, although it also included some Christians, many of them products of a Canadian Presbyterian (later United Church of Canada) missionary effort. Trinidadians of African extraction – who constituted most of the balance of the nation's population – were overwhelmingly Christian. However, some 300 dissidents, the Jamaat al-Muslimeen (Society of Muslims), had registered their dissatisfaction with western values by converting to Islam. Colonel Qaddafi's Libyans gave encouragement and lessons on subversion to the Muslimeen;[90] the Muslimeen, in turn, had minimal contact with other East Indians Muslims, let alone the Hindus and Christians.

Authorities in both Trinidad and the United States ignored the danger signals. Allies of the terrorists purchased an arsenal and stored the weapons in a Miami warehouse before transhipment to Trinidad and Tobago. U.S. authorities knew what the arms suppliers were doing but chose to take no action. Anthony Maingot observes that U.S. authorities in Miami recorded the purchase of the weapons by individuals using their real names; the goods were even shipped openly and directly to Jamaat al-Muslimeen headquarters in Port of Spain, a location that had been under "surveillance" by the Trinidad Special Branch since 1986.[91] Only after the crisis had passed did American authorities provide the Robinson government with the documentation on the Miami transfers.

For some time before the action of 27 July 1990, Muslimeen had been travelling between Trinidad and Libya via Rome, but although cabinet ministers were aware of these trips, the government of Trinidad and Tobago had not tried to stop them. For seven years, newspaper reports that the Libyan government was giving money to the Muslimeen and their arms suppliers had been so persistent that Scotland Yard offered to give Trinidad assistance with counter-intelligence.[92]

With such lax security measures, it was not surprising that the Muslimeen should have scored a rapid initial success when they struck. Heavily armed Muslimeen invaded the Red House, seized the government-owned television station, and attacked police headquarters, killing an estimated twenty-two people. They also shot Prime Minister Robinson in the legs. Their leader, Imam Yasin Abu Bakr, demanded Robinson's immediate resignation, formation of a new coalition interim government which must include the Imam, nation-wide elections within ninety days (they were not due until 1991), and an amnesty for all the Muslimeen terrorists.

Fortunately, some key members of the cabinet were out of the Red House at the time, and the armed forces remained loyal to the elected government. However, while the army focused its attention on the Red House, looting and shooting erupted elsewhere, and in the process, more people died. Estimates indicate some thirty to fifty fatalities, none of them cabinet ministers but one a Member of Parliament, as a result of the coup and the subsequent rioting.[93]

Those cabinet ministers not in captivity proclaimed a curfew and joined Deputy Prime Minister and Finance Minister Winston Dookeran, whom the terrorists had released to conduct negotiations, at Port of Spain's Hilton Hotel. Although the U.S. Ambassador, Charles J. A. Gargano, felt obliged to deny that any American experts in terrorist management had gone to Trinidad,[94] the CIA sent advisers to Port of Spain, where they assisted Dookeran. The CIA quickly installed listening devices and cameras so that the people at the Hilton knew which terrorists and which captives were in each room at the Red House and what they were saying to each other. Throughout the crisis the CIA urged a firm stand. Meanwhile, Venezuela's armed forces prepared for an invasion of Trinidad in the event that the ministers at the Hilton should lose control. There was no way that Caracas would accept a Libyan outpost only a few kilometres from Venezuela's shores.

The surrender took place the morning of 31 July, but the cabinet was not able to thank the CIA agents for their assistance. They had vanished, their rooms tidied as though they had never been there. Despite the havoc the terrorists had wreaked, courts subsequently released the Muslimeen – in large measure, it would appear, because judges were afraid of reprisals.

PNM Prime Minister Patrick Manning, elected in 1991, and his successor, Basdeo Panday of the United National Congress (UNC), an ethnic Indian party which headed a coalition government after the Trinidad and Tobago election of 1995, were highly co-operative with U.S. authorities on a range of issues of importance to both countries, in particular narcotics traffic. With the consent and support of Trinidadian authorities, the U.S. Drug Enforcement Agency has systematically sprayed marijuana crops.[95] Indicative of the degree of co-operation that evolved between the two countries when the Secretary of State,

Warren Christopher, toured parts of Latin America in 1996, Trinidad was the only Commonwealth Caribbean country on his itinerary.[96]

Haiti

As suggested in the previous chapter, the official papal visit to Haiti in March 1983 by John Paul II marked a critical turning point in the political fortunes of Jean-Claude Duvalier and in Haitian history. Speaking in Creole at François Duvalier International Airport to a crowd estimated at "hundreds of thousands," Pope John Paul articulated his social and political views:

> There must be a better distribution of goods, a fairer organization of society, with more popular participation, a more disinterested conception of service on the part of those who direct society.
>
> I appeal to all those who dispose of power, of riches, of culture, to understand their urgent responsibility towards all their brothers and sisters.[97]

In a society that took its religion and the Pope seriously, the Duvalier regime never recovered from the Pope's thinly veiled condemnation of its practices. Following the papal visit, the Roman Catholic Church's radio station, Radio Soleil, broadcast editorials critical of the Duvalier government. Clergy in their pulpits, many of them foreigners, were outspoken notwithstanding threats and actual violence against them by the Tonton-Macoutes.[98] With such external support, however, the local populace became emboldened. In 1985, Jean-Claude arranged a referendum to confirm himself as president-for-life, but more than 90 percent of the eligible electorate refused to cast a ballot. The result among those who did vote (99.98 percent affirmative) further destroyed Jean-Claude's credibility. Disgusted by his incompetence and irresponsibility, even the Haitian military and bureaucracy abandoned him.

By February 1986, Jean-Claude realized that he had a choice between the presidency or his life. Jamaican Prime Minister Edward Seaga, highly regarded by the Reagan administration, dispatched a cabinet minister to persuade him to take the second option. The Jamaican Social Security Minister, who had known Michele Duvalier and her sister, warned of the consequences at home and abroad should he try to suppress dissatisfaction with force. The U.S. Air Force then provided an aircraft stationed at Guantánamo Bay in Cuba to fly Duvalier and his entourage to exile in the south of France. The Duvalier era had ended.[99]

Following the departure of Duvalier there was an ongoing triangular struggle among the Haitian military, the Tonton-Macoutes, and the Haitian people. The Tonton-Macoutes could not regain power, but like such other paramilitary groups as the Irish Republican Army (IRA) and the Basque nationalist organization ETA, they could make life uncomfortable for everyone else.

The immediate successor to Jean-Claude Duvalier was General Henri Namphy. His provisional government took certain steps to strengthen its popularity. It replaced the black and red Duvalier flag with Haiti's traditional blue and red one. It proposed a constitution that would adopt Creole as an official language, equal to French. There was a constitutional guarantee that even if the U.S. Navy were to leave Guantánamo Bay, a new base at Môle St. Nicolas would not be available. Article 291 of the proposed new constitution barred criminal associates of the Duvaliers from political office for ten years. Namphy was supposed to arrange democratic elections as quickly as possible, and the constitution provided for an Electoral Council to guarantee their integrity. Those choosing the electoral council's nine members included, among others, the Roman Catholic Church, the Protestant Churches, the Supreme Court, the Association of Journalists, the university and the business communities. On 29 March 1987, more than 1 million Haitians voted 99.98 percent in favour of the new constitution.[100]

Despite this promising start, there were serious problems. General Namphy liked being president and did not want to step down. Potential candidates lacked party organizations or name recognition across the country, and there were too many of them. Duvalierists ran despite Article 291. Law and order collapsed, and there was no safety for life or property. Former President Carter came to Haiti and praised members of the electoral council as "dedicated and courageous men,"[101] but on 24 November 1987, five days before voting day, the Namphy government abolished the Electoral Council. Later he told a foreign diplomat, "[There is] only one [voter in Haiti]. The army. Ha ha."[102] When the Tonton-Macoutes killed thirty-three people waiting to vote plus a Dominican journalist and shot hundreds of others, the army cancelled the election on what became known as Bloody Sunday, 29 November. The Reagan administration cancelled most government-to-government aid.

Nor did the next attempt to hold elections, scheduled for 17 January 1988, proceed smoothly. This time the army organized the elections without assistance from the Electoral Council. The four leading candidates withdrew from the race and urged others to do likewise. Not all did. On voting day (a Sunday), the Roman Catholic Church cancelled mass and urged the faithful not to leave home for any reason. An estimated 15 percent of the eligible voters cast votes, 50.3 percent of which went for Leslie Manigat.[103] Manigat had spent most of the Duvalier years in exile, teaching for a short time at Yale University.[104] Manigat had the army's support, and General Namphy stepped down on 7 February.

Within months, Manigat and the army quarrelled, and on 19 June, the army ousted Manigat and restored General Namphy to the presidency. Manigat went into exile in the United States. However, without overseas support, General Namphy could not govern. The economy simply ground to a halt. There was a critical shortage of consumer goods, and government employees went without salaries. In September, it was General Namphy's turn to go into exile, and he went to the Dominican Republic. His successor, Brigadier-General Prosper Avril, survived major challenges until March 1990 when, with the help of U.S.

Ambassador Alvin Adams, he managed to escape to the United States. His successor was a civilian and a woman, Ertha Pascal Trouillot, whose task it was to disarm the Tonton-Macoutes and to hold credible elections.

Haiti's forty-third President fulfilled her mandate; on 16 December 1990, Haitian voters held what was unquestionably a fair and free election. The winner was a rather insubordinate Roman Catholic priest, Jean-Bertrand Aristide, inaugurated 7 January 1991. He accused his superior, Archbishop Ligonde, of collaboration not only with the Duvaliers but also with the Tonton-Macoutes, but in turn his superior found him too outspoken and controversial.[105] He was critical of John Paul II for doing too little too late to help the Haitian people.[106] He believed that Ronald Reagan considered him a communist, although by the time Aristide won the presidency, Bush was in the White House.[107] Although certainly no communist, there is little doubt that Aristide distrusted both France and the United States.[108]

However, Aristide's presidency did not last. In September 1991, the army removed him in a *coup d'état*, and at the time U.S. officials shed no tears at his departure. Among those hostile to Aristide was U.S. Republican Senator Jesse Helms, chairman of the Senate Foreign Relations Committee as of January 1995. Many Republicans favoured democratic elections in principle but thought that the Haitians had made a grievous error in 1990. On 3 July 1993, a representative of the military government and President Aristide met on Governors Island, New York, and signed an accord to allow the President to complete his term. Shortly thereafter, the army reneged on the arrangement.

Nevertheless, time proved to be on Aristide's side. The Soviet Union disintegrated in 1991, and the Cold War came to an end. No longer was there the slightest reason for western democracies to support anti-communist dictatorships, and dictatorships, whether in Haiti or in black Africa, became vulnerable as never before. If they wanted foreign aid at a time when investors from Japan, western Europe, and the United States had new opportunities in post-communist eastern Europe, they had to allow – and respect the results of – elections. There was a long and loud demand in western democracies that President Aristide be allowed to complete his term.

There were other factors as well. Both the OAS and the UN imposed economic sanctions against Haiti. Haiti's military tyrants governed their impoverished subjects in a most brutal manner, and the U.S. State Department indicted the human rights record of the military government. In the course of 1993 the political situation continued to deteriorate. In February, more than 200 UN and OAS human rights observers were deployed throughout the country, only to be withdrawn in October because of constant threats against their safety. That same month, Justice Minister Guy Malary was murdered in the centre of Port-au-Prince, for which the State Department blamed the Haitian military. The State Department report noted that the military government disregarded constitutional limits on its authority, made arbitrary arrests – especially of outspoken clergy, failed to protect children from those who would exploit their labour, devoted next to nothing from the national budget to health services, and eliminated collective bargaining. "Wages are generally set unilaterally by employers," said the State Department. "The majority of Haitians, who work in the agricultural sector, must survive on considerably less than the minimum wage. . . . Labor Code provisions on health and safety are not enforced."[109]

Haitians, in turn, fled in overcrowded make-shift boats to the United States, many drowning in the attempt. The Bush administration returned those who survived to Haiti, but during his successful 1992 campaign against President Bush, Democratic candidate Bill Clinton criticized Bush for this action. Black Americans voted overwhelmingly for Clinton. Once elected and inaugurated, President Clinton had two choices. He could remain true to his campaign rhetoric and antagonize large numbers of white Americans by allowing unlimited numbers of Haitians access to the United States; or, he could betray those who had supported him, and return the boat-people to Haiti. To end government by the military tyrants and restore President Aristide was more expedient. Canadian Prime Minister Brian Mulroney knew that Haitian exiles were an increasing part of the electorate in Quebec, and that it was politically expedient to end military rule there and restore President Aristide. To help the cause of Haitian democracy, Mulroney offered the services of the Royal Canadian Mounted Police to train a new type of Haitian police force.

The Haitian military proved intransigent. Despite the pleas of the U.S., Canadian, and other governments, it remained determinedly in office. Economic sanctions proved ineffective, in part because the Haitian elite could purchase what it wanted from the other side of the border in the Dominican Republic.[110] Finally, in October 1994, President Clinton had had enough. He sent his Democratic predecessor, former President Jimmy Carter, back to Haiti with a message to that country's military rulers, led by Lieutenant-General Raoul Cedras. Unless they went into exile, U.S. Marines would invade Haiti and restore President Aristide. Cedras and his military colleagues yielded, and President Aristide returned to the presidential palace, but only under the protection of a U.S.-led and dominated international peacekeeping force. The twentieth century for Haitians ended as it began, with foreign troops propping up a fragile political democracy in the most impoverished nation in the region.

Conclusion

The 1980s witnessed the most dramatic challenges and conflicts in the Caribbean basin in the twentieth century. The significance of the events in the region derived primarily from the level of superpower involvement in the region, the highest it had been since the Cuban Missile Crisis in 1962. But the tensions of the 1980s were much broader than the missile crisis had been. The regional demands for more significant social, economic and political change had finally boiled over into revolution. A successful revolution by Marxist guerrillas in Nicaragua in 1979 touched off a decade of regional conflict, in which the Nicaraguan situation also increased the fighting between insurgents and government forces in El Salvador and Guatemala. In the insular Caribbean, the New Jewel Movement in Grenada, with its ties to Castro's Cuba, combined with political instability on the island to provide the Reagan administration with justification for the first U.S. military intervention in the region in twenty years, although only the first of the decade, with the Panama invasion taking place only a few years later.

War, revolution, "freedom fighters," Contras, military intervention, drug wars, large-scale human migration as refugees were driven by war and poverty from their homelands, and the "lost decade" economically for Latin American nations as they sought to come to terms with the debt crisis – these were the main themes and challenges of the decade. Yet, above all in the regional conflict, what will remain the most significant historical development of the decade was the end of the Cold War between east and west and the opportunity that provided for a new regional reconciliation. By the beginning of the 1990s, only Cuba remained beyond the pale, isolated and embargoed by the United States and the OAS in a counter-productive U.S. policy based as much on domestic politics and historical spite as on considerations of realpolitik.

EPILOGUE

In late 1994, this author (Randall) chaired three series of symposia in the Caribbean, Central and South America organized by the Canadian International Development Agency (CIDA). Significantly, countries such as Colombia were incorporated into the South American rather than Caribbean segments of the meetings, reflective of the external perception that they belong more to the continent than to their Caribbean brethren. The participants, other than CIDA officials, included a number of prominent political, business, cultural and academic figures from the region. The objectives of those meetings were varied: to listen to the range of ideas held by the participants on the main challenges, problems and opportunities confronting their countries and regions at that moment and in the coming decades; to explore with them the most likely and viable directions in development, political and social policies; and to provide CIDA with clearer insights into the most effective development policies into which it could direct increasingly scarce development dollars.[1]

At the time these sessions took place, the Cold War was considered over; Nicaragua, El Salvador and Guatemala had emerged from civil wars and a high degree of foreign intervention; Panama had recovered from the 1989 U.S. military intervention to remove strongman Manuel Noriega from power; Haiti was still in the throes of considerable turmoil surrounding the efforts to remove the military from power and return Jean-Bertrand Aristide to the presidential office; Cuba had been cut adrift from the Soviet bloc and was struggling with deepening economic crisis; and the North American Free Trade Agreement had been in place for almost a year, and there were concerns, especially among the smaller nations in the Caribbean, about the potential impact on Central America and the Caribbean of Mexico's northern turn – the Salinas opening to the North.

Although the participants in the sessions held in the Caribbean and Central America articulated anticipated differences on a range of social, economic and political issues, what was equally striking and perhaps more significant was the degree of consensus that also existed.

In the political area, there was general agreement that the role of the state remained important but that significant reforms were required to deepen participatory democracy, particularly in still problematic regimes such as Cuba,

174

Haiti, the Dominican Republic, Guatemala and El Salvador. All participants perceived that meaningful political participation by a wider range of citizens would be difficult if not impossible to achieve without substantial economic progress and a greater degree of democratization of economic power. There was also widespread concerns that there was a deepening crisis of faith in the efficacy of democratic government, as much as it might be the desirable system, because of its perceived failure to bring about meaningful social, economic and political reforms. Several of the participants believed that problems of governance had significantly increased rather than improved in recent years; in some instances individuals argued that their societies were effectively ungovernable given the lack of basic consensus and shared values. Political confrontation, criminal violence and lawlessness were more characteristic, they argued, of their systems than civil society. Many Caribbean though less so Central American and South American participants referred to the "Africanization" of their societies, by which they meant continued massive levels of poverty, marginalization of their economies from the mainstream international system, and especially the disintegration of central civil authority, which they identified as characteristic of the situations in Somalia and Rwanda. Unless widespread poverty was alleviated, educational levels for the average citizen significantly advanced, health conditions advanced for all, substantial levels of wealth redistributed through effective tax systems, the rights of labour protected, military forces restrained especially in their internal security role, and government corruption curtailed there was little optimism that a true civil society could be achieved. For many of the countries represented, in particular but not exclusively those that had experienced recent civil wars, the problem of out-migration received considerable attention. Such migrations not only reflected the uprooting of civil wars but also was a natural response to the lack of adequate employment opportunities within the region. There was also general agreement that a strong, independent judiciary was essential to attain political and social justice; law had to be placed about privilege and powerful interest groups in the civilian and military sectors. The main objective of the political system, therefore, had to be the establishment of social solidarity, the clear identification of a common purpose of governance in the societies.

Except for the Cuban participants, there was a surprisingly high degree of agreement that a neo-liberal free market model of development was more likely to produce economic development than a highly statist one, although without exception participants suggested that the neo-liberal model tended to exacerbate rather than eliminate problems of social and economic equity. It was noted that with the exceptions of Cuba and Haiti, the current development model was a kind of "imperfectly understood" neo-liberalism imported from the developed world and urged on the region by the international funding agencies. Even those who continued to adhere to a more statist model conceded the need for a reduction in government spending, fiscal restraint, and more balance between the responsibilities assumed by the state and the private sector. As one analyst from a Caribbean island nation suggested, the private sector has to become the engine of growth in real terms, not simply in speeches designed to impress multinational funding agencies which advocate market-led-growth; as well, privatization initiatives need to become more than convenient means to balance the current account, but rather genuine attempts to motivate the private sector and stimulate economic development. The same participant was unequivocal in criticism of the unthinking role of both the state and its citizens: "The spirit of self-reliance is being systematically destroyed as we keep looking for fairy godmothers and godfathers to hold our hands and lead us to the promised land."

The same individual nonetheless contended that the state continued to have an important function. Government intervention in the economy was essential to maintain an open, competitive, investment-friendly economy, to maintain low interest rates, to encourage higher levels of domestic savings and channel those savings into productive investments, and to improve the quality and availability of public education in ways that would expand the skilled labour force and reduce unemployment. Clearly the notion of redefining the role of government and its relationship with the private sector was at the heart of this reformist vision.

Participants viewed as essential the opening of markets to foreign trade and investment, fuller integration into the world system, and closer ties to the major capitalist nations, although there was even more adamant consensus that a means had to be found to achieve a higher degree of social and economic equity under a free market system and to avoid the worst pitfalls of overly rapid structural adjustment. At the same time, participants commented on the difficulties of over-coming high levels of foreign debt, widespread poverty, with many individuals entirely outside the national and international economy, inflation, external dependency, and problems associated with attempting to attract meaningful foreign investment. One participant noted succinctly that major obstacles to development included "human resources which are inadequate in training levels and under intense pressures to migrate; poverty, joblessness, underemployment and the social exclusion of large layers of the population."

Participants were also concerned about the capacity of the region to transcend its historical past, to move beyond economies that were still tied to their colonial roots of plantation/ranching monoculture, export orientation, extractive, low value-added industries, a weak capacity of domestic consumption and saving, environmental degradation, the challenge to social order posed by international narcotics traffic, and racially based class structures with little social or economic mobility. Realistic appraisals of the future were dominant, with general recognition of the obstacles hindering domestic political and economic reform as well as the formation of regional alliances considered essential to participate more effectively in the international economy, the difficulties of a region divided by history, language, varying levels of economic and political maturity, and further hindered by their lengthy colonial heritage.

The challenges that face the region as it enters the twenty-first century are only slight variations on the dilemmas of the past century; they are not unique in either kind or magnitude. The nations of the Caribbean basin are not, of course, uniformly vulnerable to international trends nor equally incapable of shaping their own destinies. Colombia, Mexico, and Venezuela are in an entirely different category from the smaller nations of the eastern Caribbean, and Cuba for the moment at least retains its unique position in the area, and Haiti retains the distinction of being one of the hemisphere's poorest nations. This volume has suggested that the peoples of those nations whose shores are washed by the Caribbean Sea have had a common heritage and a shared future; but it is also critical to recognize that it is in many ways their divergence that has most accurately characterized the area.

NOTES

INTRODUCTION

1 Bruce B. Solnick, *The West Indies and Central America to 1898* (New York: Knopf, 1970), p. ix.
2 William G. Demas, "Foreword," in Richard Millett and W. Marvin Will (eds) *The Restless Caribbean: Changing Patterns of International Relations* (New York: Praeger, 1979), pp. vii–xvii.
3 Solnick, *West Indies*, p. ix.
4 Immanuel Wallerstein, *The Modern World-System* (New York: Academic Press, 1974); *The Capitalist World-Economy* (Cambridge: Cambridge University Press, 1979); and with Terence K. Hopkins, *World Systems Analysis: Theory and Methodology* (Beverly Hills, CA: Sage, 1982).
5 Among the many brilliant contributions by Trinidad-born V. S. Naipaul to our appreciation for and understanding of the region, the authors have found several especially illuminating: *The Middle Passage* (1962), which interweaves the history of British, French and Dutch in the West Indies and South America; *The Loss of El Dorado* (1969), which takes as its point of departure the false hopes occasioned by the quest for gold in the New World; *The Mimic Men* (1967), the fictional auto-biography of Ralph Singh, an exiled Caribbean island colonial minister.

1 THE LEGACY OF EMPIRES

1 An excellent overview of the colonial wars of the period may be found in Jan Rogozinski, *A Brief History of the Caribbean* (New York: Meridian, 1992). See also the bibliography in that volume.
2 On the British West Indies, see Michael Craton, *Testing the Chains* (Ithaca, NY: Cornell University Press, 1982); for imperialism and the Caribbean in general see Franklin Knight, *The Caribbean: The Genesis of a Fragmented Nationalism*, 2nd edn (New York: Oxford University Press, 1990).
3 Rogozinski, *Brief History*, pp. 153-7.
4 Rogozinski, *Brief History*, p. 162.
5 The classic account is by C. L. R. James, *The Black Jacobins: Toussaint L'Ouverture and the San Domingue Revolution*, 2nd edn (New York: Vintage, 1963).
6 See Knight, *The Caribbean*, pp. 112–13; Philip Curtin, *The Atlantic Slave Trade: A Census* (Madison, WI: University of Wisconsin Press, 1969).
7 Rogozinski, *Brief History*, pp. 182–4.
8 William Green, *British Slave Emancipation: The Sugar Colonies and the Great Experiment, 1830–1965* (Oxford: Clarendon Press, 1965).

9 Rogozinski, *Brief History*, p. 186; Knight, *The Caribbean*, p. 185.
10 Franklin, *The Caribbean*, p. 185; Francisco Scarano, "Labor and Society in the Nineteenth Century," in Franklin Knight and Colin A. Palmer (eds) *The Modern Caribbean* (Chapel Hill, NC, and London: University of North Carolina Press, 1989), pp. 51–84.
11 Of the many important works on this theme, see Michael Hunt, *Ideology and U.S. Foreign Policy* (New Haven, CT: Yale University Press, 1987); Edward M. Burns, *The American Idea of Mission* (New Brunswick, NJ: Rutgers, University Press, 1957).
12 The New Grenada (Colombia)–United States relationship is detailed in S. J. Randall, *Colombia and the United States: Hegemony and Interdependence* (Athens, GA: University of Georgia Press, 1992), pp. 31–5.
13 Quoted in H. C. Allen, *Great Britain and the United States* (New York: St. Martin's Press, 1955), p. 423. See also Kenneth Bourne, *The Foreign Policy of Victorian England, 1830–1902* (Oxford: Clarendon Press, 1970).
14 For the principle of no-transfer see John Quincy Adams to Hugh Nelson, 28 April 1823, *Writings of John Quincy Adams*, vol. 7: 370–81.
15 For *De Bow's Review* and discussion of Southern expansionism see Robert E. May, *The Southern Dream of a Caribbean Empire, 1854–1861* (Baton Rouge, LA: Louisiana State University Press, 1974); the De Bow reference is from Robert F. Durden, "J. D. B. De Bow: Convolutions of a Slavery Expansionist," *Journal of Southern History* 17 (Nov. 1951), p. 450.
16 Thomas G. Paterson, J. Garry Clifford and Kenneth J. Hagan, *American Foreign Policy: A History to 1914*, 2nd edn (Lexington, MA and Toronto: D. C. Heath; 1983), p. 131.
17 On Walker's ill-fated activities, see May, *Southern Dream*, pp. 77–130 *passim*.
18 On Everett, see Samuel Flagg Bemis, *American Secretaries of State and their Diplomacy*, vol. 6 (New York: Cooper Square, 1963).
19 Bruce B. Solnick, *The West Indies and Central America to 1898* (New York: Knopf, 1970), pp. 188–9.

2 HEGEMONY IN TRANSITION: THE EMERGENCE OF THE UNITED STATES, 1890–1917

1 See for instance the reports of the commanders of the *Geier* and the *Vineta* in 1900 as they made ports of call in Colón, Cartagena (to report on the Colombian civil war), Baranquilla, Curaçao, Caracas. Record Group (RG) 242, Series T-149, microfilm rolls 290, 291, National Archives of the United States (NAUS). On Germany, see Holger Herwig, *Germany's Visions of Empire in Venezuela, 1871–1914* (Princeton, NJ: Princeton University Press, 1986).
2 B. C. Richardson, *The Caribbean in the Wider World, 1492–1992: A Regional Geography* (Cambridge and New York: Cambridge University Press, 1992), p. 79.
3 The evolution of Cuban politics is ably outlined by Ramón Eduardo Ruíz, *Cuba: The Making of a Revolution* (New York: Norton, 1968). David Trask traces the history of the war itself in *The War With Spain in 1898* (New York: Macmillan, 1981).
4 Alexander E. Campbell, *Great Britain and the United States, 1895–1903* (London: Longman, 1960), p. 31.
5 The best treatment of the occupation is David F. Healy, *The United States in Cuba, 1898–1902* (Madison, WI: University of Wisconsin Press, 1963).
6 Juan Angel Silén, *Hacía una visión positiva del Puertorriqueño* (Rio Piedras: Editorial Edil, 1970), p. 89.
7 Among sources which describe the transition from Spanish to U.S. rule and the evolution of the Foraker Act see Edward J. Berbusse, *The United States in Puerto*

Rico, 1898–1900 (Chapel Hill, NC: University of North Carolina Press, 1967); Lyman J. Gould, *La Ley Foraker: raices de la política colonial de los Estados Unidos* (Barcelona: Editorial Universitaria, Universidad de Puerto Rico, 1975); Carmen I. Raffucci de Garcia, *El gobierno civil y la Ley Foraker* (Rio Piedras: Editorial Universitaria, Universidad de Puerto Rico, 1981).

8 John Gunther, *Inside Latin America* (New York: Harper and Brothers, 1941), pp. 423–35; Rexford Tugwell, *The Stricken Land: The Story of Puerto Rico* (Garden City, NY: Doubleday, 1947). For a commentary on the thoughts of respective governors about Puerto Rico, see Truman R. Clark, "The Imperial Perspective: Mainland Administrators' Views of the Puerto Rican Economy, 1898–1941," *Revista/Review Interamericana* 4, 4 (Winter 1974), pp. 505–17.

9 E. G. Peters, commander of the *Geier*, Panama, to Wilhelm II, Berlin, 21 June 1900, and Wollheim, commander of the *Vineta*, Caribbean Sea, to Wilhelm II, 15 Nov. 1900; RG 242, T-149, roll 290, NAUS, Washington, DC. See also the report from Bacher, commander of the *Stein*, written in Colón, 1 Dec. 1901 and included in a Naval Office report issued in Berlin the following day, RG 242, T-149, roll 293, NAUS.

10 E.g. Koepke, Colón, to Auswaertiges Amt, Berlin (AA), 5 Oct. 1902, RG 242, T-149, roll 291, NAUS.

11 Wollheim to Wilhelm II, 15 Nov. 1900.

12 Bacher, commander of the *Stein*, to Wilhelm II, 1 Dec. 1901, RG 242, T-199, roll 248, NAUS. In December 1901 when the German warship *Stein* arrived in Colón, several other national vessels were already in harbour: the British cruiser, *Tribune*, the French cruiser, *Suchet*, and the American cruisers, *Machias and Mariella*.

13 Richard H. Collin, *Theodore Roosevelt's Caribbean: The Panama Canal, the Monroe Doctrine and the Latin American Context* (Baton Rouge, LA: Louisiana State University Press, 1990), pp. 555–6.

14 Herwig, *Germany's Vision of Empire*, pp. 11, 150–7. Herwig indicates that German Foreign Minister Bernhard von Bulow was less inclined toward adventurism in the Caribbean than his expansionist counterpart, Tirpitz, at Admiralty.

15 Ernesto de Jesús Castillero Reyes, *La causa immediate de la emancipación de Panama* (Panama City: Imprenta Nacional, 1933), p. 99; Dwight Miner, *The Fight for the Panama Route* (New York: Octogon, 1966), p. 326. The contemporary Bogotá press gave extensive coverage to the Senate debate; see in particular *El Colombiano*. For a broad perspective on the acquisition and construction of the Panama Canal, see David McCullough, *The Path between the Seas: The Creation of the Panama Canal, 1870–1914* (New York: Simon and Schuster, 1977).

16 Philippe Bunau-Varilla, *Panama: The Creation, the Destruction, the Resurrection* (New York: McBride, 1914). See also Bunau-Varilla's papers, which are available at the Library of Congress, Washington, DC.

17 See Michael L. Conniff, *Black Labor on a White Canal: Panama, 1904–1981* (Pittsburgh, PA: University of Pittsburgh Press, 1985), pp. 3–44.

18 The translation of the quotation from the revised Panamanian constitution comes from J. H. Parry and P. M. Sherlock, *A Short History of the West Indies* (London: Macmillan, 1965), p. 283. See also Clinton V. Black, *History of Jamaica* (London: Collins, 1961 [1958]), pp. 216–18.

19 Edwin Lieuwen, *Arms and Politics in Latin America* (New York: Praeger, 1965), p. 184.

20 William Jennings Price, U.S. Minister in Panama, to Panamanian Foreign Minister Ernesto T. Lefevre, 9 May 1916, *FRUS (Papers Relating to Foreign Relations of the United States)*, 5 Dec. 1916, p. 941.

21 Von Diederichs to Head of Admiralty, Berlin, 23 Dec. 1901, RG 242, T-149, roll 248, NAUS.

22 Herwig, *Germany's Vision of Empire*, pp. 237–8.
23 Quoted in Lester D. Langley, *The United States and the Caribbean, 1900–1970* (Athens, GA: University of Georgia Press, 1980), p. 29.
24 There is an excellent summary of the Dominican debt crisis and the Roosevelt Corollary of the Monroe Doctrine in Collin, *Theodore Roosevelt's Caribbean*, pp. 341–462. See also David H. Burton, *Theodore Roosevelt: Confident Imperialist* (Philadelphia, PA: University of Pennsylvania Press, 1968), pp. 113–20; and Robert D. Crassweller, *Trujillo: Life and Times of a Caribbean Dictator* (New York: Macmillan, 1966), p. 198.
25 On the U.S. and Mexico, see Kenneth Grieb, *The United States and Huerta* (Lincoln, NB: University of Nebraska Press, 1969); Robert Quirk, *An Affair of Honor* (Lexington, KY: University of Kentucky Press, 1962); Mark Guilderhus, *Diplomacy and Revolution* (Tucson, AZ: University of Arizona Press, 1977).
26 On Haiti, see David F. Healy, *Gunboat Diplomacy in the Wilson Era* (Madison, WI: University of Wisconsin Press, 1976); Brenda Gayle Plummer, *Haiti and the United States: The Psychological Moment* (Athens, GA: University of Georgia Press, 1992).
27 Richard Millett with G. Dale Gaddy, "Administering the Protectorates: The U.S. Occupation of Haiti and the Dominican Republic," *Revista/Review Interamericana* 6, 3 (Fall 1976), p. 395. Millett and Gaddy offer a superb summary of the occupation (pp. 392–9). See also Walter C. Soderlund, "United States Intervention in the Dominican Republic 1916 and 1965," *North/South: Canadian Journal of Latin American Studies* 2, 3–4 (1977), pp. 87–95.
28 Captain Stephen M. Fuller, USMCR, and Graham A. Cosmas, *Marines in the Dominican Republic, 1916–1924* (Washington, DC: History and Museums Division, Headquarters, U.S. Marine Corps, 1974), p. 68.
29 Fuller and Cosmas, *Marines*, p. 67.
30 Bruce J. Calder, *The Impact of Intervention: The Dominican Republic during the U.S. Occupation of 1916–1924* (Austin, TX: University of Texas Press, 1982), p. 252.
31 John Bartlow Martin, *Overtaken by Events* (Garden City, NY: Doubleday, 1966), p. 29.
32 Calder, *Impact of Intervention*, pp. 238–52.
33 Conniff, *Black Labor on a White Canal*, pp. 3–4.
34 K. O. Laurence, *Immigration into the West Indies in the Nineteenth Century* (Barbados: Caribbean Universities Press, 1971), p. 26. For more about Asian indentured labour in the Caribbean, see Walton Look Lai, *Chinese and Indian Migrants to the British West Indies, 1838–1918* (Baltimore, MD: Johns Hopkins University Press, 1993).
35 Brinsley Samaroo, "The Trinidad Workingmen's Association and the Origins of Popular Protest in a Crown Colony," *Studies in Economics and Society* 21, 2 (1972), pp. 205–22. Samaroo's account is a useful corrective to Zin Henry's over-critical account of the TWA in *Labour Relations and Industrial Conflict in Commonwealth Caribbean Countries* (Trinidad: Columbus, 1972), p. 32.
36 Francis X. Marks, "Organized Labour in British Guiana," in F. M. Andie and T. G. Mathews (eds) *The Caribbean in Transition: Papers on Social, Political, and Economic Development*, (San Juan: University of Puerto Rico, 1965), pp. 224–5.
37 Henry, *Labour Relations*, p. 33.
38 B. R. Mitchell, *International Historical Statistics: The Americas, 1750–1988*, 2nd edn (New York: Stockton Press, 1993), pp. 449–50.
39 *International Historical Statistics*, pp. 495–509.
40 *International Historical Statistics*, pp. 495–509.
41 *Annual Statistical Abstract for the United Kingdom from 1893 to 1907* (London), pp. 70–7.

42 *Annual Statistical Abstract for the United Kingdom from 1908 to 1922* (London, 1924), p. 74.
43 *Annual Statistical Abstract for the United Kingdom for each of the fifteen years 1913 and 1921 to 1934* (London: Board of Trade, 1936), pp. 350–3.
44 Data cited by Herwig, *Germany's Vision of Empire*, pp. 14–15, 29.

3 THE CONSOLIDATION OF AMERICAN POWER, 1917–45

1 Zumeta, César, "El continente enfermo," *Pensamiento Politico venezolano del siglo XIX* 14, p. 121, cited in Judith Ewell, *Venezuela and the United States* (Athens, GA: University of Georgia Press, 1996), pp. 110–11.
2 The best and most recent account of these developments is Lester Langley, *The Banana Wars: United States Intervention in the Caribbean, 1898–1934* (Lexington, KY: University Press of Kentucky, 1983).
3 Secretary of State to U.S. Ambassador, 23 April 1929, *FRUS* 1929, II, 894–6.
4 Ewell, *Venezuela*, pp. 125, 127, 132, 134, 140–1. On Venezuelan oil development, see also Stephen J. Randall, *United States Foreign Oil Policy, 1919–1948* (Montreal: McGill-Queen's, 1985), p. 70.
5 Ewell, *Venezuela*, pp. 147–8.
6 On Colombian developments, see Randall, *Foreign Oil Policy*, pp. 72–4; Randall, *The Diplomacy of Modernization: Colombian–American Relations, 1920–1940* (Toronto: University of Toronto Press, 1977); and Randall, *Colombia and the United States: Hegemony and Interdependence* (Athens, GA: University of Georgia Press, 1992).
7 Randall, *Diplomacy of Modernization*, p. 4.
8 Bryce Wood, *The Making of the Good Neighbor Policy* (New York: Columbia University Press, 1961); Irwin Gellman, *Good Neighbor Diplomacy: United States Policy in Latin America, 1933–1945* (Baltimore, MD: Johns Hopkins University Press, 1979).
9 See Richard Millett with G. Dale Gaddy, "Administering the Protectorates: The U.S. Occupation of Haiti and the Dominican Republic," *Revista/Review Interamericana* 6, 3 (Fall 1976), pp. 383–402. See also Magdaline W. Shannon, "The U.S. Commission for the Study and Review of Conditions in Haiti and its Relationship to President Hoover's Latin American Policy," *Caribbean Studies* 15, 4 (Jan. 1976), pp. 53–72.
10 Hans Schmidt, *The United States Occupation of Haiti, 1915–1934* (New Brunswick, NJ: Rutgers University Press, 1971), p. 232.
11 Yvette Gindine, "Images of the American in Haitian Literature during the Occupation, 1915–1934," *Caribbean Studies* 14, 3 (Oct. 1974), pp. 37–52.
12 Schmidt, *United States Occupation of Haiti*, pp. 233–7.
13 Brenda Gayle Plummer, *Haiti and the United States* (Athens, GA: University of Georgia Press, 1992), pp. 139–41.
14 John Bartlow Martin, *Overtaken by Events* (Garden City, NY: Doubleday, 1966), p. 29.
15 Bruce J. Calder, *The Impact of Intervention* (Austin, TX: University of Texas Press, 1982), pp. 238–52.
16 Welles' opinions on the contemporary Dominican Republic are available in *Naboth's Vineyard: The Dominican Republic, 1844–1924* (New York: Arno, reprinted 1972).
17 For details of Trujillo's rise to power, see Robert D. Crassweller, *Trujillo: Life and Times of a Caribbean Dictator* (New York: Macmillan, 1966), pp. 55–72. See also R. Michael Malek, "Rafael Leonidas Trujillo: A Revisionist Critique of his Rise to Power," *Revista/Review Interamericana* 7, 3 (Fall 1977), pp. 436–45.

18 *FRUS* (1936), 5, 412–13, 421–3. France denounced the 1930 bilateral agreement in 1936. See *British and Foreign State Papers*, vol. 133, 419.

19 *FRUS* (1936), 5, 456–7.

20 For a summary of Trujillo's achievements, see Howard J. Wiarda and Michael J. Kryzanek, "Dominican Dictatorship Revisited: The Caudillo Tradition and the Regimes of Trujillo and Balaguer," *Revista/Review Interamericana* 7, 3 (Fall 1977), pp. 417–35. See also Jan Knippers Black, *The Dominican Republic: Politics and Development in an Unsovereign State* (Boston, MA: Allen and Unwin, 1986).

21 The figures are from Hubert Herring, *A History of Latin America* (New York: Knopf, 1967), p. 443.

22 Crassweller, *Trujillo*, pp. 199–200. The Haitian government requested that the U.S., Cuba and Mexico conciliate issues arising from this dispute, under the terms of the Gondra Pact of 1923. The Gondra Treaty was supplemented by the General Convention of Inter-American Conciliation of January 1929. See *FRUS* (1929), I, 653; (1937), 5, 140n.

23 U.S. Secretary of State Cordell Hull, normally an admirer of Trujillo, pressed successfully for the Dominican government to pay compensation to Haiti for the unprovoked massacre.

24 German legation (no specific signature), Ciudad Trujillo, to Auswaertiges Amt, Berlin, 1 Feb. 1937, RG 242, T-120, roll 4357, frames K215545–K215546.

25 The best general account of the Central American situation is Walter LaFeber, *Inevitable Revolutions: The United States in Central America* (New York: Norton, 1983); Neil Macaulay, *The Sandino Affair* (Chicago: Quadrangle, 1967).

26 A splendid overview of this period in Cuban history and Cuban–U.S. relations is provided by Louis A. Pérez, Jr., *Cuba and the United States* (Athens, GA: University of Georgia Press, 1990).

27 On the events of 1933 see Luis Aguilar, *1933: Prologue to Revolution* (New York: Norton, 1972).

28 Fitz A. Baptiste, *The United States and West Indian Unrest, 1918–1939* (Mona: University of the West Indies, 1978), pp. 5–7; Bonham C. Richardson, *The Caribbean in the Wider World, 1492–1992*, (Cambridge: Cambridge University Press, 1992), p. 179.

29 Baptiste, *West Indian Unrest*, p. 7.

30 Baptiste, *West Indian Unrest*, pp. 8–11.

31 Zin Henry, *Labour Relations and Industrial Conflict in Commonwealth Caribbean Countries* (Trinidad: Columbus, 1972), pp. 19–21; Richardson, *Caribbean in the Wider World*, pp. 179–80.

32 Ewell, *Venezuela*, pp. 147–8.

33 Marks, "Organized Labour in British Guiana," pp. 224–6; Henry, *Labour Relations*, pp. 34–6.

34 Brinsley Samaroo, "The Trinidad Workingmen's Association and the Origins of Popular Protest in a Crown Colony," *Studies in Economics and Society* 21, 2 (1972), pp. 213–14; W. Richard Jacobs, "The Politics of Protest in Trinidad: The Strikes and Disturbances of 1937," *Caribbean Studies* 17, 1–2 (April–July 1977), pp. 17–18.

35 Brinsley Samaroo, "The Trinidad Labour Party and the Moyne Commission, 1938," in Blanco G. Silvestrini (ed.) *Politics, Society and Culture in the Caribbean: Selected Papers of the XIV Conference of Caribbean Historians* (San Juan: University of Puerto Rico, 1983), pp. 262–4; Sahadeo Basdeo, "The Role of the British Labour Movement in the Development of Labour Organisation in Trinidad, 1929–1938," *Social and Economic Studies*, 31, 1 (1982), pp. 42–52.

36 Basdeo, "Role of the British Labour Movement," pp. 42–8. On the Labour

government in Britain, see John Stevenson and Chris Cook, *The Slump: Society and Politics during the Depression* (London: Quartet, 1979), pp. 94–113.

37 Sahadeo Basdeo, "Walter Citrine and the British Caribbean Workers Movement during the Moyne Commission Hearing, 1938–1939," in Silvestrini, *Politics, Society and Culture in the Caribbean*, pp. 239–55; John Gaffar La Guerre, "The Moyne Commission and the Jamaican Left," *Social and Economic Studies* 38 (1982), pp. 59–94.

38 Ken Post, *Arise Ye Starvelings: The Jamaican Labour Rebellion of 1938 and its Aftermath* (The Hague: Martinus Nijhoff, 1978).

39 George Eaton, *Alexander Bustamente and Modern Jamaica* (Kingston: Kingston Publishers, 1975).

40 Henry, *Labour Relations*, pp. 43–5; Knowles, *Trade Union Development and Industrial Relations in the British West Indies*, pp. 69–72; W. L. Cumiford, "The Political Role of Organized Labor in the Caribbean," *Journal of Third World Studies* 4, 1 (1987), p. 122.

41 G. Arosemena and A. Diogenes, *Documentary Diplomatic History of the Panama Canal* (Panama City: Imprenta Nacional, 1961), pp. 343–6, 360–5.

42 On the Colombian experience, especially the aviation issue, see Randall, *Colombia and the United States*.

43 This is the turning point indicated by Rexford Tugwell, U.S. Governor of wartime Puerto Rico; Rexford Guy Tugwell, *The Stricken Land* (Garden City, NY: Doubleday, 1947), pp. 400–1, 408.

44 David Murray, "Garrisoning the Caribbean: A Chapter in Canadian Military History," *Revista/Review Interamericana* 7, 1 (Spring 1977), pp. 73–4.

45 The German Minister in Panama City to AA, 19 March 1940, RG 242, T-120, roll 1279, frame 485954, NAUS (Washington).

46 Ladislas Farago, *The Game of the Foxes: The Untold Story of German Espionage in the United States and Great Britian during World War II* (New York: David McKay, 1971); see also Julio (a Panamanian spy) to Abwehrm Hamburg, 20 June 1940; also Winter (Julio's superior) to Abwehr, 3 July 1940, File R102046, Auswartiges Amt, Bonn.

47 Press Statement of Secretary of State Cordell Hull, 16 Oct. 1941, and other documents, RG 59, Series 819.000, Box 3728, NAUS (Washington, DC).

48 Fitz Andre Baptiste, *War, Cooperation and Conflict: The European Possessions in the Caribbean, 1939–1945* (New York: Greenwood Press, 1988), pp. 1–34.

49 Baptiste, *European Possessions*, pp. 34–83, *passim*.

50 William Shirer, *The Collapse of the Third Republic: An Inquiry into the Fall of France in 1940* (New York: Simon and Schuster, 1969), p. 854.

51 Baptiste, *European Possessions*, pp. 51–61.

52 William Langer, *Our Vichy Gamble* (New York: Knopf, 1947).

53 U.S. Secretary of State to the Chiefs of Diplomatic Missions in the American Republics, 17 June 1940, *FRUS* (1940), V, 180–1.

54 The Minister in Haiti (Mayer) to the U.S. Secretary of State, 18 June 1940, *FRUS* (1940) , V, 181–2.

55 The Chargé in Caracas to the U.S. Secretary of State, 2 July 1940; Venezuelan Ambassador (Washington) to U.S. Secretary of State, 3 July 1940; U.S Secretary of State to the Ambassador in Rio de Janeiro (Caffery), 22 June 1940; Secretary of State to Ambassador in Rio de Janeiro (Caffery), 21 June 1940, *FRUS* (1940), V, 191, 194, 209–11.

56 Ambassador in Havana (Messersmith) to the Secretary of State, 18 June 1940, *FRUS* (1940), V, 183–8.

57 The Chargé in Caracas (Scott) to the Secretary of State, 13 July 1940, *FRUS* (1940), V, 224.

58 Chargé in Guatemala (Cabot) to the Secretary of State, *FRUS* (1940), V, 252. See also Memorandum of the First Secretary of the Embassy (Beaulac) to Messersmith, 17 July 1940 (cited hereafter as Beaulac Memorandum), pp. 231–3.

59 Ambassador in Argentina (Armour) to the Secretary of State, 21 June 1940, *FRUS* (1940), V, 192–3; see also Beaulac Memorandum, p. 233.

60 The Minister in Uruguay (Wilson) to the Secretary of State, 10 July 1940, *FRUS* (1940), V, 214–15.

61 Acting Secretary of State (Welles) to the Ambassador in Peru (Norweb), 20 June 1940, *FRUS* (1940), V, 189.

62 The Minister in Bolivia (Jenkins) to the Secretary of State, 10 July 1940, *FRUS* (1940), V, 215.

63 Memorandum by Philip Bonsal, division of the American Republics, to the Chief of the Division (Duggan), 5 July 1940, *FRUS* (1940), V, 212. Ambassador in Peru to the Secretary of State, 9 July 1940, pp. 213–14.

64 Langer, *Our Vichy Gamble*.

65 The Minister in Uruguay (Wilson) to the Secretary of State, 9 July 1940, *FRUS* (1940), V, 213.

66 Ruhi Bartlett, *The Record of American Diplomacy: Documents and Readings from the History of American Foreign Relations* (New York: Knopf, 1964), p. 558.

67 Baptiste, *European Possessions*, pp. 63–74.

68 Baptiste, *European Possessions*, pp. 72–4, 115–44 *passim*.

69 Tugwell, *Stricken Land*, pp. 239–42, 273, 360–4.

70 Tugwell, *Stricken Land*, pp. 72, 96–100, 148–9, 158, 183–5, 209–11, 240, 360, 365–70.

71 Baptiste, *European Possessions*, pp. 171–220.

72 Murray, "Garrisoning the Caribbean," p. 77.

73 Murray, "Garrisoning the Caribbean," pp. 83–4.

74 Edward Chester, *The United States and Six Atlantic Outposts* (Port Washington, NY: Kennikat, 1980), pp. 70–1.

75 Murray, "Garrisoning the Caribbean," pp. 73–86.

76 Ralph de Boissiere, *Rum and Coca-Cola* (London: Allison and Busby, 1984 [1956]).

77 Bernardo Vega, *Nazismo, Fascismo y Falangismo en la Republica Dominicana* (Santo Domingo: Fundación Cultural Dominicana, 1985), pp. 381–90.

78 Mayer, Port-au-Prince, to the Secretary of State, Washington, 24 March 1939, *FRUS* (1939), 5, p. 638.

79 Mayer to the Secretary of State, 5 July 1939, *FRUS* (1939), 5, pp. 640–1.

80 J. Kenly Bacon, U.S. chargé d'affaires, Port-au-Prince, to the Secretary of State, 3 Sept. 1939, *FRUS* (1939), 5, pp. 645–6.

81 Hull to Mayer, 30 March 1939, *FRUS* (1939), 5, pp. 638–69.

82 Hull to Mayer, 14 July 1939, *FRUS* (1939), 5, p. 644.

83 Mayer to Hull, 21 June 1940, *FRUS* (1940), 5, pp. 126–7. For correspondence concerning Vincent's pressure and wants and the State Department's response, see *FRUS* (1940), 5, pp. 122–9.

84 Intercepted letter of Vincent to Lescot, 26 June 1940, *FRUS* (1940), 5, pp. 889–91.

85 The Secretary of State to the Chargé in Haiti, 7 Oct. 1940; the Chargé in Haiti to the Secretary of State, 12 Oct. 1940, *FRUS* (1940), 5, pp. 919–20.

86 Press release issued by the Department of State, 13 April 1942, *FRUS* (1940), 5, pp. 467–8. More extensive correspondence on U.S. assistance to Haiti in 1942 appears in *ibid.*, pp. 460–77.

4 FROM WAR TO REVOLUTION, 1945–59

1 Jay Mandle, "British Caribbean Economic History," in Franklin W. Knight and Colin A. Palmer (eds.) *The Modern Caribbean* (Chapel Hill, NC, and London: University of North Carolina Press, 1989), p. 247. Brenda Gayle Plummer, *Haiti and the United States* (Athens, GA: University of Georgia Press, 1992), pp. 130, 131. A. Curtis Wilgus (ed.) *The Caribbean: Its Culture.* (Gainesville, FL: University of Florida Press, 1955) does not mention tourism.

2 Anthony P. Maingot, *The United States and the Caribbean* (London: Macmillan, 1994), p. 52.

3 On Colombia see S. J. Randall, *Colombia and the United States* (Athens, GA: University of Georgia Press, 1992). The broader issue of American anti-Communist policies in the Eisenhower years is thoroughly examined by Stephen Rabe, *Eisenhower and Latin America* (Chapel Hill, NC: University of North Carolina Press, 1988).

4 *FRUS* (1952–4), III, 1372.

5 *The Times*, 24 Nov. 1948, p. 3.

6 *The Times*, 27 Nov. 1948, p. 5.

7 *FRUS* (1947), I, 323–4.

8 Jan Rogozinski, *A Brief History of the Caribbean* (New York: Meridian, 1992), p. 256.

9 Department of State Briefing paper, 29 April 1953, *FRUS* (1952–4), IV, 147–9.

10 "General Policy Toward Latin America," *FRUS* (1952–4), IV, 14–15.

11 The best studies of the events in Guatemala and their larger context are: Walter LaFeber, *Inevitable Revolutions* (New York: Norton, 1983); Stephen Kinzer and Stephen Schlesinger, *Bitter Fruit* (New York: Doubleday, 1982); Richard Immerman, *The CIA in Guatemala: The Foreign Policy of Intervention* (Austin, TX: University of Texas Press, 1982).

12 *FRUS* (1952–4), II, Part II, 1821. *The Times*, 27 Feb. 1954, p. 7.

13 "General Policy Toward Latin America," *FRUS* (1952–4), IV, 14–15.

14 *The Times*, 1 March 1954, p. 4.

15 *The Times* 3 March 1954, p. 8.

16 *The Times* 5 March 1954, p. 6; 6 March 1954, p. 5; 10 March 1954, p. 6; 13 March 1954, p. 5.

17 F. S. Northedge, *Descent from Power: British Foreign Policy, 1945–1973* (London: Allen and Unwin, 1974) stresses the basic differences in Cold War orientation between the United States and Great Britain. On Guatemala see p. 203.

18 R. Eduardo Ruíz, *Cuba: The Making of a Revolution* (New York: Norton, 1968), pp. 141–63.

19 Franklin W. Knight, *The Caribbean, Genesis of a Fragmented Nationalism* (New York: Oxford University Press, 1978), pp. 191–4.

20 Knight, *The Caribbean*, p. 194.

21 See Louis A. Pérez, Jr., *Cuba and the United States* (Athens, GA: University of Georgia Press, 1990), p. 234.

22 Robert D. Crassweller, *Trujillo: Life and Times of a Caribbean Dictator*, (New York: Macmillan, 1966), pp. 218–313; Bernardo Vega, *Eisenhower y Trujillo* (Santo Domingo: Fundación Cultural Dominicana, 1991), especially pp. 207–8 ; Canada, Department of External Affairs, *Documents on Canadian External Affairs*.

23 Crassweller, *Trujillo*, pp. 270–3.

24 James Alan Clark, *The Church and the Crisis in the Dominican Republic* (Westminster, MD: Newman Press, 1967), pp. 2–3. See also Crassweller, *Trujillo*, pp. 382–94.

25 Crassweller, *Trujillo*, p. 382.

26 Clark, *The Church*, pp. 2–3.

27 Summary of document DR-1, summarized in *FRUS (1958–60)*, 5, 806.

28 Stephen E. Ambrose, *Eisenhower the President* (New York: Simon and Schuster, 1984), p. 556. That 1958 was a pivotal year is also the opinion of Dominican historian Bernardo Vega, *Eisenhower y Trujillo*, pp. 207–15. See the summary of Document DR-25 in *FRUS*, pp. 807–8.

29 The quotation comes from document DR-20, quoted in *FRUS*, p. 807. The preceding material comes from documents 16–20, summarized in *FRUS*, pp. 806–7.

30 For an assessment of the sanctions, see C. Lloyd Brown-John, "Economic Sanctions: The Case of the OAS and the Dominican Republic, 1960–1962", *Caribbean Studies* 15, 2 (July 1975), pp. 73–105.

31 Crassweller, *Trujillo*, p. 428.

32 Office of the High Commissioner, Canada House, London, to the Secretary of State for External Affairs (SSEA), Ottawa, 6 March 1959, RG 25, Box 6845, File 3493–40, part 2, National Archives of Canada (NAC).

33 Re: the British arms embargo, report from Canada House, London. Re: the Canadian refusal to sell the Vampire jets, Chargé d'Affaires, Ciudad Trujillo, to SSEA, Ottawa, 6 Feb. 1959, RG 25, Box 6845, File 3493–40, part 2, NAC.

34 McVittie to Selwyn Lloyd, "Dominican Republic: Annual Review for 1958," RG 25, Box 6845, File 3493–40, part 2, NAC.

35 McVittie, "Dominican Republic: Annual Review for 1958," W.W. McVittie to Selwyn Lloyd, "Dominican Republic: Annual Review for 1959," *ibid.*

36 L. Hudon, Chargé d'affaires, Canadian Embassy, Ciudad Trujillo, to the SSEA, Ottawa, 17 Feb. 1959, RG 25, Box 6845, File 3493–40, part 2, NAC.

37 Hudon, Ciudad Trujillo, to the SSEA, Ottawa, 11 June 1959, RG 25, Box 6845, File 3493–40, part 2, NAC.

38 Plummer, *Haiti and the United States*.

39 Plummer, *Haiti and the United States*, pp. 164–5.

40 For an account of the 1957 election, see Bernard Diederich and Al Burt, *Papa Doc: The Truth about Haiti Today* (New York: McGraw-Hill, 1969), pp. 3–18.

41 Graham Greene, "Foreword" to Diederich and Burt, pp. viii–ix. Anselme Remy, another commentator on François Duvalier, agrees that he resorted to tyranny and terror after 1961 in a manner unknown in the earlier years; Anselme Remy, "The Duvalier Phenomenon," *Caribbean Studies*, 14, 2 (July 1974), pp. 38–65.

42 Elizabeth Abbott, *Haiti: An Insider's History of the Rise and Fall of the Duvaliers* (New York: Simon and Schuster, 1990), p. 120. The author is sister-in-law to General Henri Namphy, immediate successor to Jean-Claude Duvalier as President of Haiti.

43 *FRUS* (1952–4), IV, 1394–5.

44 Acheson to President Truman, 17 Jan. 1952, *FRUS* (1952–4), III, 1391.

45 *FRUS* (1952–4), IV, 1395.

46 Michael L. Conniff, *Black Labor on a White Canal: Panama, 1904–1981* (Pittsburgh, PA: University of Pittsburgh Press, 1985), pp. 101–9; Walter LaFeber, *The Panama Canal: The Crisis in Historical Perspective* (Oxford: Oxford University Press, 1979 [1978]), pp. 98–120.

47 Conniff, *Black Labour on a White Canal*, pp. 110–15; LaFeber, *Panama Canal*, pp. 120–31; John Major, *Prize Possession: The United States and the Panama Canal, 1903–1979* (Cambridge: Cambridge University Press, 1993), pp. 329–33.

48 National Security Council (NSC) 6026, "U.S. Policy on the Panama Canal and a Future Inter-Oceanic Canal in Central America," *Presidential Directives on National Security from Truman to Clinton* (Washington, DC: National Security Archive, 1994), item 627.

49 United Nations Resolution 748 (VIII), adopted 27 Nov. 1953.

50 Roberta A. Johnson, "The 1967 Puerto Rican Plebiscite: The People Decide," *Revista/Review Interamericana* 5, 1 (Spring 1975), pp. 27–46. See also Angel Calderon Cruz, "The Puerto Rican Status Question," *Revista/Review Interamericana* 6, 1 (Spring 1976), pp. 18–22. For a commentary on economic considerations related to the status question, see Carmen Gautier Mayoral, "Interrelation of U.S. Poor Relief, Massive Unemployment and Weakening of 'Legitimacy' in Twentieth Century Puerto Rico," *Caribbean Studies* 19 , 3–4 (Oct. 1979/Jan. 1980), pp. 5–46. For information about Puerto Rican migration to the United States mainland, see Jose Hernandez, "La Migracion Puertorriquena Como Factor Demográfico: Solución y Problema," *Revista/Review Interamericana* IV, 4 (Winter 1974–5), pp. 526–34. See also Guy T. Ashton, "Migration and the Puerto Rican Support System," *Revista/Review Interamericana* 12, 2 (Summer 1981), pp. 228–42.

51 *FRUS* (1952–4), III, 1370. Surinam was the leading supplier of bauxite to the United States in the 1950s. On British policy, see Northedge, *Descent from Power*, p. 284.

52 *Keesing's Contemporary Archives*, 10–17 Oct. 1953, pp. 13,177.

53 *Keesing's Contemporary Archives*, pp. 13,177–9.

54 Steins, Georgetown, to U.S. consulate-general, Port of Spain, 10 Nov. 1953, 841D.2569/11–1053; and 27 Jan. 1954, 841D.2569/1–2754; U.S. National Archives and Records Center, College Park, Maryland.

55 These quotations are from documents in the British Guiana collection at the archives of the Aluminum Company of Canada, Montreal.

56 Cheddi Jagan, *The West on Trial* (London: Michael Joseph, 1966); *Keesing's Contemporary Archives*.

57 Michael Kaufman, *Jamaica under Manley: Dilemmas of Socialism and Democracy* (London: Zed Books; Westport, CT: Lawrence Hill, 1985).

58 Kaufman, *Jamaica under Manley*, p. 49.

59 For more information on the political developments of 1946, see Brinsley Samaroo, "The Making of the 1946 Trinidad Constitution," *Caribbean Studies* 15, 4 (January 1976), pp. 5–27.

60 Nicholas Mansergh (ed.) *Documents and Speeches on Commonwealth Affairs, 1952–1962* (London: Oxford University Press, 1963), pp. 163–83.

61 Elisabeth Wallace, *The British Caribbean: From the Decline of Colonialism to the End of Federato* (Toronto: University of Toronto Press, 1977), p. 48. For further information about politics and the constitution see Douglas G. Anglin, "The Political Development of the West Indies," *The West Indies Federation* (New York: Columbia University Press, 1961), pp. 35–62.

62 Dawn Marshall, "The International Politics of Caribbean Migration," in R. Millett and W. M. Will (eds.) *The Restless Caribbean: Changing Patterns of International Relations* (New York: Praeger, 1979), pp. 42–50.

63 Kari Levitt and Alistair McIntyre, *Canada–West Indies Economic Relations* (Montreal: McGill Centre for Developing Area Studies, 1967), pp. 95–101.

64 Marshall, "International Politics of Caribbean Migration," p.45.

65 Sidney Mintz, "Puerto Rican Emigration: A Threefold Comparison," *Caribbean Studies* 4, 4 (1955), 311–25; Joseph Fitzpatrick, *Puerto Rican Americans: The Meaning of Migration to the Mainland* (Englewood Cliffs, NJ: Prentice Hall, 1971); Orlando Patterson, "Migration in Caribbean Societies: Socioeconomic and Symbolic Resource," in William H. McNeill and Ruth S. Adams (eds) *Human Migration: Patterns and Policies* (Bloomington, IN: University of Indiana Press, 1978).

66 Aaron Lee Segal (ed.) *Population Policies in the Caribbean* (Lexington, MA: Lexington Books, 1975), p. 219.

67 Colin Brock (ed.) *The Caribbean in Europe: Aspects of the West Indian Experience in Britain, France and the Netherland* (London: Frank Cass, 1986), p. 11.

68 Segal, *Population Policies*, p. 219. Brock, *Caribbean in Europe*.

69 U. S. Naipaul, *The Middle Passage* (Harmondsworth: Penguin, 1969), p. 73.

70 G. Tidrick, "Some Aspects of Jamaican Migration to the United Kingdom, 1953–1962," *Social and Economic Studies* 15, 1 (1966), 26.

5 THE CUBAN REVOLUTION AND CARIBBEAN BASIN RELATIONS, 1960–79

1 Timothy Ashby, *The Bear in the Back Yard: Moscow's Caribbean Strategy* (Lexington, MA: Lexington Books, 1987), ix.

2 *Miami Herald*, 29 May 1977, 25 Jan. and 3 Feb. 1978.

3 *Miami Herald*, 30 July 1980.

4 Gerard T. Rice, *The Bold Experiment: JFK's Peace Corps* (Notre Dame, IN: University of Notre Dame Press, 1985).

5 Rex Nettleford, "Cultivating a Caribbean Sensibility: Media, Education and Culture," *Caribbean Review* 15 (Winter 1987), pp. 4–8, 28.

6 Nettleford, "Cultivating a Caribbean Sensibility," p. 8.

7 Ashby, *Bear in the Back Yard*, pp. 28–30. Memorandum of Discussion at the 467th Meeting of the National Security Council, Augusta, Georgia, 17 November 1960, *FRUS* (1958–60), 5, 453–4.

8 Philip W. Bonsal, *Cuba, Castro and the United States* (Pittsburgh, PA: University of Pittsburgh Press, 1971); one of the author's (Randall) discussion with Bonsal, Washington, DC, 1980. On Fulbright, see Arthur M. Schlesinger, Jr., *A Thousand Days* (Boston, MA: Houghton Mifflin, 1965), p. 252.

9 Nikita S. Khrushchev, *Khrushchev Remembers: The Glasnost Tapes*, edited by Jerrold Schecter and Vyacheslav V. Luchkov (Boston, MA: Little, Brown, 1990), pp. 170–1, 509.

10 *Khrushchev Remembers*, p. 172. The best first-hand account remains that of Robert F. Kennedy, *Thirteen Days: A Memoir of the Cuban Missile Crisis* (New York: Norton, 1969).

11 *Khrushchev Remembers*, pp. 177, 511.

12 *Khrushchev Remembers*, p. 511n.

13 Ashby, *Bear in the Back Yard*, p. x.

14 Tad Szulc in *Esquire* (Feb. 1974), cited in *Khrushchev Remembers*, p. 510n.

15 Ashby, *Bear in Back Yard*, p. 43.

16 Ashby, *Bear in the Back Yard*, pp. 45–53, 70–1.

17 Judith Ewell, *Venezuela and the United States* (Athens, GA: University of Georgia Press, 1996); S.J. Randall, *Colombia and the United States* (Athens, GA: University of Georgia Press, 1992); J. H. Thompson and S. J. Randall, *Canada and the United States* (Athens: University of Georgia Press, 1994).

18 McGeorge Bundy, National Security Adviser, to Dean Rusk, Secretary of State, 13 Feb. 1961, *Presidential Directives on National Security from Truman to Clinton* (Washington, DC: National Security Archive, 1994), item 653.

19 Schlesinger, *A Thousand Days*, p. 769. For a summary of other opinion in print, see C. Lloyd Brown-John, "Economic Sanctions: The Case of the OAS and the Dominican Republic, 1960–1962)," *Caribbean Studies* 15, 2 (July 1975), p. 75, note 7. See also Bernard Diederich, *Trujillo: The Death of the Goat* (Boston, MA: Little, Brown, 1978), p. 263; Piero Gleijeses, *The Dominican Crisis*, translated by Lawrence Lipson (Baltimore, MD: Johns Hopkins, 1978), pp. 303–7.

20 Bundy to National Security Administration, 13 May 1962, *Presidential Directives*, item 859; John Bartlow Martin, *Overtaken by Events* (Garden City, NY: Doubleday, 1966).

21 Dean Rusk, *As I Saw It* (New York: Norton, 1990), pp. 368–77; Gleijeses, *Dominican Crisis*, pp. 125, 284, 287.

22 Numbers regarding the Marines and the paratroops who went to the Dominican Republic came from Warren I. Cohen, *Dean Rusk* (Towota, NJ: Cooper Square, 1980), p. 265; Rusk, *As I Saw It*, p. 377.

23 Lyndon Baines Johnson, *The Vantage Point: Perspectives of the Presidency, 1963–1969* (New York: Popular, 1973), pp. 187–205.

24 Lawrence A. Yates, *Power Pack: U.S. Intervention in the Dominican Republic, 1965–1966* (Fort Leavenworth, KS: Combat Studies Institute, U.S. Army Command and General Staff College, 1988), p. 9.

25 Tad Szulc, *Dominican Diary* (New York: Delacorte Press, 1965).

26 Rusk, *As I Saw It*, pp. 368–77, especially p. 373.

27 Cohen, *Dean Rusk*, pp. 265–8.

28 Abraham F. Lowenthal, *The Dominican Intervention* (Cambridge, MA: Harvard University Press, 1972), p. v.

29 Gleijeses, *Dominican Crisis*, p. 125.

30 Gleijeses, *Dominican Crisis*, p. 259.

31 Gleijeses, *Dominican Crisis*, p. 293.

32 One source says that foreign investment doubled between 1966 and 1978; José Antonio Moreno, *The Dominican Revolution Revisited*, Monograph no. 7 (Pittsburgh, PA: Northwest Pennsylvania Insitute for Latin American Studies, 1978), p. 32.

33 Graeme S. Mount, "Aspects of Canadian Economic Activity in the Spanish-speaking Caribbean," *Laurentian University Review* 5, 1 (Nov. 1972), pp. 93–6.

34 For more information on banking in the Dominican Republic, see Mount, *Laurentian Review*, pp. 89–90.

35 Frank Moya Pons, *El Pasado Dominicano* (Santo Domingo: Fundación J. A. Caro Alvarez, 1986), p. 335 (translation the author's).

36 Rockefeller Report to President Nixon, 1969, RG 4, Box 97, File: Presidential Mission, Dominican Republic, Rockefeller Archives Center, North Tarrytown, New York.

37 Kissinger to Patrick J. Hillings, a Los Angeles lawyer, 11 Feb. 1971, White House Central Files, Country Files, CO 44, File 1/1/71–31/12/72, Nixon Collection, US National Archives and Record Center, College Park, Maryland. (cited hereafter as Nixon Collection).

38 For an analysis of the 1978 election in the Dominican Republic, see Michael J. Kryzanek, "The 1978 Election in the Dominican Republic: Opposition Politics, Intervention and the Carter Administration," *Caribbean Studies* 19, 1–2 (April–July 1979), pp. 51–73.

39 *Special National Intelligence Estimate*, 10 March 1959, *FRUS* (1958–60), 5, 363.

40 John Major, *Prize Possession: The United States and the Panama Canal, 1903–1979* (Cambridge: Cambridge University Press, 1993), p. 309.

41 *National Intelligence Estimate*, 10 March 1959, *FRUS* (1958–60), 5, 368–9, 370–1.

42 *Presidential Directives*, items 764, 841–8, 850–8, 879–83, 885–91.

43 *Presidential Directives*, item 884.

44 National Security Action Memorandum (NSAM) 164, 20 Jan. 1964, *Presidential Directives*, item 893.

45 Johnson, *Vantgage Point*, pp. 180–4.

46 Cohen, *Dean Rusk*, pp. 228–9. See also LaFeber, *Inevitable Revolutions*, pp. 142, 146, 191, 216.

47 *Presidential Directives*, item 1112.

48 Rockefeller Report to President Nixon, 1969, RG 4, Box 100, File: Presidential Mission, Panama; also Rockefeller to Torrijos, 11 Nov. 1969, RG 4, Box 122, File: Panama: VIP correspondence, Rockefeller Archives Center, Tarrytown, New York.

49 Michael L. Conniff, *Black Labor on a White Canal: Panama, 1904–1981* (Pittsburgh, PA: University of Pittsburgh Press, 1985), p. 128.

50 *Presidential Directives*, item 1209.

51 National Security Decision Memorandum (NSDM) 115, *Presidential Directives*, item 1247.

52 The Statement of Principles is part of *Presidential Directives*, item 1537.

53 NSDM 131, 13 Sept. 1971, *Presidential Directives*, item 1259.

54 NSDM 302, 18 Aug. 1975, *Presidential Directives*, item 1313.

55 A review of the negotiations before President Carter's inauguration is available in *Presidential Directives*, item 1537.

56 Presidential Review Memorandum/NSC 1, 21 Jan. 1977; *Presidential Directives*, item 1536.

57 Robert A. Pastor, *Whirlpool: U.S. Foreign Policy Toward Latin America and the Caribbean* (Princeton, NJ: Princeton University Press, 1992), p. 3.

58 Major, *Prize Possession*, p. 344.

59 Conniff, *Black Labor on a White Canal*, p. 135; Pastor, *Whirlpool*, p. 8.

60 *FRUS* (1958–60), 5, 817–19.

61 Elizabeth Abbott, *Haiti: An Insider's History of the Rise and Fall of the Duvaliers* (New York: Simon and Schuster, 1990) p. 114.

62 McGeorge Bundy (National Security Director) to the Secretary of State, the Secretary of Defense, and the Director of Central Intelligence, NSAM 246, 23 May 1963, National Security Archive, *Presidential Directives* (Washington, DC, 1994), item 993.

63 Abbott, *Haiti*, p. 114.

64 Abbott, *Haiti*, p. 153.

65 Kissinger to the Secretary of State and the Administrator, AID, 13 Nov. 1970, NSDM 94, *Presidential Directives*, item 1234.

66 One of the authors (Mount) visited Haiti in 1976 and observed many of these points.

67 Nixon to Jean-Claude Duvalier, 2 Oct. 1973, White House Central Files, Box 34, CO 61 (Haiti) Nixon Collection.

68 Abbott, *Haiti*, p. 192.

69 Abbott, *Haiti*, p. 234.

70 Abbott, *Haiti*, pp. 255–7.

71 Abbott, *Haiti*, pp. 254–5.

72 See Brenda Gayle Plummer, *Haiti and the United States* (Athens, GA: University of Georgia Press, 1992), pp. 193–209.

73 Sloan, Washington, to Feliciano, Culebra, 14 April 1970, White House Central Files, Puerto Rico, Box 20, File EX ST 51–2, Nixon Collection, National Archives of the USA, College Park, Maryland. Cited hereafter as Nixon Collection.

74 Nixon, Washington, to Ferre, San Juan, 15 Dec. 1970, and J. Bruce Whelihan to White House Press Secretary Ronald L. Ziegler, 7 Jan. 1971, Nixon Collection. From those two letters, it is possible to understand what Ferre had written to Nixon. The quotation comes from the Nixon letter.

75 Brooke to Nixon, 29 March 1971, Nixon Collection. There is another letter in the collection from Congressman Abner J. Mikva to Nixon, 29 March 1971.

76 Laird to Nixon, 1 April 1971, Nixon Collection. For more information on the Culebra controversy, see Graeme S. Mount, "Canada and the 1971–1972 Culebra Controversy," *Revista/Review Interamericana* 5, 3 (Fall 1975), pp. 378–90.

77 Nixon sent Ferre a letter of thanks "for all the work you did for our cause during the campaign;" Nixon to Ferre, 20 Nov. 1972, Nixon Collection.

78 For information on the Puerto Rican economy since World War II, see Henry Wells, "Development Problems of the 1970s in Puerto Rico," *Revista/Review Interamericana* 7, 2 (Summer 1977), pp. 169–92.

79 Information on the Ford administration and Puerto Rico is based on an article by Michael D. Stevenson, "The Compact of Permanent Union and the 1977 Puerto Rico Statehood Proposal," *Revista/Review Interamericana* 23 (1993), pp. 7–25.

80 Cheddi Jagan, *The West on Trial* (London: Michael Joseph, 1966); *Keesing's Contemporary Archives*.

81 Schlesinger, *A Thousand Days*, pp. 774–9.

82 Pearson Visit Briefing Book, 1/21–22/64, National Security File (NSF) Country File, Canada, Box 167, items 18z and 58; Memorandum of Conversation, 22 Jan. 1964, NSF Country File, Canada, Box 167–8, Folder: Canada-Pearson Visit, item 22a, Lyndon Baines Johnson Presidential Archives, Austin, Texas.

83 Pearson Visit Briefing Book, 1/21–22/64, NSF Country File, Canada, Box 167, items 18z and 58; Memorandum of Conversation, 22 Jan. 1964, NSF Country File, Canada, Box 167–8, Folder: Canada-Pearson Visit, item 22a, Lyndon Baines Johnson Presidential Archives, Austin, Texas.

84 One of the authors (Mount) heard Dr. Moore make this statement before an audience in Sudbury, Ontario, when students from the University of Guyana visited Laurentian University in the autumn of 1974. See also the book by Janet Jagan (Cheddi's wife), *Army Intervention in the 1973 Elections in Guyana* (Georgetown: People's Progressive Party, 1973).

85 For an interpretation of Burnham's foreign policy, see Festus Brotherson, Jr., "The Foreign Policy of Guyana, 1970–1985: Forbes Burnham's Search for Legitimacy," *Journal of Inter-American Studies and World Affairs* 31, 3 (Fall 1989), pp. 9–35.

86 Noted by Graeme Mount during an interview with Burnham, Feb. 1974.

87 Ashby, *Bear in the Back Yard*, pp. 143–5.

88 Ivelow L. Griffith, "The Military and the Politics of Change in Guyana," *Journal of Inter-American Studies and World Affairs* 23, 2 (Summer 1991), p. 160.

89 Frank Shakespeare, USIA, to Nixon, 11 Aug. 1970, White House Country Files, Box 42, CO 74 (Jamaica), File EX CO 74, 1969–70, National Archives and Research Center, College Park, MD. Cited hereafter as Nixon Project.

90 DLC (probably Dwight L. Chapin), "Note for December file," 12 Aug. 1970, White House Country File, Box 42, File EX CO 74, 1969–70, Nixon Project.

91 George Crawford to Moorhead Kennedy, 8 March 1972, White House Country File, Box 42, File EX CO 74, 1971–2, Nixon Project. Other U.S. companies included Alcoa, Anaconda, and Revere.

92 Carlton Davis, *Jamaica in the Aluminum Industry, 1938–1973*, vol. 1 (Kingston: Jamaica Bauxite Industry, 1989), p. 53.

93 Duncan C. Campbell, *Global Mission: The Story of Alcan* (Montreal: Alcan, 1989), p. 276.

94 Randy Jayne, White House, for Jamie McLaine, 13 June 1974, White House Country File, Box 42, File EX CO 74, File 1973–4, Nixon Project.

95 Mount interview with Burnham, Georgetown, Guyana, 3 March 1974.

96 *New York Times*, 16 May 1975.

97 The meeting with Rockefeller seems not to have taken place. Kissinger, however, spent a few days in Jamaica over the Christmas break and spoke with Manley and others. Telephone interview (Mount) with archivist John Leglouhec, Rockefeller Archive Center, North Tarrytown, New York, 13 Nov. 1995. *New York Times*, 25 Dec. 1975.

98 *New York Times*, 16 and 17 Dec. 1976.

99 *New York Times*, 21 Jan. 1977.

100 *New York Times*, 16 June 1977.

101 *New York Times*, 31 May 1977.

102 *New York Times*, 9 Nov. 1977.

103 *New York Times*, 17 Dec. 1977.

104 Elizabeth Mitchell, White House, to Fran and Phil, 21 Nov. 1977, WHCF, CO 77, Carter Presidential Archives, Atlanta.
105 *New York Times*, 10 Feb. 1978.
106 New York Times, 19 Oct. 1979, 5 Feb., 16 April, 11, 14, and 30 May, 5 June, 30 June 1980; *Financial Times*, 24 Oct. 1979.
107 Al Stern to Stu Eizenstat, 21 Nov. 1978, WHCF CO 77, CPA.
108 *New York Times*, 5 March, 11 May 1980.
109 *New York Times*, 1 Nov. 1980.
110 *New York Times*, 2 Nov. 1980.
111 *New York Times*, 1 Dec. 1980, 15 April 1981.
112 *New York Times*, 20 Jan. 1981.
113 *New York Times*, 22 Jan. 1981.
114 *New York Times*, 30 Jan. 1981.
115 *New York Times*, 31 March 1981.
116 *New York Times*, 5 May 1981.
117 For a review of the foreign policy of the PNM governments under Eric Williams and George Chambers, see Jacqueline A. Braveboy-Wagner, "The Regional Foreign Policy of Trinidad and Tobago: Historical and Contemporary Aspects," *Journal of Inter-American Studies and World Affairs* 31, 3 (Fall 1989), pp. 37–61.
118 William Demas, "Foreword," in R. Millett and W. M. Will (eds) *The Restless Caribbean: Changing Patterns of International Relations* (New York: Praeger, 1979), p. ix.

6 FROM REVOLUTION TO THE END OF THE COLD WAR

1 Robert A. Pastor, *Whirlpool: U.S. Foreign Policy Toward Latin America and the Caribbean* (Princeton, NJ: Princeton University Press, 1992).
2 For population statistics on Belize, see D. A. G. Waddell, *British Honduras: A Historical and Contemporary Survey* (London: Oxford University Press, 1961), pp. 64–6; Narda Dopson, *A History of Belize* (Hong Kong: Longmans Caribbean, 1973), p. 251. Information on Belize–Guatemala–British relations are drawn from the Belize government publication, *The New Belize*, and from the personal observations in 1978 of one of the authors (Mount). See also Thomas J. Spinner, Jr., "Belize, Guatemala, and the British Empires," *Revista/Review Interamericana* 6, 2 (Summer 1987), pp. 282–90; Tony Thorndike, "The Conundrum of Belize: An Anatomy of a Dispute," *Revista/Review Interamericana* 11, 2 (Summer 1981), pp. 159–82; Anthony J. Payne, "The Belize Triangle: Relations with Britain, Guatemala, and the United States," *Journal of Interamerican Studies and World Affairs* 32, 1 (Spring 1990), 120–35.
3 Pastor, *Whirlpool*, p. 53.
4 Pastor, *Whirlpool*, pp. 54–5.
5 Pastor, *Whirlpool*, pp. 56–7.
6 U.S. Government, *Weekly Compilation of Presidential Documents*, 21 (11 Feb. 1985), 145.
7 There has been a great deal of controversy over the question of Nicaraguan support for the FMLN-FDR. Although there were clearly exaggerations by Reagan administration officials, we find credible Robert Pastor's account of the 1980–1 events in *Whirlpool*, p. 59. For an opposing view see Thomas Walker, "Nicaraguan–U.S. Friction: The First Four Years, 1979–1983," in Kenneth Coleman and George C. Herring (eds) *The Central American Crisis: Sources of Conflict and the Failure of U.S. Policy* (Wilmington, DE: Scholarly Resources, 1985), pp. 157–92.

8 Report of the National Bipartisan Commission on Central America (Kissinger Report) (Washington: GPO, 1984), p. 126.

9 Pastor, *Whirlpool*, pp. 68–9. Fortunately cooler heads prevailed in the NSC, where repeatedly Haig advocated direct action against what he argued was the source of the Central American insurgency – Cuba.

10 Pastor, *Whirlpool*, p. 76.

11 James Rochlin, *Discovering the Americas: The Evolution of Canadian Foreign Policy Towards Latin America* (Vancouver: University of British Columbia Press, 1994), pp. 157–8.

12 The following discussion draws heavily on the excellent work by Jan S. Adams, *A Foreign Policy in Transition: Moscow's Retreat from Central America and the Caribbean, 1985–1992* (Durham, NC, and London: Duke University Press, 1992). Other important accounts include: Howard J. Wiarda and Mark Falcoff, *The Communist Challenge in the Caribbean and Central America* (Washington, DC: American Enterprise Institute for Public Policy Research, 1987); Bruce Larkin (ed.) *Vital Interests: The Soviet Issue in U.S. Central American Policy* (Boulder, CO, and London: Lynne Rienner, 1988); G.W. Sand, *Soviet Aims in Central America: The Case of Nicaragua* (New York: Praeger, 1989); S.N. MacFarlane, "Superpower Rivalry and Soviet Policy in the Caribbean Basin," Occasional Papers no. 1, (Ottawa: Canadian Institute for International Peace and Security, 1987); Eusebio Mujal-León, (ed.) *The USSR and Latin America: A Developing Relationship* (Boston, MA: Unwin Hyman, 1989); Dennis Bark, (ed.) *The Red Orchestra: Instruments of Soviet Policy in Latin America and the Caribbean* (Stanford, CA: Hoover Institution Press, 1986). For a good corrective to the Bark volume, see Wayne S. Smith (ed.) *The Russians Aren't Coming: New Soviet Policy in Latin America* (Boulder, CO, and London: Lynne Rienner, 1992).

13 Adams, *Moscow's Retreat*, p. 107.

14 Adams, *Moscow's Retreat*, p. 108.

15 Adams, *Moscow's retreat*, p. 136.

16 Adams, *Moscow's Retreat*, pp. 110–12.

17 *New York Times* (4 Dec. 1989), pp. 10–11.

18 Adams, *Moscow's Retreat*, pp. 114, 117–18, 124–5.

19 Interestingly, Japan had the largest representation among the UN electoral observers in the February 1990 elections. Author's note. See also Adams, *Moscow's Retreat*, pp. 119–20.

20 Adams, *Moscow's Retreat*, pp. 129–30.

21 Adams, *Moscow's Retreat*, pp. 140–3.

22 Pastor, *Whirlpool*, p. 99.

23 Pastor's account of U.S.–Grenadian relations during the Carter administration appears in Robert A. Pastor, *U.S. Foreign Policy Toward Latin America and the Caribbean* (Princeton, NJ: Princeton University Press, 1992), pp. 145–67. President Reagan gave specific orders to study the captured documents; "Processing and Disposition of Documents Acquired by US Forces in Grenada," 15 Nov. 1983, National Security Archive, *Presidential Directives for National Security from Truman to Clinton* (Washington, DC: 1994), item 1763. Cited hereafter as *Presidential Directives*.

24 Pastor, *Whirlpool*, p. 157.

25 The NJM quotation is repeated in "Grenada: The New Jewel Movement and Religion," 2 Feb. 1984, *Presidential Directives*, item 1765.

26 "Address to the Nation on Events in Lebanon and Grenada," 27 Oct. 1983, *Public Papers of the Presidents: Ronald Reagan, 1983* (cited hereafter as *Public Papers*), p. 1, 517.

27 George P. Shultz, *Turmoil and Triumph: My Years as Secretary of State* (New York: Scribner's, 1993), pp. 323–45.

28 "Address to the Nation . . . ," *Public Papers*, p. 1,520.
29 *New York Times* (citing Prime Minister Bishop himself), 5 June 1983. See also Margaret Thatcher, *The Downing Street Years* (New York: HarperCollins, 1993), p. 166.
30 *New York Times*, 29 Oct., 4 and 5 Nov. 1983. For further information about Communist influence in Grenada, see Robert A. Pastor, "Does the U.S. Push Revolutions to Cuba?: The Case of Grenada," *Journal of Inter-American Studies and World Affairs* 28, 1 (Spring 1986), pp. 1–34.
31 Oleg Kalugin, *The First Directorate: My 32 Years in Intelligence and Espionage Against the West* (New York: St. Martin's Press, 1994), pp. 174–5.
32 J. Bowyer Bell, *The Secret Army: The IRA, 1916–1979* (Dublin: Poolbeg, 1989), p. 417; Patrick Bishop and Eamonn Mallie, *The Provisional IRA* (London: Corgi, 1988), pp. 246, 305–6.
33 *New York Times*, 8 Nov. 1983.
34 Bob Woodward, *Veil: The Secret Wars of the CIA* (New York: Simon and Schuster, 1993), p. 290.
35 In an "Address Before a Joint Session of the Congress on Central America" delivered 27 April 1983, President Reagan mentioned Libyan cargo aircraft which had recently refueled in Brazil so that they could deliver what were supposed to be medical supplies to Nicaragua; *Public Papers*, p. 601.
36 *New York Times*, 26 Oct. 1983.
37 Shultz, *Turmoil and Triumph*, p. 327.
38 Shultz, *Turmoil and Triumph*, pp. 331, 336; Thatcher, *Downing Street Years*, pp. 328–35.
39 *New York Times*, 30 Oct. 1983.
40 Pastor, *U.S. Foreign Policy*, p. 158. See also Lars Schoultz, *National Security and United States Policy toward Latin America* (Princeton, NJ: Princeton University Press, 1987), p. 243.
41 Schoultz, *National Security*, p. 242.
42 "Remarks of the President and Prime Minister Eugenia Charles of Dominica Announcing the Deployment of United States Forces in Grenada," 25 Oct. 1983, *Public Papers*, p. 1506. Shultz, *Turmoil and Triumph*, pp. 324–5.
43 "Letter to the Speaker of the House and the President Pro Tempore of the Senate on the Deployment of United States Forces in Grenada," 25 Oct. 1983, *Public Papers*, pp. 1,512–13.
44 *New York Times*, 30 Oct. 1983.
45 "Address to the Nation on Events in Lebanon and Grenada," 27 Oct. 1983, *Public Papers*, p. 1,521.
46 *New York Times*, 31 March 1983; 2 Nov. 1983.
47 For difficulties in connection with existing runway facilities on Grenada, see Schoultz, *National Security*, pp. 240–1.
48 *New York Times*, 26 Oct. 1983.
49 *New York Times*, 25 Oct. 1983.
50 *New York Times*, 27 Oct. 1983.
51 *New York Times*, 27 Oct. 1983.
52 *New York Times*, 26, 27 Oct. 1983.
53 Defense Department figures, reported in the *New York Times*, 16 Dec. 1983.
54 *New York Times*, 1 Nov. and 16 Dec. 1983.
55 *New York Times*, 29 Oct. 1983.
56 *New York Times*, 3 Nov. 1983.
57 *New York Times*, 27 Oct. 1983.
58 *New York Times*, 6 Nov. 1983.
59 *New York Times*, 29 and 30 Oct. 1983.

60 *New York Times*, 27 Oct. 1983.
61 *New York Times*, 25 Oct. 1983.
62 *New York Times*, 26 Oct. 1983.
63 These words appear in most volumes of the United Nations Treaty Series.
64 An unidentified member of the United Nations Secretariat made this point to the *New York Times*; *New York Times*, 2 Nov. 1983. A search by one of the authors through the *United Nations Treaty Series* could find no reference to the treaty in question.
65 *New York Times*, 27 Oct. 1983.
66 *New York Times*, 27 Oct. 1983.
67 National Security Archives, *The U.S. Intelligence Community, 1947–1989* (Washington, DC), item 00630.
68 Margaret E. Scranton, *The Noriega Years: U.S.–Panamanian Relations, 1981–1990* (Boulder, CO: Lynne Rienner, 1991), p. 13.
69 For a profile of Manuel Noriega, see John Dinges, *Our Man in Panama: The Shrewd and Brutal Fall of Manuel Noriega* (New York: Random House, 1991).
70 Scranton, *Noriega Years*, p. 12.
71 Michael L. Conniff, *Black Labor on a White Canal: Panama 1904–1981* (Pittsburgh, PA: University of Pittsburgh Press, 1985), p. 151.
72 Scranton, *Noriega Years*, pp. 204, 215.
73 Pastor, *U.S. Foreign Policy*, p. 93.
74 Conniff, *Black Labor on a White Canal*, p. 168. See also the speculative article by Richard L. Millett, "The Aftermath of Intervention: Panama 1990," *Journal of Inter-American Studies and World Affairs* 32, 1 (Spring 1990), pp. 1–15.
75 S.J. Randall, *Colombia and the United States* (Athens, GA: University of Georgia Press, 1992), pp. 246–51.
76 Pastor, *Whirlpool*, p. 91.
77 *New York Times*, 16 Feb. and 24 July 1990.
78 *Keesing's Contemporary Archives, 1986*, p. 34,401.
79 Howard J. Wiarda and Michael J. Kryzanek, *The Dominican Republic: A Caribbean Crucible* (Boulder, CO: Westview, 1992), p. 82.
80 Wiarda and Kryzanek, *Caribbean Crucible*, p. 87.
81 Wiarda and Kryzanek, *Caribbean Crucible*, p. 141.
82 For a survey of the contemporary Dominican economy, see Wiarda and Kryzanek, *Caribbean Crucible*, pp. 79–94, 113–32. The birthrates' statistic comes from p. 123.
83 U.S. State Department, "Background Note: Dominican Republic," *U.S. Foreign Affairs on CD-ROM, January 1990–September 1994* (cited hereafter as CD-ROM) 30 Dec. 1991, #40.
84 U.S. State Department, "Dominican Republic: Announcement of Balaguer Victory," *CD-ROM*, 22 Aug. 1994, #30. U.S. State Department, "Dominican Republic Human Rights Practices, 1993," *CD-ROM*, 31 Jan. 1994, #46.
85 Wiarda and Kryzanek, *Caribbean Crucible*, p. 139.
86 White House Readout on the visit of President Balaguer of the Dominican Republic, 25 March 1988, retrieved at the National Security Archive, George Washington University, Washington, DC.
87 Wiarda and Kryzanek, *Caribbean Crucible*, p. 137.
88 For a review of the foreign policy of the PNM governments under Eric Williams and George Chambers, see Jacqueline A. Braveboy-Wagner, "The Regional Foreign Policy of Trinidad and Tobago: Historical and Contemporary Aspects," *Journal of Interamerican Studies and World Affairs* 31, 3 (Fall 1989), pp. 37–61.
89 Sahadeo Basdeo, "Cuba in Transition: Socialist Order Under Siege," *Canadian Journal of Latin American and Caribbean Studies* 18, 36 (1993), pp. 107–39.
90 *Keesing's Record of World Events, 1990*, pp. 37,606–7.

91 Anthony P. Maingot, *The United States and the Caribbean* (London, Macmillan, 1994), p. 52.

92 Anthony P. Maingot, "The Internationalization of Corruption and Violence: Threats to the Caribbean in the Post-Cold War World," in Jorge I. Dominguez, Robert A. Pastor and R. Delisle Worrell (eds), *Democracy in the Caribbean: Political, Economic, and Social Perspectives* (Baltimore, MD: Johns Hopkins University Press, 1993), p. 52.

93 *New York Times*, 29 July 1990. Also *Keesing's Record of World Events*, 1990, pp. 37,606–7. *Keesing's* places the death toll for five days of violence at thirty, the *New York Times* (31 July) at fifty.

94 *New York Times*, 1 Aug. 1990.

95 *Daily Express* (Port of Spain), 17 Feb. 1996.

96 *Trinidad Guardian*, 24 Feb. 1996.

97 Abbott, *Haiti*, p. 262 (for the estimate of the crowd size) and p. 262 (for the papal quotation).

98 Abbott, *Haiti*, pp. 281–3.

99 For an assessment of Haitian history until the presidency of Jean-Claude Duvalier, see O. Ernest Moore, "The Tragic Island," *Revista/Review Interamericana* 10, 3 (Fall 1980), pp. 305–19.

100 Abbott, *Haiti*, pp. 337–44.

101 Abbott, *Haiti*, p. 354.

102 Abbott, *Haiti*, pp. 358–60.

103 Abbott, *Haiti*, p. 365.

104 Manigat, Yale, to Henry Kissinger, Washington, 4 July 1971, Nixon Collection.

105 Jean-Bertrand Aristide, *An Autobiography* (Maryknoll, NY: Orbis, 1993), pp. 45, 79–81.

106 Aristide, *An Autobiography*, pp. 181–2.

107 Aristide, *An Autobiography*, p. 79.

108 Aristide, *An Autobiography*, p. 180.

109 U.S. State Department, "Haiti Human Rights Practices, 1993," *U.S. Foreign Affairs on CD ROM, January 1990–September 1994*, Item #47.

110 U.S. State Department, "U.S.–CARICOM Efforts to Support UN Security Council Resolution 940," 5 Sept. 1994, *CD-ROM*, item 31.

EPILOGUE

1 The sessions were held in Bridgetown, Barbados, San José, Costa Rica, and Santiago, Chile under the direction of CIDA Vice-President for the Americas, Pierre Racicot. They concluded with a roundtable discussion at the Inter-American Dialogue in Washington, DC.

BIBLIOGRAPHY

Abbott, E. (1990) *Haiti: An Insider's History of the Rise and Fall of the Duvaliers.* New York: Simon and Schuster.

Adams, J. S. (1992) *A Foreign Policy in Transition: Moscow's Retreat from Central America and the Caribbean, 1985–1992.* Durham, NC, and London: Duke University Press.

Aguilar, L. (1972) *1933: Prologue to Revolution.* New York: Norton.

Allen, H. C. (1955) *Great Britain and the United States.* New York: St. Martin's Press.

Ambrose, S. E. (1984) *Eisenhower the President.* New York: Simon and Schuster.

Ameringer, C. D. (1982) "The Tradition of Democracy in the Caribbean: Betancourt, Figueres, Muñoz and the Democratic Left," *Caribbean Review* 11, 2 (Spring): 28–31.

Angel Silén, J. (1970) *Hacía una visión positiva del Puertorriqueño.* Rio Piedras: Editorial Edil.

Antonio Moreno, J. (1978) *The Dominican Revolution Revisited.* Monograph no. 7, Pittsburgh, PA: Northwest Pennsylvania Institute for Latin American Studies.

Aristide, J.-B. (1993) *An Autobiography.* Maryknoll, NY: Orbis.

Arosemena, G. and Diogenes, A. (1961) *Documentary Diplomatic History of the Panama Canal.* Panama City: Imprenta Nacional.

Ashby, T. (1987) *The Bear in the Back Yard: Moscow's Caribbean Strategy.* Lexington, MA: Lexington Books.

Azéma, J.-P. and Bédarida, F. (eds) (1992) *Vichy et les Français.* Paris: Fayard.

Azicri, M. (1980) "Cuba and the US: On the Possibilities of Rapprochement," *Caribbean Review* 9 (Winter): 26–9.

Bajeux, J.-C. (1994) "An Embarrassing Presence," *New York Review of Books* 3 November: 37–8.

Baptiste, F. A. (1973) "The Seizure of the Dutch Authorities in Willemstad, Curaçao by Venezuelan Political Exiles in June 1929, viewed in Relation to the Anglo-French Landings in Aruba and Curaçao in May 1940," *Caribbean Studies* 13 (April): 37–41

—— (1978) *The United States and West Indian Unrest, 1918–1939.* Mona: University of the West Indies.

—— (1988) *War, Cooperation and Conflict: The European Possessions in the Caribbean, 1939–1945.* New York: Greenwood Press.

Bark, D. (ed.) (1986) *The Red Orchestra: Instruments of Soviet Policy in Latin America and the Caribbean.* Stanford, CA: Hoover Institution Press.

Basdeo, S. (1993) "Cuba in Transition: Socialist Order Under Siege," *Canadian Journal of Latin American and Caribbean Studies* 18, 36: 107–39.

Bell, J. B. (1989) *The Secret Army: The IRA, 1916–1979.* Dublin: Poolbeg.

Bemis, S. F. (1963) *American Secretaries of State and their Diplomacy*, vol. 6. New York: Cooper Square.

Berbusse, E. J. (1967) *The United States in Puerto Rico, 1898–1900*. Chapel Hill, NC: University of North Carolina Press.

Bethell, L. (ed.) (1995) *Cambridge History of Latin America, Part I, Latin America Since 1930, vol. 6, Economy, Society and Politics*. Cambridge: Cambridge University Press.

—— (1995) *Cambridge History of Latin America, Part II, Latin America Since 1930, vol. 6, Economy, Society and Politics*. Cambridge: Cambridge University Press.

Bishop, P. and Mallie, E. (1988) *The Provisional IRA*. London: Corgi.

Black, C. V. (1961 [1958]) *History of Jamaica*. London: Collins.

Black, J. K. (1986) *The Dominican Republic: Politics and Development in an Unsovereign State*. Boston, MA: Allen and Unwin.

Bloomfield, L. M. (1953) *The British Honduras–Guatemala Dispute*. Toronto: Carswell.

Bonsal, P. (1971) *Cuba, Castro and the United States*. Pittsburgh, PA: University of Pittsburgh Press.

Bourne, K. (1970) *The Foreign Policy of Victorian England, 1830–1902*. Oxford: Clarendon Press.

Braveboy-Wagner, J. A. (1989) "The Regional Foreign Policy of Trinidad and Tobago: Historical and Contemporary Aspects," *Journal of Inter-American Studies and World Affairs* 31, 3 (Fall): 37–61.

Brotherson, Jr., F. (1989) "The Foreign Policy of Guyana, 1970–1985: Forbes Burnham's Search for Legitimacy," *Journal of Inter-American Studies and World Affairs* 31, 3 (Fall): 9–35.

Brown-John, C. L. (1975) "Economic Sanctions: The Case of the OAS and the Dominican Republic, 1960–1962," *Caribbean Studies* 15, 2: 73–105.

Bunau-Varilla, P. (1914) *Panama: The Creation, the Destruction, the Resurrection*. New York: McBride.

Burns, E. M. (1957) *The American Idea of Mission*. New Brunswick, NJ: Rutgers University Press.

Burton, D. H. (1968) *Theodore Roosevelt: Confident Imperialist*. Philadelphia, PA: University of Pennsylvania Press.

Calcott, W. H. (1942) *The Caribbean Policy of the United States, 1890–1920*. Baltimore, MD: Johns Hopkins University Press.

Calder, B. J. (1982) *The Impact of Intervention: The Dominican Republic during the U.S. Occupation of 1916–1924*. Austin, TX: University of Texas Press.

Calderon Cruz, A. (ed.) (1979) *Problemas del Caribe Contemporaneo*. Rio Piedras, PR: Instituto de Estudios del Caribe.

Campbell, A. E. (1960) *Great Britain and the United States, 1895–1903*. London: Longman.

Campbell, D. C. (1989) *Global Mission: The Story of Alcan*. Montreal: Alcan.

Castillero Reyes, E. (1933) *La causa immediate de la emancipación de Panama*. Panama City: Imprenta Nacional.

Charnowitz, S. (1985) "Varieties of Labor Organization: The Caribbean and Central America Compared," *Caribbean Review* 14, 2 (Spring): 14–17.

Chester, E. (1980) *The United States and Six Atlantic Outposts*. Port Washington, NY: Kennikat.

Clark, J. A. (1967) *The Church and the Crisis in the Dominican Republic*. Westminster, MD: Newman Press.

Clark, T. R. (1974/5) "The Imperial Perspective: Mainland Administrators' Views of the Puerto Rican Economy, 1898–1941," *Revista/Review Interamericana* 4, 4: 505–17.

Cohen, W. I. (1980) *Dean Rusk*. From the series *American Secretaries of State and their Diplomacy*. Towota, NJ: Cooper Square.

Collin, R. H. (1990) *Theodore Roosevelt's Caribbean: The Panama Canal, the Monroe Doctrine, and the Latin American Context*. Baton Rouge, LA: Louisiana State University Press.

Conniff, M. L. (1985) *Black Labor on a White Canal: Panama, 1904–1981*. Pittsburgh, PA: University of Pittsburgh Press.

Crassweller, R. D. (1966) *Trujillo: Life and Times of a Caribbean Dictator*. New York: Macmillan.

Craton, M. (1982) *Testing the Chains*. Ithaca, NY: Cornell University Press.

Cumiford, W. L. (1987) "The Political Role of Organized Labor in the Caribbean," *Journal of Third World Studies* 4, 1: 119–27.

Curtin, P. (1969) *The Atlantic Slave Trade: A Census*. Madison, WI: University of Wisconsin Press.

Davis, C. (1989) *Jamaica in the Aluminum Industry, 1938–1973*, vol. 1. Kingston: Jamaica Bauxite Industry.

de Boissiere, R. (1984 [1956]) *Rum and Coca-Cola*. London: Allison and Busby.

de Kadt, E. (ed.) (1972) *Patterns of Foreign Influence in the Caribbean*. London: Royal Institute of International Affairs.

Diederich, B. (1978) *Trujillo: The Death of the Goat*. Boston, MA: Little, Brown.

Diederich, B. and Burt, A. (1969) *Papa Doc: The Truth about Haiti Today*. New York: McGraw-Hill.

Dinges, J. (1991) *Our Man in Panama: The Shrewd and Brutal Fall of Manuel Noriega*. New York: Random House.

Durden, R. F. (1951) "J. D. B. De Bow: Convolutions of a Slavery Expansionist," *Journal of Southern History* 17: 441–61.

Eduardo Ruíz, R. (1968) *Cuba: The Making of a Revolution*. New York: Norton.

Ewell, J. (1996) *Venezuela and the United States: From Monroe's Hemisphere to Petroleum's Empire*. Athens, GA: University of Georgia Press.

Fagen, R. (1982) "The Real Clear and Present Danger: A Critique from the Left," *Caribbean Review* 11, 2 (Spring): 18–20.

Farago, L. (1971) *The Game of the Foxes: The Untold Story of German Espionage in the United States and Great Britain during World War II*. New York: David McKay.

Farley, E. L. (1976) "Puerto Rico: Ordeals of an American Dependency during World War II," *Revista/Review Interamericana* 6, 2: 202–10.

Fuller, S. M. and Cosmas, G. A. (1974) *Marines in the Dominican Republic, 1916–1924*. Washington, DC: History and Museums Division, Headquarters, U.S. Marine Corps.

Gindine, Y. (1974) "Images of the American in Haitian Literature during the Occupation, 1915–1934," *Caribbean Studies* 14, 3: 37–52.

Gleijeses, P. (1978) *The Dominican Crisis: The 1965 Constitutionalist Revolt and American Intervention*, translated by Lawrence Lipson. Baltimore, MD: Johns Hopkins University Press.

Gonzales, A. P. (1984) "The Future of CARICOM: Collective Self-Reliance in Decline?" *Caribbean Review* 13, 4 (Fall): 8–11.

Gould, L. J. (1975) *La Ley Foraker: raices de la política colonial de los Estados Unidos*. Barcelona: Editorial Universitaria, Universidad de Puerto Rico.

Green, W. (1965) *British Slave Emancipation: The Sugar Colonies and the Great Experiment, 1830–1965*. Oxford: Clarendon Press.

Griffith, I. L. (1991) "The Military and the Politics of Change in Guyana," *Journal of Inter-American Studies and World Affairs* 23, 2 (Summer): 141–74.

Gunther, J. (1941) *Inside Latin America*. New York: Harper and Brothers.

Hamshere, C. (1972) *The British in the Caribbean*. Cambridge, MA: Harvard University Press.

Healy, D. F. (1963) *The United States in Cuba, 1898–1902*. Madison, WI: University of Wisconsin Press.

Henry, Z. (1972) *Labour Relations and Industrial Conflict in Commonwealth Caribbean Countries*. Trinidad: Columbus.

Herring, H. (1967) *A History of Latin America*. New York: Knopf.

Herwig, H. (1986) *Germany's Visions of Empire in Venezuela, 1871–1914*. Princeton, NJ: Princeton University Press.

Hiller, H. (1978) "Sun Lust Tourism in the Caribbean," *Caribbean Review* 7 (October–December): 12–15.

Hunt, M. (1987) *Ideology and U.S. Foreign Policy*. New Haven, CT: Yale University Press.

Immerman, R. (1982) *The CIA in Guatemala: The Foreign Policy of Intervention*. Austin, TX: University of Texas Press.

Ince, B. (ed.) (1978) *Contemporary International Relations of the Caribbean*. St. Augustine, Trinidad: University of the West Indies.

Jacobs, W. R. (1977) "The Politics of Protest in Trinidad: The Strikes and Disturbances of 1937," *Caribbean Studies* 17, 1–2 (April–July): 5–54.

Jagan, C. (1966) *The West on Trial*. London: Michael Joseph.

Jagan, J. (1973) *Army Intervention in the 1973 Elections in Guyana*. Georgetown: People's Progressive Party.

James, C. L. R. (1963) *The Black Jacobins: Toussaint L'Ouverture and the San Domingue Revolution*, 2nd edn. New York: Vintage.

Johnson, H. (1975) "Oil, Imperial Policy and the Trinidad Disturbances, 1937," *Journal of Imperial and Commonwealth History* 4: 5–54.

Johnson, L. B. (1973) *The Vantage Point: Perspectives of the Presidency, 1963–1969*. New York: Popular.

Kalugin, O. (1994) *The First Directorate: My 32 Years in Intelligence and Espionage Against the West*. New York: St. Martin's Press.

Kennedy, R. F. (1969) *Thirteen Days: A Memoir of the Cuban Missile Crisis*. New York: Norton.

Khrushchev, N. S. (1990) *Khrushchev Remembers: The Glasnost Tapes*, edited by J. Schecter and V. V. Luchkov. Boston, MA: Little, Brown.

Kinzer, S. and Schlesinger, S. (1982) *Bitter Fruit*. New York: Doubleday.

Knight, F. W. (1978) *The Caribbean, Genesis of a Fragmented Nationalism*. New York: Oxford University Press.

—— (1990) *The Caribbean: The Genesis of a Fragmented Nationalism*, 2nd edn. New York: Oxford University Press.

Knowles, W. H. (1959) *Trade Union Development and Industrial Relations in the British West Indies*. Berkeley, CA: University of California Press.

Krenn, M. L. (1990) *US Policy toward Economic Nationalism in Latin America, 1917–1929*. Wilmington, DE: Scholarly Resources.

Kryzanek, M. J. (1977) "Diversion, Subversion and Repression: The Strategies of Anti-Opposition Politics in Balaguer's Dominican Republic," *Caribbean Studies* 17, 1–2: 83–103.

—— (1979) "The 1978 Election in the Dominican Republic: Opposition Politics, Intervention and the Carter Administration," *Caribbean Studies* 19, 1–2: 51–73.

Lacouture, J. (1990–2) *De Gaulle: The Rebel (1890–1944)*. New York: Norton.

Lael, R. (1987) *Arrogant Diplomacy: U.S. Policy toward Colombia, 1903–1922*. Wilmington, DE: Scholarly Resources.

LaFeber, W. (1979) *The Panama Canal: The Crisis in Historical Perspective*. New York: Oxford University Press.

—— (1983) *Inevitable Revolutions: The United States in Central America*. New York: Norton.

Langer, W. (1947) *Our Vichy Gamble*. New York: Knopf.

Langley, L. D. (1976) *Struggle for the American Mediterranean: United States–European Rivalry in the Gulf–Caribbean, 1776–1914*. Athens, GA: University of Georgia Press.

—— (1980) *The United States and the Caribbean, 1900–1970*. Athens, GA: University of Georgia Press.

—— (1983) *The Banana Wars: United States Intervention in the Caribbean, 1898–1934*. Lexington, KY: University Press of Kentucky.

—— (1989) *The United States and the Caribbean in the Twentieth Century*, 4th edn. Athens, GA: University of Georgia Press.

Larkin, B. (ed.) (1988) *Vital Interests: The Soviet Issue in U.S. Central American Policy*. Boulder, CO, and London: Lynne Rienner.

Laurence, K. O. (1971) *Immigration into the West Indies in the Nineteenth Century*. Barbados: Caribbean Universities Press.

Lieuwen, E. (1965) *Arms and Politics in Latin America*. New York: Praeger.

Linton, N. (1970–71) "Regional Diplomacy of the Commonwealth Caribbean," *International Journal* 26: 401–17.

Liss, S. B. (1978) *Diplomacy and Dependency: Venezuela, the United States and the Americas*. Salisbury, NC: Documentary Publications.

Look Lai, W. (1993) *Chinese and Indian Migrants to the British West Indies, 1838–1918*. Baltimore, MD: Johns Hopkins University Press.

Lowenthal, A. F. (1972) *The Dominican Intervention*. Cambridge, MA: Harvard University Press.

McCann, T. (1976) *An American Company: The Tragedy of United Fruit*. New York: Crown.

McCullough, D. (1977) *The Path between the Seas: The Creation of the Panama Canal, 1870–1914*. New York: Simon and Schuster.

MacFarlane, S. N. (1987) "Superpower Rivalry and Soviet Policy in the Caribbean Basin," Occasional Papers no. 1. Ottawa: Canadian Institute for International Peace and Security.

Maingot, A. P. (1993) "The Internationalization of Corruption and Violence: Threats to the Caribbean in the Post-Cold War World," in J. I. Dominguez, R. A. Pastor and R. D. Worrell (eds) *Democracy in the Caribbean: Political, Economic, and Social Perspectives* Baltimore, MD: Johns Hopkins University Press.

—— (1994) *The United States and the Caribbean*. London: Macmillan.

Major, J. (1993) *Prize Possession: The United States and the Panama Canal, 1903–1979*. Cambridge: Cambridge University Press.

Malek, R. M. (1977) "Rafael Leonidas Trujillo: A Revisionist Critique of his Rise to Power," *Revista/Review Interamericana* 7, 3: 436–45.

Marks, F. X. (1965) "Organized Labour in British Guiana," in F. M. Andie and T. G. Mathews (eds) *The Caribbean in Transition: Papers on Social, Political, and Economic Development*, San Juan: University of Puerto Rico.

Martin, J. B. (1966) *Overtaken by Events*. Garden City, NY: Doubleday.

May, R. E. (1974) *The Southern Dream of a Caribbean Empire, 1854–1861*. Baton Rouge, LA: Louisiana State University Press.

Millett, R. L. (1990) "The Aftermath of Intervention: Panama 1990," *Journal of Inter-American Studies and World Affairs* 32, 1 (Spring): 1–15.

Millett, R. with Gaddy, G. D. (1976) "Administering the Protectorates: The U.S. Occupation of Haiti and the Dominican Republic," *Revista/Review Interamericana* 6, 3: 383–402.

Millett, R. and Will, W. M. (eds) (1979) *The Restless Caribbean: Changing Patterns of International Relations*. New York: Praeger.

Miner, D. (1966) *The Fight for the Panama Route*. New York: Octogon.

Mitchell, B. R. (1993) *International Historical Statistics: The Americas, 1750–1988*, 2nd edn. New York: Stockton Press.

Mitchell, H. (1963) *Europe in the Caribbean*. Edinburgh: W. and R. Chambers.

Moore, O. E. (1980) "The Tragic Island," *Revista/Review Interamericana* 10, 3 (Fall): 305–19.

Mount, G. S. (1972) "Aspects of Canadian Economic Activity in the Spanish-speaking Caribbean," *Laurentian University Review* 5, 1: 93–6.

—— (1975) "Canada and the 1971–1972 Culebra Controversy," *Revista/Review Interamericana* 5, 3: 378–90.

Moya Pons, F. (1986) *El Pasado Dominicano*. Santo Domingo: Fundación J. A. Caro Alvarez.

Mujal-León, E. (ed.) (1989) *The USSR and Latin America: A Developing Relationship*. Boston, MA: Unwin Hyman.

Munro, D. (1934) *The United States and the Caribbean Area*. Boston, MA: World Peace Foundation.

—— (1964) *Intervention and Dollar Diplomacy in the Caribbean, 1900–1921*. Princeton, NJ: Princeton University Press.

Murray, D. (1977) "Garrisoning the Caribbean: A Chapter in Canadian Military History," *Revista/Review Interamericana* 7, 1: 73–77.

Needler, M. C. (1982) "Hegemonic Tolerance: International Competition in the Caribbean and Latin America," *Caribbean Review* 11, 2 (Spring): 32–4.

Nettleford, R. (1987) "Cultivating a Caribbean Sensibility," *Caribbean Review* 15 (Winter): 4–8, 28.

Northedge, F. S. (1974) *Descent from Power: British Foreign Policy 1945–1973*. London: Allen and Unwin.

Parry, J. H. and Sherlock, P. M. (1965) *A Short History of the West Indies*. London: Macmillan.

Pastor, R. A. (1986) "Does the U.S. Push Revolutions to Cuba?: The Case of Grenada," *Journal of Inter-American Studies and World Affairs* 28, 1 (Spring): 1–34.

—— (1992) *Whirlpool: U.S. Foreign Policy Toward Latin America and the Caribbean*. Princeton, NJ: Princeton University Press.

Paterson, T. G., Clifford, J. G., and Hagan, K. J. (1983) *American Foreign Policy: A History to 1914*, 2nd edn. Lexington, MA and Toronto: D.C. Heath.

Pérez, Jr., L. A. (1990) *Cuba and the United States: Ties of Singular Intimacy*. Athens, GA: University of Georgia Press, 1990.

Plummer, B. G. (1992) *Haiti and the United States: The Psychological Moment*. Athens, GA: University of Georgia Press.

Rabe, S. (1988) *Eisenhower and Latin America*. Chapel Hill, NC: University of North Carolina Press.

Radosh, R. (1969) *American Labor and United States Foreign Policy*. New York: Random House.

Raffucci de Garcia, C. I. (1981) *El gobierno civil y la Ley Foraker*. Rio Piedras: Editorial Universitaria, Universidad de Puerto Rico.

Randall, S. J. (1992) *Colombia and the United States: Hegemony and Interdependence*. Athens, GA: University of Georgia Press.

Remy, A. (1974) "The Duvalier Phenomenon," *Caribbean Studies* 14, 2: 38–65.

Richardson, B. C. (1992) *The Caribbean in the Wider World, 1492–1992: A Regional Geography*. Cambridge: Cambridge University Press.

Rochlin, J. (1994) *Discovering the Americas: The Evolution of Canadian Foreign Policy Towards Latin America*. Vancouver: University of British Columbia Press.

Rogozinski, J. (1992) *A Brief History of the Caribbean*. New York: Meridian.

Rosenberg, E. (1982) *Spreading the American Dream: American Economic and Cultural Expansion, 1890–1945*. New York: Hill and Wang.

Rusk, D. (1990) *As I Saw It*. New York: Norton.

Samaroo, B. (1972) "The Trinidad Workingmen's Association and the Origins of Popular Protest in a Crown Colony," *Studies in Economics and Society* 21, 2: 205–22.

Sand, G. W. (1989) *Soviet Aims in Central America: The Case of Nicaragua*. New York: Praeger.

Scarano, F. (1989) "Labor and Society in the Nineteenth Century," in F. Knight and C. A. Palmer (eds) *The Modern Caribbean*, Chapel Hill, NC and London: University of North Carolina Press.

Scranton, M. E. (1991) *The Noriega Years: U.S.–Panamanian Relations, 1981–1990*. Boulder, CO: Lynne Rienner.

Schlesinger, Jr., A. M. (1965) *A Thousand Days: John F. Kennedy in the White House*. Boston, MA: Houghton Mifflin.

Schmidt, H. (1971) *The United States Occupation of Haiti, 1915–1934*. New Brunswick, NJ: Rutgers University Press.

Shannon, M. W. (1976) "The U.S. Commission for the Study and Review of Conditions in Haiti and its Relationship to President Hoover's Latin American Policy," *Caribbean Studies* 15, 4: 53–72.

Shultz, G. P. (1993) *Turmoil and Triumph: My Years as Secretary of State*. New York: Scribner's.

Slater, J. (1976) *La Intervención Americana: Los Estados Unidos y la Revolución Dominicana*. Santo Domingo: Editorial de Santo Domingo.

Smith, W. S. (ed.) (1992) *The Russians Aren't Coming: New Soviet Policy in Latin America*. Boulder, CO and London: Lynne Rienner.

Soderlund, W. C. (1977) "United States Intervention in the Dominican Republic 1916 and 1965," *North/South: Canadian Journal of Latin American Studies* 2, 3–4: 87–95.

Solnick, B. B. (1970) *The West Indies and Central America to 1898*. New York: Knopf.

Stevenson, M. D. (1993) "The Compact of Permanent Union and the 1977 Puerto Rico Statehood Proposal," *Revista/Review Interamericana* 23: 7–25.

Szulc, T. (1965) *Dominican Diary*. New York: Delacorte Press.

Thatcher, M. (1993) *The Downing Street Years*. New York: HarperCollins.

Thompson, J. H. and Randall, S. J. (1994) *Canada and the United States: Ambivalent Allies*. Athens, GA: University of Georgia Press.

Trask, D. (1981) *The War With Spain in 1898*. New York: Macmillan.

Tugwell, R. G. (1947) *The Stricken Land: The Story of Puerto Rico*. Garden City, NY: Doubleday.

United Kingdom (1856–1940). *Annual Statistical Abstract for the United Kingdom*. London: Board of Trade.

United States (1985) *Weekly Compilation of Presidential Documents*, 21 (11 February), Washington, DC.

Vega, B. (1985) *Nazismo, Fascismo y Falangismo en la Republica Dominicana*. Santo Domingo: Fundación Cultural Dominicana.

—— (1991) *Eisenhower y Trujillo*. Santo Domingo: Fundación Cultural Dominicana.

Waddell, D. A. G. (1967) *The West Indies and the Guianas*. Englewood Cliffs, NJ: Prentice Hall.

Walker, T. (1985) "Nicaraguan–U.S. Friction: The First Four Years, 1979–1983," in K. Coleman and G. C. Herring (eds) *The Central American Crisis: Sources of Conflict and the Failure of U.S. Policy*. Wilmington, DE: Scholarly Resources.

Wallerstein, I. (1974) *The Modern World-System*. New York: Academic Press.

—— (1979) *The Capitalist World-Economy*. Cambridge: Cambridge University Press.

—— with T. K. Hopkins (1982) *World Systems Analysis: Theory and Methodology*. Beverly Hills, CA: Sage.

Welles, S. (1972 [1928]) *Naboth's Vineyard: The Dominican Republic, 1844–1924*. New York: Arno.

Wells, H. (1977) "Development Problems of the 1970s in Puerto Rico," *Revista/Review Interamericana* 7, 2: 169–92.

Wiarda, H. J. and Falcoff, M. (1987) *The Communist Challenge in the Caribbean and Central America*. Washington, DC: American Enterprise Institute for Public Policy Research.

Wiarda, H. J. and Kryzanek, M. J. (1977) "Dominican Dictatorship Revisited: The Caudillo Tradition and the Regimes of Trujillo and Balaguer," *Revista/Review Interamericana* 7, 3: 417–35.

—— (1992) *The Dominican Republic: A Caribbean Crucible*. Boulder, CO: Westview.

Wilgus, A. C. (ed.) (1952) *The Caribbean: Peoples, Problems, Prospects*. Gainesville, FL: University of Florida Press.

—— (1953) *The Caribbean: Contemporary Trends*. Gainesville, FL: University of Florida Press.

—— (1955) *The Caribbean: Its Culture*. Gainesville, FL: University of Florida Press.

—— (1957) *The Caribbean: Contemporary International Relations*. Gainesville, FL: University of Florida Press.

—— (1967) *The Caribbean: Its Hemispheric Role*. Gainesville, FL: University of Florida Press.

Woodward, B. (1993) *Veil: The Secret Wars of the CIA*. New York: Simon and Schuster.

Woodward, R. L. (1976) *Central America: A Nation Divided*. New York: Oxford University Press.

Writings of John Quincy Adams. John Quincy Adams to Hugh Nelson, 28 April 1823, vol. 7: 370–81.

Yates, L. A. (1988) *Power Pack: U.S. Intervention in the Dominican Republic, 1965–1966.* Fort Leavenworth, KS: Combat Studies Institute, U.S. Army Command and General Staff College.

Young, R. C. (1976) "Political Autonomy and Economic Development in the Caribbean Islands," *Caribbean Studies* 16 (April): 86–114.

Archival sources

Canada

National Archives of Canada

RG 25 -Records of the Department of External Affairs

United States

National Archives of the United States

RG 242, Records of Imperial and Weimar-Nazi Germany (Microfilm)
RG 59, General Records of the Department of State

Presidential Papers

Jimmy Carter Presidential Archives, Atlanta, Georgia
Lyndon Baines Johnson Presidential Library, Austin, Texas
Richard Nixon Collection, United States National Archives and Record Center, College Park, Maryland

Nelson A. Rockefeller, Personal, Presidential Mission, 1969, RG 4, Rockefeller Archive Center, Tarrytown, New York

Nelson A. Rockefeller, Vice-Presidential papers, RG 26, Rockefeller Archive Center, Tarrytown, New York

Printed government documents

National Security Archive, *The U.S. Intelligence Community*, 1947–1989 (Washington, DC: National Security Archive, 1990)

Presidential Directives (Washington, DC: National Security Archives 1994)

United States Department of State, *Papers Relating to the Foreign Relations of the United States* (Washington, DC, 1890–)

Germany

German Foreign Office Archives

File R102046, Auswaertiges Amt, Bonn

Interviews

Sahedeo Basdeo (Mount), Kelowna, Canada, 1995–6
Forbes Burnham (Mount), Georgetown, Guyana, 3 March 1974
Lawrence Chewning (Mount), 13 May 1996
Robert DuBose (Mount), Harpers Ferry, 17 May 1996
Cheddi Jagan (Mount), Georgetown, Guyana, 2 March 1974

Newspapers

Chicago Tribune
Christian Science Monitor
Daily Express (Port of Spain)
Financial Time
Globe and Mail (Toronto)
Journal of Commerce
Le Monde
Los Angeles Times
Miami Herald
New York Times
Newsweek
San Juan Star
St. Petersburg Times
Sun Sentinal (Fort Lauderdale)
The Times
Trinidad Guardian
Wall Street Journal
Washington Post

Journals

Caribbean Yearbook of International Relations (Trinidad various years)

INDEX

208